What's the Point of Parenting?

What's the Point of Parenting?

How to Turn Your Child into a Responsible Adult

Sherry Rhodes

Graceful Heart Publishing

Colorado Springs, Colorado

GRACEFUL HEART
PUBLISHING

What's the Point of Parenting?
How to Turn Your Child into a Responsible Adult.

Copyright © 2012 by Sherry Rhodes.

For more information contact

Graceful Heart Publishing
P.O. Box 25519
Colorado Springs, CO 80936
www.GracefulHeartPublishing.com

All rights reserved. No part of this book may be transmitted or reproduced in any form or by any electronic or mechanical means including information storage and retrieval systems without written permission of the publisher, except by reviewers who may quote short passages for a review.

Although the author and publisher have made every effort to ensure the accuracy of the information provided in this book, we assume no responsibility for errors, inaccuracies, omissions, or any inconsistency herein.

ISBN 970-0-98510-340-8

Library of Congress Control Number: 2012935006

Library of Congress Cataloging-in-Publication Data

Rhodes, Sherry.
    What's the point of parenting? : how to turn your child into a responsible adult / Sherry Rhodes.
    p. cm.
    Includes bibliographical references and index.
    LCCN 2012935006
    ISBN 978-0-9851034-0-8 (Soft cover)
    ISBN 978-0-9851034-1-5 (Hard cover)
    ISBN 978-0-9851034-2-2 (ePub)
    ISBN 978-0-9851034-3-9 (Audio Book)
    ISBN 978-0-9851034-4-6 (Mobi)

    1. Child rearing.   I. Title.

HQ769.R46 2012   649'.1
                  QBI12-600064

Printed in the United States of America
First printing 2012

Edited by Susan Hindman
Cover and interior design by Kerrie Lian,
under contract with MacGraphics Services

Dedication

Thanks to my husband, Pat; our three wonderful sons, who made our parenting journey so much fun; their amazing wives; and their beautiful children. Thanks, too, to my sister, Lisa, for always encouraging me to continue.

Most importantly, thanks to my Lord and Savior, Jesus Christ, who insisted I write this book, and to my "Holy Ghost writer," who gave me guidance and direction.

Contents

Introduction xi
About the Author xiii

PART ONE—YOUR CURRICULUM GUIDE 1

Chapter 1: What Is the Point of Parenting? 3
Needs of Children 4
Every Interaction Teaches Your Child Something 11
The Eight-to-One Rule 14
Parenting Is More Than a Part-Time Job 15
Reactive vs. Proactive Parenting 20

Chapter 2: Attitude 25
You Can Choose Your Attitude 25
Confidence vs. Shyness 28
Dealing with Disappointment and Frustration 36
Dealing with Teasing and Bullying 39
An Attitude of Gratitude 40
The Power of Forgiveness 43
Likability 44

Chapter 3: Education 47
Resistance 49
Sneakiness 51
How to Sell the Importance of Education 51
How to Motivate Students 52
Learning Styles 56
How to Help Them Succeed in School 59
English 70
How Do They Know When They're Successful? 70
Senioritis 72

Chapter 4: Life Skills 75
- Chores 75
- Goal Setting 77
- Problem Solving 78
- Perseverance and Commitment 79
- Decision Making 81
- Creativity 86
- Spirituality/Religion 87
- Helping Others 88
- Communication and Listening 90
- Conflict Resolution 94
- What to Look For in a Potential Spouse 98

Chapter 5: Consequences 105
- Identify Your Expectations 108
- Discipline vs. Punishment 110
- Natural and Logical Consequences 120
- Finding the Right Consequences 122
- Early Training Is Important 123
- But It's Hard! 125
- Encouragement 127
- Enabling 128

Chapter 6: Respect 131
- Why Respect Is So Important 132
- You're Their Number-One Teacher 133
- Ways to Model Respect 138
- Trust 140
- Respect for Others 140
- Respect for Authority 142
- Respect for Family Members 143
- Self-Respect 145
- How to Be Respectful with Difficult People 146
- How to Sell Respect to Your Children 147

Chapter 7: Ethics 149
- Lying 150
- Stealing 158
- Cheating 163

Work Ethic	167
Job Interviews	174

Chapter 8: Social Skills ... 179
Manners	179
Traits of Socially Successful People	185
Class	188
Where Have All Our Standards Gone?	194
How to Sell Propriety (Classiness) to Your Children	197

Chapter 9: Safety ... 199
Physical Safety for Small Children	200
Bullies	204
Driving	205
Emotional and Moral Safety	210
Dating	222
Sex	223

Chapter 10: Finances ... 229
Why Should We Teach Money Skills?	230
Getting Started	232
The Plan	235
Should Allowance Be Tied to Chores?	241
Strategies for Controlling Overspending	242
Budgeting	244
Online Banking	246
Online Spending	246
How to Sell Money Management to Your Children	247

Chapter 11: A Healthy Lifestyle ... 251
The Standard American Diet	253
Plant-Based vs. Animal Foods	254
Some Advice about Medical Advice	255
Why did the American Diet Change?	256
A Healthy Weight	256
Disease Facts	258
Three Types of Nutrients	259
Problem Foods	261
Easy Changes to Make	264

Exercise 267
Sleep 268
Resources for Healthy Living 271

Chapter 12: Illegal Substances 273
Drugs 274
Alcohol 278
Smoking 280
Other Talking Points Regarding Illegal Substances 282

Part Two—Your Lesson Plans 283

Ages 1–3 285
Age 4 286
Ages 5–7 288
Ages 8–10 290
Ages 11–13 292
Ages 14–18 295
After Age 18 298
Appendix 299
Index 301

Introduction

A New Kind of Parenting Book

What's the Point of Parenting? guides parents through the process of raising children over the course of eighteen or so years. It was designed to cover the things children need to learn before they leave the nest, so it's more about what to teach than how to make children "behave," whatever that means. Part One is your curriculum guide—all those things that need to be taught. Part Two consists of lesson plans: what to teach at each stage of development.

Some of this I learned as I was raising my three boys and teaching middle school and high school; the rest is based on extensive research. This is the book I wish I'd had when our first bundle of joy was born. It's my sincere hope that this book will be a reference for you and that you'll read it many times as you raise your children.

With apologies to my wonderful oldest son, it's been said that children are like pancakes: everybody messes up the first one. There may be a grain of truth to that. Many of us, including myself, start out relatively clueless as to what our job description should be, but we learn more with each successive child. I finally asked myself, wouldn't it be nice to have that knowledge from the beginning?

As a teacher, I realized that too many students weren't learning important skills, such as study skills, financial management, and consequences, from their parents. I finally figured out why: parents are often too busy, too tired, or too preoccupied to remember to teach these things.

Sometimes parents assume it's the school's job to teach their children everything they need to know. The reality is that the most important lessons your child will learn—attitude, values, and respect, to name a few—will be learned from parents first, then from popular media (TV, movies, music). Parents *must* take an active role in teaching these things. I hope this book will help.

About the Author

Sherry Rhodes graduated from California State University, Northridge with a bachelor's degree in mathematics and from Minot State University with bachelor's degrees in both computer science and secondary education.

Sherry started teaching when she was twelve, assisting her father with swimming lessons each summer through the Los Angeles County Aquatics program. She later enjoyed teaching wherever she and her husband Pat were stationed—across the country and in Department of Defense schools around the world, including Okinawa, Japan; Lakenheath, England; Alconbury, England; and Ramstein, Germany. She taught both middle school and high school, as a substitute teacher when her children were young and as a full-time teacher when they got older. She currently teaches computer classes and maintains the computer lab at a nonprofit organization in Colorado Springs.

She and her husband Pat live in Colorado Springs and enjoy visiting their three sons, Travis, Justin, and Daniel, and their families.

Part I

Your Curriculum Guide:

All the Things Children Need to Learn

Chapter 1

What Is the Point of Parenting?

Today it seems parents are busier than ever. As we struggle to remember who has soccer practice tonight and which day we need to send treats to school, it's easy to forget our ultimate goal as parents. Our primary focus should be to teach our children the skills needed to take their place in society. We want them to develop a number of traits such as having a good work ethic, being financially responsible, and showing respect for others. In addition, there are other skills we can teach them that will make their lives (and the lives of those around them) easier, including practicing good manners, living within their means, and doing what's right. Of course, we also need to keep them safe, fed, and clothed, and send them to school, but for some reason it's the life skills that seem to get lost in the chaos.

When you first learned you (meaning both of you) were pregnant, you probably realized your life was about to change forever. Middle-of-the-night feedings and a houseful of toys would soon become your new reality. Did you ever stop to wonder what life would be like in ten years? Fifteen? I certainly didn't.

When we brought home our first little bundle of joy, I assumed we'd take things one day at a time, tackling problems as they came up. I didn't realize that this was the classic model of reactive parenting. Over time, we learned that life was easier if we planned ahead for potential problems and discussed them with the kids. "Now that you're in middle school, you'll find that a lot of kids cheat. Let's talk about why you don't want to do that." Or "Now that you have your driver's license, you may be tempted to speed. Here is a list of reasons why you shouldn't, and a list of consequences for breaking the law."

Did you ever talk to your spouse about what to teach your little cherub? What your role as parent should be? I never did. We had a vague idea of what we wanted from our children—we wanted them to be polite and respectful, and to do well in school—but never thought much beyond that. It wasn't until our kids got older (and we realized we were outnumbered) that we started becoming more proactive as parents.

NEEDS OF CHILDREN

In the mid-twentieth century, Dr. Abraham Maslow created a now famous hierarchy of human needs. His theory was that all humans have basic requirements, which he sorted into five groups: physiological, security, social, esteem, and self-actualization. He went on to rank these needs because people can't worry about things such as personal growth if they're starving or afraid.

Using Maslow's hierarchy, we can identify the needs of our children.

1. **Physiological needs (the most basic for survival):**
- **Food, water,** and **adequate sleep** are the most obvious.
- **Physical contact.** In a well-known series of experiments, Harry Harlow discovered that baby rhesus monkeys, separated from their mothers at birth, developed fierce attachments to the cloth lining of their cages and reacted violently when the cloth was removed for cleaning. When raised in a cage with a bare floor, many of the baby monkeys died within the first five days. Harlow offered the monkeys a choice of two surrogate mothers: one made of a wire frame that provided nourishment, and the other made of terry cloth that provided no nourishment. The

monkeys routinely clung to the terry cloth mother, only going to the wire surrogate when they needed food. When frightened, monkeys who were raised with a terry cloth surrogate clung to it and eventually calmed down; those monkeys raised only with a wire mesh surrogate cowered on the floor, screaming in terror. Monkeys raised without the tactile comfort of the cloth "mother" showed developmental delays and social ineptitude that continued into adulthood.

In 1989, a team of foreign doctors visited the overcrowded orphanages in Romania. The overworked staff struggled just to keep up with the feeding and diaper changing; there was no time for cuddling or interacting with the infants. Babies were often fed from a propped-up bottle and almost never left their cribs. The team of doctors found these infants to have "grossly delayed" mental and motor skills, and later in life displayed seemingly insurmountable social ineptness. Since then, Maternal Deprivation Syndrome has been defined as a failure to thrive due to neglect (either intentional or unintentional) by the primary caregiver.

Touch deprivation has been linked to many physiological and social problems, including increased stress, physical violence, cardiovascular disease, sleep difficulties, decreased immune response, and a reduction in levels of growth hormone in children. Hug your kids every day.

Hug your kids every day

2. **Security needs (physical and emotional safety):**
- **Physical safety.** They don't need to know the gory details of all the evil in the world, but they do need to know that bad guys exist. Your job is to protect them from bad guys and other dangers. That's why there are rules about using the Internet, talking to strangers, and playing with matches.

- **Trust**. All children need to be able to trust their parents both physically and emotionally. If they can't trust their parents, they never learn to trust anyone. You can build trust with your family members by:
  - *Keeping your word and not making promises if you're not sure you can keep them.*
  - *Doing everything you can to lift up their self-esteem instead of tearing it down.*
  - *Keeping their confidences.*
  - *Never ever embarrassing them, especially in public.*
  - *Hanging on to your patience. When parents lose their temper frequently, it frightens children and may cause emotional scars.*
  - *Avoiding physical punishment whenever possible. Physical abuse is never okay.*
  - *Avoiding excessive teasing.*
- **Boundaries and limits**. Once babies become mobile, they can start learning physical boundaries. "Dog food is not for eating; streets are for cars, not children; hitting is not allowed." As they get older, you'll add others: "Ask permission before using or taking someone's things." You can also start adding social (nonphysical) boundaries. "Don't repeat things you were told in confidence; don't ask personal questions unless you're very close to the person."
- **Stability**. Children who see their parents fighting all the time live in constant fear their world is about to fall apart.

3. Social needs:
- **Unconditional love**. This seems obvious, but it's not always demonstrated. It's not enough to tell them they're loved, because as the saying goes, actions speak louder than words. Hugs and smiles speak volumes about your love for them. When we're angry, children internalize that to mean we don't love them. We

need to remind them frequently that there's nothing they can do to make us stop loving them.

Kids are, well, kids, and as parents we must understand that they *will* make mistakes, they *will* disobey authority occasionally (sometimes intentionally, sometimes accidentally), and they *will* sometimes make us angry. Through all of this, we have to make it clear that while we may not like a certain behavior, we will always love them. When we correct their behavior, it's *because* we love them, even though we don't love the behavior.

When we're angry, it's especially important to choose our words carefully. Name-calling and put-downs may make us feel better temporarily, but will become a permanent part of how your child sees himself. Disrespectful comments make children feel unloved. If you struggle with this, memorize the following sentence: I love you with all my heart, but your behavior right now is unacceptable, and we need to correct it. This simple statement avoids any character assassination and tells the child you're correcting the behavior because you love him. Saying "We need to correct it" implies you expect cooperation.

Don't forget to tell each kidlet "I love you" every day and follow those words with actions.

- **To fit in and be accepted.** This need is greater for some children than for others, but most kids have some fear of being seen as different.

When I was in seventh grade, the big fad was white majorette boots. (Hey, it was the sixties.) Everyone was wearing them, and I absolutely *had* to have a pair. I'm still grateful my mother understood how important it was for me to have those boots.

Sometimes the essential fashion item is a $200 pair of shoes or a $300 phone. If your child feels he can't live without something that's outside your budget, your family will have to talk it over to try to find an alternate plan. Perhaps Junior can pay for half the cost or find a suitable, less expensive substitute.

Parents and children often argue over TV programs or current movies. I don't recommend compromising your values in this area. If you feel a certain program is unsuitable, stick to your guns. There were several shows our kids weren't allowed to watch because they encouraged what we consider antifamily values. We frequently heard how "everybody else" got to watch the shows and how unfair we were, but our boys survived. All three have since told us that while they didn't like the rule, they now understand the reasons for it.

- **Social skills.** Every society has certain mores and rules to make social interaction as pleasant as possible. See Chapter 8.

4. **Esteem needs:**

- **Praise.** Children need to be praised for their efforts as well as their accomplishments.
- **Encouragement.** Being little is hard work—there's *so* much to learn. Physical skills (walking, talking, throwing a ball, riding a bike), social skills (manners, respect for others), school—the list seems endless. We need to encourage effort and progress, not just praise successes. Encouragement tells children we believe in them and helps them believe in themselves. It also teaches them that success often comes through persistence.
- **Self-worth.** Babies generally start with healthy egos, but a constant barrage of negative comments from parents and siblings can quickly eradicate their self-esteem. Encourage their talents and interests, and tell them every day how much they mean to you.

- **Patience and understanding.** Kids are not short adults. They're not born knowing what the rules are in the grown-up world. They don't know what's expected of them unless we tell them, and they rarely learn anything the first time we teach it. Learning takes practice. Lots of practice.
- **Empathy.** Things unimportant to us are devastating to them. A dead goldfish barely registers on our radar screen yet can seem like the loss of a best friend to a small child. When a favorite stuffed animal gets lost at naptime, it can cause a major melt-

down—and no other toy can take its place. <u>Remember to look at the world through their eyes.</u>

- **Attention.** Even when we're tired or busy, our offspring need our attention.

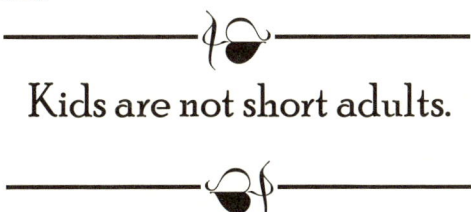

Kids are not short adults.

5. **Self-actualization needs (personal growth):**

- **Education**, both formal and informal. Knowledge is power. Often kids will ignore their schoolwork either because they don't feel like doing it or to punish their parents for something. Teach your children that education is something they do for themselves. We adults know that the more education they get, the better their chances are of acquiring a high-paying job—and that a poor education almost always guarantees a low-paying job. Try to explain that to them in terms they'll understand.

  Tell them why you want them to do well in school. It's certainly not for your benefit, unless you expect them to support you in your golden years. They need the education so they <u>can get a job that pays enough to allow them to buy all those toys they want.</u> I used to have a poster in my classroom that showed an array of expensive sports cars. The caption read "Justification for Higher Education."

  Informal education is the learning that occurs outside of school—tap dancing, soccer, or reading about something that interests them.

To Maslow's list, I would add the following other needs that are also important:

- **A childhood.** Kids are always in a hurry to grow up. They want to emulate Mom or Dad and all the "cool" people they see in the media. There's plenty of time to be a grown-up. <u>Children should be allowed to enjoy the freedom and innocence of youth.</u>

Responsibilities should be commensurate with age, and having too many responsibilities is just as bad as not having any. I've seen fourteen-year-olds acting as the parent in charge, doing all the cooking, cleaning, and supervising of younger siblings because Mom and Dad were never home. I've also seen nine-year-old girls dressed like streetwalkers, wearing more makeup in a day than most women wear in a month. Why?

- **A healthy lifestyle**. Allowing a child to become obese is child abuse, plain and simple. It ruins their self-esteem, causes them to be the object of teasing, and puts them at risk for myriad health problems. Even if their weight is in the normal range, allowing kids to subsist on junk food and empty calories will ultimately cause health problems. See Chapter 11.

- **Two parents**. I know this isn't a politically correct statement, but there were reasons God decided it should take two people to create a baby. Raising small children is a full-time job, and providing for a family is also a full-time job. In addition, boys need a male role model, and girls need a female role model.

    Obviously, this isn't always possible. Divorce happens. It's been shown repeatedly, however, that children from a loving, stable, two-parent home are better adjusted than children of divorce.

    Both parents in a divorce should work to keep their relationship with their kids strong and healthy, and make it clear that the divorce has nothing to do with the children's behavior. It's never okay to put children in the middle of adult battles.

    If your spouse is not a good role model, or has little contact with the children, seek out a trusted friend or family member to provide that relationship in your children's lives. Someone who makes them feel special and will reinforce the values you are teaching them.

- **Happy memories**. Unhappy events tend to stick in our brain more easily than happy events, so it's important to create many happy memories. Family vacations are great, but even a family game night or movie night or camping in the backyard can do the trick. Make a point to do something fun with the kids each week.

- **Great role models.** We can preach to our children all day long, but most of the time they'll use our behavior as their guide. You and your spouse *must* demonstrate the values and traits you want your kids to embrace consistently. Lead by example.
- **Patience.** Small children will forget the rules; older children will test the rules. Both will strain the boundaries of your patience. Knowing these things makes it easier to stay calm.

In addition to meeting the needs listed above, parents have a few other job requirements:

- *Teach the skills children need for adulthood.*
- *Improve each generation.*
- *Be their parent, not their friend.*
- *Say no when you need to and stick to your guns.*
- *Do what's best for the child, not what's convenient for you.*
- *Admit your parenting mistakes and apologize when necessary. It's okay to be human.*

EVERY INTERACTION TEACHES YOUR CHILD SOMETHING

Studies have shown repeatedly that the greatest influence in a child's life is the same-sex parent. Girls usually grow up to be like Mom, and boys will follow in Dad's footsteps. Who's their second most important role model? You guessed it—the other parent. It only makes sense since they have watched both of you since the day they were born. Kids learn facts and figures at school, but learn most of their behavioral traits at home. If you're not teaching the kids, then the bachelors on *Two and a Half Men* probably are.

If you're a parent, then you're a teacher, like it or not. It's important, when making decisions that involve them, to ask yourself if you're teaching them the right thing.

Are you teaching them that communication means calling names and yelling at the top of your lungs, or that it means calmly listening to the other person's point of view? Are they learning it's okay to swear because everybody else does it, or that swearing is not allowed in your house? Teaching by example is infinitely more powerful than telling them they shouldn't do something. Screaming "Don't talk to me that way, you little jerk!" sends a very confusing message.

Every interaction you have with your children teaches them something, good or bad.

If you allow your daughter to skip class so she can get her hair done, or let your son go to a party Friday night even though he was "too sick" to go to school that day, you're teaching them that school isn't as important as looking pretty or having fun. If you consistently ignore their bad behavior in the hopes that they'll outgrow it, what you're really teaching them is that bad behavior is tolerable. If you let them stay home because they forgot to study for a test, they learn that deadlines can be ignored. As you make these decisions, even if it's "just this once," ask yourself if this is a trait that will serve your child well in society.

Often (okay, usually) it's much easier to give in to a request than to argue. Your daughter wants to sleep over at a friend's house tonight, but you've never met the friend or her parents. In your heart, you know this is not a good idea, but wouldn't it be nice to have a quiet evening tonight? You've had a hard day and don't feel up to the pouting and/or temper tantrum that will ultimately occur if you say no to her request. What to do?

Even seemingly minor exchanges with kids have a message. Giving them a hug and a smile when they get home from school tells them that they're loved and you missed them. Stopping what you're doing and crouching down to look at the pretty rock they brought you says you respect their thoughts and feelings, and you appreciate their love. Asking for their help tells them they're a valuable member of the family team.

I spent many years as a substitute teacher, and I quickly learned that if a sub lets a student out of the room at the start of class, that student may never come back. As soon as I'd walk into a classroom, there would be at least one cherub planning such an escape. "Teacher, can I have a pass to, uh, my locker? Yeah, that's it—I need something out of my locker." I had a policy to never give anyone a pass in the first half hour of class.

Often students would ask, "How come you never let us go anywhere?"

My standard answer, even to kids I'd never seen before, was, "Because I miss you when you're gone." I was always surprised at the number of kids who would give me a look as though I was the only person who had ever said I missed them. They just sort of melted and returned to their seat.

On the other hand, ignoring our children or snapping at them when they ask a question teaches them they're a bother. Laughing at them when they're struggling with something indicates their feelings are unimportant, and therefore *they* are unimportant.

And then there's the self-fulfilling prophecy. When we start telling a child she's forgetful, the label begins to stick. Subconsciously, the child tells herself, "I can't help it. I'm a forgetful person." She has no reason to try to remember things because Mom and Dad already know she can't. The label gives her a convenient excuse, so the forgetting just gets worse.

When my kids were small, I decided to learn sign language, and I taught it to our boys as well. Actually, I taught them sign language so I could "yell" at them in church, but they quickly learned not to look at me during the service. Anyway, now and then (not at church) I'd catch their eye and sign "You're cute." They'd respond by signing "You're funny." The signs are similar, and they'd always pretend it was an honest mistake while I pretended to be offended. When you're in public, signing "I love you" is less embarrassing to them than saying it out loud, and it's an easy way to remind them how you feel. We still do it, and it still makes us smile.

The Eight-to-One Rule

It's an unfortunate fact of human nature that we internalize negative events and comments much more readily than positive ones. If one friend says she likes your dress, and a second friend says it makes you look fat, which comment do you focus on? The same is true for our children. Some child psychologists advise parents and educators to work on a ratio of at <u>least four positive comments for each negative one</u>. Some advocate more than that—as many as <u>eight to one</u>.

Each negative comment should be counterbalanced with at least four positive ones. Eight is better.

Often our interactions with children are negative simply because we need to give advice or correct behavior: "Don't drop your plate." "Don't run in the house." "Don't forget your backpack." They're all little negatives to be sure, but they add up. Other negative events include frowning, yelling, and, heaven forbid, name-calling. I have to confess it was hard for me to break the name-calling habit. My mother was a name-caller, as was her mother, and I have vivid memories of being called an ungrateful brat, lazy slob, and more. I know just how hurtful those labels are and how they can destroy self-esteem. I vowed never to do that to my own kids, but when we're angry we fall back on old patterns of behavior.

To help break away from those old patterns, I started using other words such as *hooligan* and *twit*. It's hard for those labels to become self-fulfilling prophecies, but they do still have a negative ring to them. If I had it to do over, I'd go with something cute, because it's nearly impossible to stay angry when you're yelling, "Get in here right now, you little bunny rabbit!" I'm not condoning name-calling, but calling them cute names is a step toward no name-calling at all.

One way to overcome these negative comments is to rephrase them: "I'm glad you're being careful with your plate." "Thank you for not running in the house" (even if, in fact, they are running). "Do you have everything?" (as they're leaving for school).

Positive events don't necessarily have to be verbal. Hugs, smiles, a kiss on the head (never in public, I'm told, at least for boys), saying thank you, and giving praise for a job well done are all happy events. Telling a friend about a significant accomplishment when your child is within earshot is especially effective. "Johnny made his bed all by himself today!" Of course, your friend will look suitably impressed, and now there are two adults proud of him.

PARENTING IS MORE THAN A PART-TIME JOB

Too many people today treat parenting as a hobby (or a chore), something they do when they have the time. It doesn't usually start out that way; it just seems to happen. You'd like to talk to your first grader about what to do when the mean kid in her class picks on her, but you really need to iron something for work tomorrow. Your fifteen-year-old just got dumped by his girlfriend and is feeling pretty low, but you're in the middle of watching the big game and the score is tied. You plan on talking to him later, but by then he's gone off to his friend's house.

There's a reason it takes two people to conceive a child—God knew it would take at least two people to raise one. In the old days, the entire tribe or village was responsible for raising the children. Even when Dad was off hunting for dinner, Mom had other people around to help teach the values of the community. Sort of a tribal day care center. Grandparents and other mature members of the society were available to offer advice and moral support to new parents. In addition, the entire group looked out for all children. Youngsters were less likely to misbehave because they would suffer the wrath of the entire clan. In today's mobile society, we've gotten away from the extended family. Families have become more isolated, and the communal advice that was once widely available becomes harder to find.

If you're feeling isolated, find resources in your community. Often churches or community centers will have support groups for parents, such as MOPS (Mothers of Preschoolers), or offer parenting classes. When our eldest was four, my husband and I took a STEP (Systematic Training for Effective Parenting) class at our church. We not only learned a great deal, but also took comfort in the fact that other people were struggling with the same issues.

Brian was a ninth-grade student of mine who was well known in the school as a troublemaker. He enjoyed disrupting classes, sassing teachers, and bullying classmates. One day, he was making no effort to hide the fact that he was handing a note to the student next to him. As I walked over to take the note, Brian snatched it back and refused to give it to me. Since I couldn't physically force him to hand over the note, I started to send him to the office when he unfolded the note, stood up, and showed the class it wasn't a note—it was the homework handout I had given out earlier. He smirked at me and shouted, "Now don't you feel stupid?"

That afternoon, as the principal and I were speaking with Brian's mother about the importance of appropriate classroom behavior, she began to explain why Brian and his sister were out of control. "His father travels quite a bit on business. I work from eight to five and go to school until ten o'clock three days a week. On weekends I have to do the housework, laundry, and shopping. I'm just too tired to be disciplining them all the time."

I looked at her and asked, "So who exactly is raising your children? Who is teaching them values, checking their homework, meeting their friends?"

That's when I realized the problem: Brian and his sister were raising themselves, and not doing a very good job of it. Unfortunately, they are not alone—there are thousands of children across the country who are raising themselves, at least part of the time. When they don't get the attention they need at home, many students look for attention in other ways. Brian was willing to get into trouble in order to look cool in front of his peers. Angry with parents for not "being there" for them, children turn their anger not only toward Mom and Dad, but toward other adults in their lives as well. Authority figures become targets.

All children need attention, and negative attention is better than none at all. When we only interact with them when they're "bad," they learn that being bad is a good thing. Getting in trouble is better than being invisible.

I wish I could say this was an isolated case, but the problem is growing. Too many parents are too tired to teach values and priorities. It's the Scarlett O'Hara theory of child-raising: "I'll think about it tomorrow."

Of course, no one plans to have their kids raise themselves. It's just that by the end of the day, we're often exhausted, and if no major problems have cropped up, we're happy to kiss the little angels good night and crawl into bed ourselves.

Somewhere between the ages of ten and twelve, children become responsible enough to stay home alone for a few hours—however, this does not mean home alone all the time. Old enough to not burn the house down is not old enough to raise themselves. There's so much we need to teach our munchkins, but if we're not physically there, the teaching doesn't happen. More to the point, when kids are home alone, they often turn to the "electric babysitters" for entertainment: TV, music, or the Internet. Not always the best sources of moral guidance. (Let me hop up on my soapbox for a moment: parents should never ever allow children access to the Internet without supervision. See Chapter 9.)

The National PTA recommends that parents spend at least twenty minutes each day talking one-on-one with each child. Twenty minutes doesn't sound like much, but I can tell you it's a challenge. For some families, just eating dinner together is a major accomplishment.

Now look at it from your child's perspective: the two people you love more than anything can't or won't even spend a third of an hour alone with you. It's no wonder some kids misbehave to get attention. They're desperate.

I once took an informal poll among my high school students: "What's the one thing you want from your parents?" The overwhelming response was, "I wish they'd spend more time with me."

Working Parents

There are many compelling reasons for a woman to work full-time, not the least of which is her mental health. I was feeding our cat one day when I heard myself ask him, "Can you say 'thank you'?" That's when I knew I had to get out more and find some adult conversation. As soon as my youngest started first grade, I went back to work part-time, and when he got to junior high I found a full-time job.

At the time, I thought my kids didn't need me as much since they were teenagers and pretty self-reliant. I was wrong. Teens need their parents as much as younger children do, just for different reasons. Hormones, new schools, more teachers, more homework, more classmates, learning to drive, and dating all weigh heavily on the hearts of our young adults. I was extremely fortunate to get a teaching job at their school. I had essentially the same hours they did and was able to see them during the day. It was the perfect job. I knew their friends, and I saw them more than if I wasn't working. I wish all mothers could work at their child's school.

> Teens need their parents as much as younger children do, just for different reasons.

When parents work full-time, spending twenty minutes a day alone with each child seems as doable as climbing Mount Everest. Even without the twenty-minute one-on-one time, kids still require a lot of attention. When you choose to become a parent, though, you are choosing to take on a huge responsibility. You're taking a brand-new human being and molding that person into a responsible adult. When they're in the car with you, turn off the electronics and talk to them. Make an effort to have everyone eat breakfast and dinner together. When they're watching TV, watch it with them and talk to them about the program.

We've all seen articles on the importance of taking time for yourself, and while I agree with the premise, I feel strongly that our children's needs come first. Your child is totally dependent on you for everything. Don't let her down. Nobody ever regrets the time spent with their kids. After they grow up and move away, you'll have lots of happy memories.

If you're a full-time working mom, ask yourself if you can find a way to cut back. A friend of mine, Amy, was telling me one day that she was jealous of me because I was able to be a stay-at-home mom when my kids were little. Her daughter was three, and Amy dearly wanted to stay home and raise her. I was confused, because as near as I could tell, Amy was working so they could afford to pay the gardener, dog walker, pool maintenance company, cleaning lady, dog groomer, the guy who detailed their car every month or so, the lady who did their ironing, and, of course, their day care provider. Not to mention they had two enormous car payments. I pointed out that if she quit paying all those people and downsized the cars, she could do the work herself and be able to stay home with her daughter. "Oh, no," she said. "My husband would never let me do that." To Amy and her husband, their lifestyle was more important than their daughter. How sad.

I admit I was very blessed to be able to stay home with our boys before they started school. If you're not able to do that, at least choose a caregiver with values similar to yours and make sure you spend time with your kids as often as you can.

Job Sharing

Job sharing is when two people each work half-time to cover a full-time job. Sometimes one will work two days a week, and the other three, or whatever fits their situation. The advantage is that if one is sick, the other can cover for that person. The advantage to the employer is that the work continues seamlessly when someone is out sick. The disadvantage to the employees is that the employer may not offer benefits (medical and dental) to part-time workers. If you have some other source of medical benefits, then job sharing may be a good option.

REACTIVE VS. PROACTIVE PARENTING

Over the last few decades, the American approach to parenting has changed. The dramatic increase in the number of two-income families and single working parents means parenting has become a part-time endeavor for many. The busier we get, the more we tend to shoot from the hip ("react") when responding to our kids. We do whatever's convenient at the moment. Worse, we do whatever it takes to avoid conflict with them. All too often, we give in to their demands because we want them to be happy, we don't feel like arguing, and we feel guilty for not spending more time with them.

Proactive parenting, on the other hand, requires some forethought but has several benefits. Most importantly, it helps prevent problems before they occur. By thinking ahead to possible trouble spots, you can let your cherubs know in advance what the consequences will be for poor choices or anticipate how to deal with a difficult situation. "If you lose the cell phone, you don't get another one." "If I catch you with drugs, I'll be the one to call the police."

Preschoolers don't have the cognitive skills to understand "if-then" statements. When you say something like, "If you hit the baby, then you'll get a time-out," what they hear is closer to, "Blah blah blah **hit the baby** blah blah blah." Thus for small children, a more direct statement is best. "Babies are not for hitting."

Proactive parenting is also helpful when your little ones are facing a new situation. It tells little ones that you care about their feelings, alleviates some of their fears of the unknown, and lets them know what's expected of them. It's much easier for them to deal with a new situation if you explain ahead of time what may happen. Starting school, moving, doctor visits, sleepovers, and new siblings are all unknowns for children. Talk openly and honestly about upcoming events. For example:

- Before going to a friend's birthday party for the first time, explain to your daughter that it's not her turn to open the presents or blow out the candles, but she will probably get some ice cream and cake, and maybe play a few games.

- Before dropping off your son at a new day care provider, arrange a meeting so they can get to know each other. Have the provider explain the rules; show your son where the bathroom is and which rooms are off-limits.

- Before the new sibling arrives, explain what to expect. "The new baby will take a lot of our time, and we will need your help." Think of some ways your older child can assist you. Perhaps he can bring Mom a glass of water when she nurses the baby, or he can rock the crib when Baby is fussy. My older boys would dance and sing for the youngest while I fixed dinner.

Indicators of a Reactive Parenting Style

- Reactive parents live in the moment. Everything seems fine, so they don't ask any questions or rock the boat. It's so much easier to assume everything is going well instead of taking time to make sure. People tend to believe what they want to believe. If our little angel says everything is fine, we really want to believe her.

  I overheard Julie, a tenth grader, talking to her friend one day about the shoes she had just purchased. When asked where she got the money, she explained, "I steal stuff from my sister's room and sell it to my friends."

  I was curious. "Doesn't your mother wonder where you get the money for the things you buy? Doesn't your sister wonder where her stuff is going?"

  Julie laughed. "My mother is so dumb. I tell her my boyfriend is buying me presents. When my sister accuses me of stealing her things, I tell Mom she's lying."

  I thought about it for a moment. "So, let me get this straight. Your mother trusts you to be a good person, and you think that makes her dumb?"

  "Of course," she replied. "If your kids told you that story, would you believe it?" Clearly it was easier for Julie's mother to believe the story and hope for the best, than to dig deeper and get to the truth. And that was just fine with Julie.

- When children need or want something, reactive parents say yes if it doesn't inconvenience them; otherwise, they say no "because I said so."
- When their child gets into trouble, reactive parents either ignore the problem because they're tired or punish him too severely to make sure it never happens again. It's easy to forget that it's unfair to punish mistakes made in ignorance. We got our son Justin a cell phone when he was in high school in Germany but forgot to explain about roaming charges. When Justin went to England for a wrestling tournament, he spent a good part of the weekend talking to his girlfriend. I nearly had heart failure when we got the bill, but I knew we couldn't punish him. We had dropped the ball.
- They will engage in parenting by intimidation. When they're angry, they'll do a lot of shouting, which cuts down on the back talk.
- Often, rules exist only in the reactive parent's head, because the parent forgot to explain them to the children:
    "You can't go to Fred's house because you haven't cleaned your room."
    "You didn't tell me to clean my room."
    "It doesn't matter. I want it clean right now!"
- Reactive parents ignore bad or annoying behavior until they can't take it anymore and then they snap. Boy, could I snap. It took me a few years before I realized I should give them some warning. "I've asked you nicely twice to stop teasing your brother. I'm getting angry. Do I need to help you find something else to do?"

Indicators of a Proactive Parenting Style

- Proactive parents practice empathy. They look at situations through a child's eyes. Missing a favorite TV show means having to wait a whole week to see it. That's almost a lifetime in kid years. Think back to your childhood about things that were important to you.

- They explain the rules and expectations, as well as the consequences for breaking the rules, because they realize they can't punish mistakes made in ignorance.
- They anticipate a child's concerns and explain what to expect in new situations. Fear of the unknown can be paralyzing for children, especially shy ones.
- Proactive parents respect the child's feelings so he'll respect theirs. When your son says he doesn't want to take swim lessons because he's afraid of the water, you talk to him about the importance of knowing how to swim and discuss ways to make him feel more comfortable. (One of our boys, age six, refused to take lessons because he didn't know how to swim. He insisted I teach him how before he'd go to swim class. He later got a job as a lifeguard. Go figure.)
- They discipline with love and respect. "I love you, but your behavior was unacceptable and needs to be corrected." Or, "I love you and that's why I can't let you act this way."
- They honor each child's individuality. One child loves fish for dinner, the other gags at the sight of it. One is an amazing athlete, the other excels at poetry.
- They're consistent in the enforcement of the rules, even when they're tired, busy, or distracted, because they know it's important to send clear messages to children.
- They understand the importance of communicating with the little ones on a daily basis, beyond the usual "How was school? / Fine. I'll be in my room" exchange after school. Proactive parents ask leading questions, such as "What do you think about…" or "What should we do this weekend?" or "Tell me about your English teacher. I hear she's a lot of fun." They may not have heard anything of the sort, but it's a conversation starter.

- They listen attentively when a child is speaking to them because it's important to keep the lines of communication open. If your child is comfortable talking about day-to-day issues, he'll probably feel comfortable coming to Mom or Dad when he has a major problem to work through.
- Proactive parents know how important it is to do what's best for the child, not what's easiest for them.

Proactive parents do what's best for the child, not what's easiest for the parents.

Being proactive means taking time to teach things to children instead of hoping someone else does the teaching. It takes a great deal more energy than simply reacting on an as-needed basis. The benefits are enormous and absolutely worth the effort. Your life will be more peaceful, your kids will be happier, and your family will have more of a "team spirit" attitude. Even better, your children will pick up these skills and pass them on to future generations.

Most of us fall somewhere in the middle of the reactive-proactive continuum; there's always room for improvement. It took Pat and me several years to get good at being proactive, but if we can do it, you can, too.

Chapter 2

Attitude

A good attitude will get each of us through hard times, make our life easier, and will make the lives of those around us better.

You Can Choose Your Attitude

I once asked our boys what they considered the most important life lessons we'd taught them, and each of them put "choosing your attitude" in the top three. We can't necessarily choose how we feel about a given situation. Coworkers make us angry occasionally; family members make us feel frustrated. When we suffer disappointment, we're sad for a while. While we can't choose our feelings, we *can* decide how we react to those feelings. We can choose our attitude.

> We can't necessarily choose how we feel about a given situation. We <u>can</u> decide how we react to those feelings.

I discovered this one day when the boys and I were clearing the yard before planting grass. We were removing rocks from the top layer of dirt, and there were millions of rocks. As an incentive,

I paid each kid a penny a rock, but one of my cherubs still had an attitude problem. Every rock that went into the wheelbarrow had a complaint that went with it. "I HATE this. This is STUPID! WHY do we have to do this? I DON'T want to do this!" The whining got old after about ten rocks.

We had a little talk about attitude adjustment. He could either complain the whole time (to himself) and get angrier with every rock, or start thinking about what he wanted to buy with the money he was earning.

As with any new skill, it took practice, but he caught on quickly. In fact, one day I was in a snit about something, and my formerly whiny son reminded me that I could choose my attitude. He was right. I was reluctant to give up my rant but knew I had to set a good example, so I gritted my teeth and quit complaining.

Examples:

- If the hose breaks and soaks you from head to toe, you can use every swear word you ever learned, or you can laugh about how funny it probably looked.
- If some thoughtless jerk cuts you off in traffic, you can yell and shake your fist and be angry for hours, or you can say a prayer that he doesn't injure anyone and give thanks he didn't injure you.
- If your youngster wants something they can't have—a toy, a boyfriend, a new car—they can pout for days, or they can say "Oh well" and move on.
- If your best friend moves away, or the dog dies, of course you'll grieve; but ask yourself how long you'll allow yourself to suffer before getting on with life. Then stick to that time frame.
- If you have a flat tire on the way to work and are now twenty minutes late, you can fume, or you can breathe deeply and remind yourself that "it is what it is." Raising your blood pressure won't get you to work any faster.
- If your husband forgets to pick up milk on his way home from work, you can yell at him about how inconvenienced you are, or you can remind yourself that the kids will be fine if they drink water tonight.

- If your son is angry because his teacher assigned a book report, he might pout and stomp his feet, delaying the inevitable. Help him set manageable goals instead by having him read one or two chapters each day and telling you the highlights.
- If your daughter has been having a great time at a friend's house, but is throwing a tantrum now that it's time to go, try telling her something like this: "I'm glad you had so much fun, but we need to go home and have dinner. You can cry and make a lot of noise so that these folks will be glad you're leaving, or you can thank them for inviting you."

I used to have our boys figure out the solution to this question: "If you cry and scream when it's time to leave your friend's house, guess what happens?" Even the youngest one knew the answer: you don't get to come back. Kids are surprisingly good at connecting cause and effect.

We have a "five-year rule" at our house: will whatever we're upset about matter in five years? Will we even remember why we were mad five years from now? Usually the answer is no. If it won't matter five years from now, it's probably not worth ruining your day over (or anyone else's day for that matter). Of course, for preschool-age children, you'll have to use a time frame they can relate to.

Will whatever we're upset about matter in five years?

One day I was substituting in a high school history class. One of the students had been teasing another from the moment they both walked into the room. Before I had a chance to separate them, George jumped out of his chair and took a swing at his tormenter. I took him out into the hallway and asked, "Do you like that guy? Is he your friend?"

"Of course not!" was the quick reply.

"Then don't let someone you don't like ruin your day. There are hundreds of students in this school. Find some who have the same interests as you, and ignore the ignoramuses who are looking for entertainment at your expense. You're smarter than they are."

I could literally see the light bulb come on over George's head. He spent the rest of the hour cheerfully ignoring the other student. I would see him from time to time after that, and he looked much happier.

We've all known people who seem to be perpetually angry. Every perceived slight sets off a tirade, and they lash out at whoever is around. Wouldn't it be nice if they used all that negative energy for something more positive? Think of all the good they could do instead of dragging down the rest of us.

Some people say they're afraid of acting like a phony, pretending to be cheerful. Wouldn't you rather spend time with someone pretending to be cheerful than someone who is genuinely angry?

Confidence vs. Shyness

Most children go through a shy phase during the toddler years, and while the majority of them grow out of it over time, it's painful to watch them struggle socially.

There is a big difference between shy and reserved. Quiet children are not necessarily shy. Some are just reserved—they watch what's going on around them, taking it all in. They only join the conversation when they feel they have something of value to add. These children are comfortable around peers but don't feel the need to be the star of the show.

Shy children suffer from social anxiety. They're afraid that everyone is laughing at them and thus try hard to be invisible. They avoid eye contact with strangers and maybe even with people they know, sometimes to the point of always staring at the ground. They have trouble making friends because they don't want to join in the group. Sometimes the shyness is situational. They're comfortable with friends but not strangers.

Causes

Shyness has a host of possible causes, most notably:

- **Learned behavior.** If Mom or Dad is shy, then Junior probably will be, too. There's a genetic predisposition to a timid personality ("nature"), while kids also learn to "hang back" from watching Mom and Dad ("nurture").
- **Low self-esteem.** Are his parents hypercritical? Do they embarrass him in public or in private? Do all statements of praise end in "but"? "I'm glad you got a ninety-five on your test, but you should have gotten a hundred."
- **Isolation.** A child who doesn't often get to interact with others may feel uncomfortable around strangers. Sometimes they feel as though everybody knows the rules but them.
- **Fear.** Children who live with excessive criticism often have many fears: of failure, of the unknown, of being laughed at, of being singled out. Some want to avoid all attention, even good attention.

Coping Strategies

Before you can help conquer your child's shyness, you need to be sure you aren't part of the cause. If you're uncomfortable in social situations, you may as well start practicing these strategies along with your child. Make eye contact, say hello to strangers, shake hands and say "So nice to meet you." Give others a gracious smile, one that says your day is better for having met them. In other words, model confident behavior.

Conversely, the opposite of a timid parent is an overbearing one. Make sure you aren't always speaking for a child who's old enough to speak for himself. It implies you don't think he's capable. And never embarrass or demean him intentionally, especially in public. When you accidentally embarrass him, be sure to apologize.

We recently met a new family at church—a young mother with ten-year-old twin boys. As we were chatting, she started telling a story that was clearly intended to embarrass the boys. She pointed to one and laughed, saying, "Watch his cheeks turn pink." I'm sure she loves her boys, but she doesn't realize how hurtful it is when parents stomp on their children's feelings. I think sometimes we tell "cute" stories about our kids because we don't know what else to say. Better to say nothing than hurt little egos.

If your toddler is always hiding behind you, don't worry—it's fairly normal at that stage. He's starting to realize that he doesn't know what to do, so the safest thing is to do nothing. When my kids were little, I didn't feel completely dressed without a child hanging on to my pant leg.

As they get older and their verbal skills improve, start talking to them about what they're thinking. Help them put words to their feelings: "Is it scary when grown-ups talk to you?" By the way, if the answer to this question is yes, you can help by crouching down to their level when another adult is speaking to them, and by encouraging the other adult to do the same. It's hard being little, surrounded by a forest of grown-ups. In addition, ask *why* it's scary and what you can do to help make it easier.

One of the most effective means of overcoming shyness is to do some role-playing, also known as "let's pretend." It's helpful to have both parents for this, but if you're the only parent around, you can play both roles (the parent and the other adult you'll be introducing Suzie to). Start with baby steps, so to speak. Your shy child is not going to suddenly step forward, make eye contact, and say "Nice to meet you" as she shakes hands. Pretend that someone Suzie knows has just walked up, said "hi" to you, then "hi" to Suzie. See if you can get Suzie to lean out from behind you and say "hi" back. If that's too much at first, see if she can just lean out and smile, or even stick out a hand and give a little finger wave. Let her choose which of these she's most comfortable with, and praise all forward progress—in private, of course. "Mrs. Smith looked happy when you waved at her this morning." Praising her in front of others in this case draws attention to her shyness. The goal is to replace the scary feeling with warm fuzzy ones.

Over time, Suzie can progress from waving to smiling to saying "hi" to actually shaking hands. It's important not to force her into something she's not ready for. It only makes matters worse. In addition, you don't want to label your child ("She's always been shy") because you run the risk of creating a self-fulfilling prophecy.

Often, bashful children are so focused on what others are thinking about them that they don't realize the negative effect their behavior has. Talk about irony. They're afraid people won't like them, so they come across as rude. A conversation I had with our shy child went something like this:

"When someone says hello to you and you ignore them, it hurts their feelings," I said. "When you come running up to me and say 'Hi Mom,' what do I do?"

"You say 'hi' back."

"Okay. Pretend you say 'Hi Mom,' and I just turn my back to you and walk away. How would you feel? You'd probably wonder if I was mad at you. Now pretend we're at the store and you see your friend Tommy. What if you waved and said, 'Hi Tommy,' but Tommy just looked at you and then looked away. Would your feelings be hurt?"

My shy child agreed that being ignored would feel hurtful.

"That's how other people feel when they greet you and you ignore them.

"You're a wonderful kid, and I know you don't want to hurt people's feelings. That's why it's important that we practice saying 'hi' back to people. We'll start by pretending we're meeting someone you know, and later we'll get a friend to help us practice. I'll let you choose who you want to practice with."

As the two of you are practicing (or three of you, if your spouse is helping), you can make it more fun by putting on a silly hat or speaking in a goofy voice every time you play the role of the person Suzie is to say "hi" to. You could even use a puppet to play that person. Getting a kid to smile is the best way to lower their stress level. As Suzie gets older, teach her that she doesn't always have to *be* confident, but it helps to *act* as if she's confident.

> We can't always <u>feel</u> confident, but if we <u>act</u> as if we're confident, people will treat us as though we <u>are</u> confident.

Other strategies for helping a bashful child:

- Foster their self-esteem by encouraging their talents. All kids need to have something they excel at, whether it's art, math, cooking, poetry, storytelling, or even map reading. Having a skill gives them a feeling of accomplishment and a reason to stand a little taller.

  God may have given them a talent that they haven't discovered yet, so your job is to get them to try new things. They won't be good at, or even enjoy, everything, but it can be fun trying.

  When I was a math major in college, I was required to take a computer programming class for graduation. I kept putting it off because I knew nothing about computers (this was back when computers were relatively new), and all my friends told me how hard it was. I finally took the class during the last semester of my senior year and was surprised to find I loved it. I later went back to school to major in computer science. My favorite job ever was teaching high school computer classes, and now I teach adult classes and run the computer lab at a local nonprofit organization. The moral of the story is: it's important to try new things.

- When your children are learning a new skill, remind them of past successes. "Remember how hard you worked to learn to ride your bike? If you can do that, I know you can teach yourself to roller-skate."

- Listen to their fears. *You* know that no one will laugh at them when they draw a picture, but *they* don't know that.

  I think bashful children overreact when adults laugh at their cuteness. We need to remind them often that adults laugh because the child is adorable. When a little one tells us "I wike pasghetti" (I like spaghetti), we can't help but giggle because they're so cute. The outgoing child will think "That was fun" and say it again. The shy child will think "I'm a moron" and go hide.

  When they're fearful, ask them, "What's the worst thing that can happen?" The fear of the unknown can be paralyzing for many of us, adults as well as children, and talking it over with you can put things in perspective. Perhaps your son is afraid to give his oral report because everyone will think he's "dumb." Telling him "Don't be ridiculous" just proves his point: you think that the last thing he said was dumb.

  Instead, you could ask him some questions:

  - *Why will they think you're dumb?*
  - *Do you listen to everyone else's speech? Do you think they're dumb? Why or why not?*
  - *If someone actually told you "That was the dumbest report I ever heard," what could you say back to that person?*
  - *What can we do to help you get through this? Be realistic—the teacher won't let me give your report for you. How about if you practice giving it to me?*
  - *Do you think anybody else is afraid or nervous about giving a report? Maybe you could find someone who is and then make a deal with that person: after class, tell each other "good job!"*

- In new social situations, tell your child you'll stay for a while until she is settled in. The first day of gymnastics class, for example, tell your daughter you'll stay and watch. The second day, you'll stay for half the class, then wave good-bye and wait out in the hall. Keep decreasing the amount of time you're in the room with her until she feels comfortable saying good-bye at the door when you drop her off.

If she refuses to let you leave her sight, don't despair. Eventually she'll get over this clingy stage. No college student (or high school student, for that matter) ever insisted Mom come along to class.

- At parties, whether in your home or someone else's, try to find a task for your cherub. Younger children can circulate a plate of hors d'oeuvres as long as they're tall enough to keep the food out of the dog's reach. Or maybe they could be stationed at the door to ask newcomers to fill out a name tag. Older children can fetch drinks or coffee for guests, or keep an eye on the food trays, refilling them as needed.

  Having a job to do makes kids feel trusted and important. It gives them a safe topic of conversation ("Would you like a meatball?"), and at the same time it keeps the conversation short ("I'd better see if anyone else wants one"). It also allows adults to pay sincere compliments ("It's so nice of you to help out").

- Remind your child that she can choose her attitude. This is her chance to be an actress instead of a drama queen. Being shy is okay; letting it paralyze you is not. If she acts in a confident manner, she'll not only put others at ease, but the others will admire her confidence. I read in a psychology book one time about the benefits of "acting as if." In this case, Suzie will be acting as if she's already confident. It's also known as "fake it until you make it." The theory is that as you get in the habit of projecting confidence, over time you actually feel more confident. You become the person you were pretending to be.

  We've all seen speakers who look terrified. As they stumble through their speeches, voices quivering, we feel our own heart rate increasing. We literally feel for these speakers. It's hard to focus on their message—we just want them to be done. When they finally finish, we're relieved.

  Let's say that speaker is followed by one who is just the opposite. This next speaker appears calm and self-assured, smiling and making eye contact with the audience. We'd much rather listen to this person because we can relax and focus on what he's saying.

This holds true not just for public speaking but for most social interactions as well. We gravitate toward people who look at ease and happy. Better to pretend to be at ease than appear genuinely frightened.

- Teach them to focus on putting others at ease. Your daughter won't be the only bashful child in her class or at the birthday party. Help her practice some conversation starters for when she finds someone to chat with.
    - *What's your favorite kind of cake?*
    - *How's the punch?*
    - *That's a really cute top. Where'd you get it?*
    (For more conversation starters, see Chapter 8.)

    Starting a conversation with a sincere compliment usually puts the other person at ease and makes you sound like a nice person to hang out with. Clearly you have great taste since you like her dress, or whatever. Saying something positive about a third person has the same effect. ("Mary Jane has a nice house," or "That guy is a great skateboarder."). Putting people down may lift our spirits by making us feel superior but doesn't win us many friends. We need to remind children to focus on the positive things in life.

- Have your child invite a friend over for a specific activity. This gives her the home-turf advantage; she'll be more relaxed in her own house, with you nearby. Having an activity planned eases the burden of conversation, creates an opportunity to bond, and provides a specific time frame for the day. If she isn't having fun, at least she knows it'll be over at four o'clock when her friend goes home. If things go well, the kids can arrange to do it again.

    Some ideas: watch a video (G-rated, I hope), bake and decorate cookies, play basketball, build a model house using all the Legos, or make a bunch of flowers out of tissues or round coffee filters and decorate a room with them.

Dealing with Disappointment and Frustration

Too many parents want to shield children from negative emotions. I know this because I was one of those parents. I never wanted my boys to be unhappy. How realistic is that? Then one day I was chatting with a friend at the high school where I taught. She was waiting for her daughter to finish cheerleading tryouts. I told her I was glad I didn't have a daughter because I didn't think I could handle cheerleading tryouts. "What if she doesn't get picked?" I asked. "What do you do?"

Nancy said, "Learning to deal with disappointment is an important part of life. If she doesn't make the squad, I'll hug her and remind her of all the things she's good at. I'll be sad with her for a day or two, then help her move on." What great advice.

Too many parents want to shield children from negative emotions.

We never want to ignore our child's feelings. Losing a boyfriend or not making the team can feel like the end of the world to kids, and they need to know that we understand their pain. Even the captain of the football team needs hugs from Mom and Dad now and then. Adults have experienced many disappointments over the years, but these feelings are new to our children. We have to help them learn to cope, and the first step is critical: validate their feelings. "I know it hurts, sweetie."

The second step, of course, is to help them deal with those feelings. There are always at least two choices: dwell on the pain until they are swimming in a pool of anger and despair, or find a bright side to focus on.

I liked Nancy's advice about being sad with her daughter for just a day or two. Some people want to hang on to the hurt forever, which just isn't healthy. If your child has trouble letting go, ask her how long she plans to stay upset. A week? A month? A year? Until she's thirty? Help her put the pain in perspective and allow a reasonable amount of time for the "pity party." Talk about ways to move on. With small children, empathize with them and then play the "I wish" game. "I wish your best friend could live next door to us instead of clear across town" or "I wish we could go to Disneyland every single day." This validates their feelings and lets them know you're on their side.

Sometimes it's helpful to take the approach that it could always be worse:

- I know you're not happy that we're moving to Florida (or wherever), but at least we're not moving to Antarctica. They *will* have a mall where we're going.
- I know you're disappointed that you got the flu the day before the band concert that you practiced so hard for. At least you didn't get the flu during the concert. You might have thrown up in front of the whole school.

Of course, you'll want to do this exercise after you've validated their feelings; otherwise, it sounds like you're insensitive.

Small children have a harder time choosing their attitude because they don't have the vocabulary to express themselves. They throw tantrums so that we will know how terribly upset they are. If we don't acknowledge their feelings, the tantrum may go on for some time. It helps to teach them words to describe their feelings.

In addition to disappointment, frustration is a part of life, yet the inability to deal with it is a major problem in our society. Frustration often leads to anger: we can't have our way, so we get even by throwing some sort of tantrum, or worse. It can involve something as trivial as a friend not answering their phone or as earthshaking as an insurance company refusing to pay for lifesaving treatment. Causes include:

- Physical limitations
    - *Little fingers unable to tie a shoelace*
    - *Bad cell phone reception*
    - *The inability to verbalize what's bothering them*
- Interpersonal conflict

- A team member in an important class project who isn't doing any work
- A friend who always makes plans to meet but then cancels at the last minute
- A friend who was told something in private but made it public on the Internet

- Unrealistic expectations, also known as the "should" or "It's not fair" mentality
  - I should have gotten an A on that paper.
  - All my friends get a Mercedes for their sixteenth birthday, and I should, too.
  - I really want to go on the field trip, but I forgot to turn in the permission slip on time. The teacher should let me go anyway.
  - My older sister gets to stay up until nine o'clock. I should, too.
  - My little brother should have to do as many chores as I do.

There are several methods for helping children cope with frustration. First, have them stop and take a deep breath or two to calm down. Chanting "In with the good air, out with the bad" may get a smile out of them. Acknowledge what they're feeling and then help adjust their attitude:

- Can you take a different approach? If you can't rearrange the furniture by yourself, is there someone around who can help? If cleaning the room seems overwhelming, can you break it into parts?
- Are your expectations realistic? Do you really think your parents should provide alcohol for your party?
- Do you need to change your attitude? Instead of "I hate cleaning my room every week," try "I sure like having a clean room and being able to find the things I need." Instead of "I hate putting all this stuff away," try "I'm grateful for my stuff."

Dealing with Teasing and Bullying

My mind-set has always been that teasing is bad, period—probably because I grew up in a house where people teased unmercifully. There are two types of teasing, however: the good-natured kidding we engage in with close friends, and the mean-spirited type that can leave emotional scars on little egos.

Friendly Teasing

Many child psychologists see this type of interaction as a bonding experience. We all know that when a little boy punches a girl's shoulder or pulls her hair, it means he likes her. The same goes for gentle teasing. Children kid around when they feel safe with someone.

Occasionally someone will cross a line and offend another person unintentionally. When that happens, the victim can reply simply with "You teased too hard" or "You hurt my feelings." We need to teach our children to stand up for themselves. As Dr. Phil says, we teach people how to treat us. If your child is the one who has caused the offense, she needs to take responsibility for it. Just as with physical roughhousing, <u>kids need to stop and apologize when someone gets hurt.</u>

Sometimes it's hard for children to know where the line is. If little brother is sensitive about his height, calling him Shorty crosses the line. If sister has a weight problem, teasing her about it will surely produce tears. The rule of thumb is, never tease anyone about something they can't change in the next ten minutes. Height, weight, glasses, handicaps, and so forth are all off-limits. Conversely, if your child seems hypersensitive when teased, <u>help him understand that it's okay to laugh at himself</u>. Don't forget to model this attitude as well.

Mean-Spirited Teasing

This type of teasing is a form of bullying. It's a deliberate intent to cause fear or psychological harm.

A child bullies because:

- He feels inferior. Putting others down says "See, you're even worse off than I am."
- She's unhappy. Misery loves company, so let's make others just as unhappy.
- He wants to fit in or appear "cool." If teasing another child gets a laugh from his friends, that's a pretty powerful reward. He probably knows bullying is wrong, but the need to fit in overrides those guilt feelings.
- She doesn't understand the concept of "teasing too hard."
- He is being bullied by someone else in his life, possibly a sibling or someone at school.

I point out these reasons in case your child is ever accused of bullying. By determining the underlying reason, you'll be better able to correct the problem.

If you learn that your child has been teasing someone, talk to him about empathy:

- "Why were you teasing Mary?"
- "How do you think Mary felt when you teased her?"
- "If you were Mary, what would you tell the kids who were teasing you?"

If that doesn't seem to be getting through to your child, you may want to seek the help of a counselor to address the problem. See also Chapter 9 for tips on dealing with bullies.

An Attitude of Gratitude

Busy parents tend to do more and buy more stuff for their kids than necessary, out of guilt. They ask little of their children, either because of a mistaken need to be Super Parent or because they feel that they, the adults, give little to their family. "I can't ask the kids to clean their rooms if I never clean mine." "We'll use paper plates since we never have time to do dishes." "I missed Chelsea's birthday, so I'd better buy her plenty of gifts." "I can't make it to the soccer playoffs, so I'll pick up that new MP3 player she's been wanting." This parental behavior is especially prevalent in a divorce environment.

When you add a lack of discipline to the mix, you get kids who have an overwhelming sense of entitlement. They've grown up expecting to receive all the toys and gadgets everyone else has. They know they don't have to help around the house because Mom and Dad won't make them. They go off to school knowing they needn't worry about classroom rules because there are no rules at home. In extreme cases, they feel they should get everything they want in life, that the world "owes" them.

Make a habit of counting your blessings.

We all do things for our children because we love them, and that's the way it should be. We must be careful, however, not to let it get one-sided. When adults do all the giving, it means the kids do all the taking. That's fine for newborns, not teenagers. Children gradually need to learn to be loving, giving adults. You provide food, shelter, clothing, and transportation; toys and spending money are privileges. Kids need to acknowledge what's done for them and give back without complaining. Each family member is part of the team. The answer to "Why do I have to do this chore?" is "Because you're a member of this family, and we all need to work together as a team."

Gratitude is more than just returning favors, however. It's giving heartfelt thanks for everything you have. There are millions of people in the world who are grateful to get a piece of bread for lunch. Surely our kids can be grateful for their cell phones, computers, cars, and TVs. I personally am especially grateful for my car. I'm so happy to know that if I need to run to the store, I don't have to spend an hour hitching horses to a wagon first.

A friend of mine is a social worker, married to a very successful accountant. Their children rarely went without anything they wanted, and Maggie made sure they stayed aware of how fortunate they were. Every now and then, when the "gimmies" got out of hand, she piled them in the car and they spent the day volunteering at a homeless shelter. The first time they went, her children were shocked to learn there were people in their own community without a place to live, without anywhere to put their stuff, and without any stuff, for that matter. The kids immediately realized how much they had to be thankful for—especially when Maggie threatened to donate all nonessential stuff to the thrift store.

One way to foster gratitude is to make a habit of counting your blessings. Some families do this every Thanksgiving, but families with thankful hearts do it weekly or even daily. One family I know started a list of all their blessings, beginning with the names of their children. They put the list up in the family room and go over it regularly. Every family member is encouraged to add to it, and visitors enjoy reading it as well. They joke about it being their favorite wallpaper.

As you're counting your blessings, don't forget to thank the One who provides it all. Daily prayers should start with "Thank you for…" continue with "Forgive me for…," and only then end with "I need help with…" Another way to think of it is to remember the mnemonic ACTS:

Adoration, **C**onfession, **T**hankfulness, **S**upplication.

Another step in the process is to say thank you to people whenever you can, especially to strangers. It makes people feel appreciated and makes the world a nicer place. Thank the person who cleans the restrooms where you work or shop. When you get a traffic ticket, thank the officer for making your city a safer place. When you see a celebrity, instead of asking for an autograph, simply tell them how much you enjoy their work.

The Power of Forgiveness

When I was growing up, I was taught that when someone said "I'm sorry," I should respond with "It's okay." This created a lot of confusion in my little brain, because even though the other person was sorry, what they did really *wasn't* okay. In a way, I felt as though I was giving permission for that person to do it again. Needless to say, I rarely could forgive anyone. It wasn't until the last few years that I've come to realize that forgiveness is not about saying "It's okay."

Forgiveness is generally defined as the process of letting go of resentment or anger, and ceasing to desire punishment or restitution. It's a lofty goal, so how do you actually achieve it, much less teach it to children? Some will say you just let go of the hurtful incident. Some think of it as turning the incident over to God to do the punishing. We still may want revenge, but we'll let God take care of it for us. Others adopt Christ's attitude as He was dying on the cross: He asked God to forgive those who had hurt Him, because they were acting out of ignorance.

People who say they can't let something go often mean they don't *want* to let it go. Righteous indignation is a powerful emotion. When you don't forgive someone, however, you put yourself in a prison of sorts. Whenever you think of the incident, you get angry, vengeful, resentful, and bitter. That's a lot of negative energy! All that anger works to create some harmful physiological reactions. According to recent research on the subject, unforgiveness can cause increased blood pressure and hormonal changes, which, in turn, can contribute to both cardiovascular disease and lessened immunity.

When you choose to forgive someone, you are, in reality, setting yourself free. You let go of all the anger and negative energy. You're not saying what happened is okay, you're just choosing not to let it control you. You can choose your attitude. Instead of continuing to fret over the incident, you acknowledge that we all make mistakes—it's part of being human. Even when someone wrongs us intentionally, we can forgive him because he hasn't learned yet to be a nice person. He acted out of ignorance.

In other words, forgiveness is something we do for ourselves as much as for our offender. We choose peace instead of ongoing hostility. We choose not to live in the role of a victim. It doesn't mean we condone what happened, allow the abuse to continue, or that we should forget about it. It doesn't mean the wrongdoer should not be punished if the situation calls for it. It *does* mean we can stop plotting our revenge and get on with our life.

> Forgiveness is something we do for ourselves as much as for our offender.

LIKABILITY

I've often thought that one of the critical skills parents should teach is likability. Difficult, rude, and arrogant people just make life harder on themselves. Difficult students are judged more harshly by teachers and administrators, and often don't do as well academically as they could. This is partly because teachers are unlikely to ever give them the benefit of the doubt and partly because arrogant students often feel entitled to better grades than they actually earned.

Unlikable youngsters generally grow up to be unlikable adults. They have trouble making and keeping friends, and may find it hard to get hired. They may lose one or more jobs because they're not team players. They're destined to have marital problems. None of this describes the future that parents would choose for their child.

Likability is not the same as popularity. Popularity generally refers to your peer group. Often it's the "cool" kids who are popular, and while a popular student may be likable, it's not always the case.

Likable people get along with other people, even with the difficult ones. Their lives are easier because they're not fighting with everyone.

Components of Likability

- **A cheerful attitude.** Remember, you can choose your attitude, so choose a good one.
- **Respect for others.** This means genuine respect for the rights and feelings of others, not just telling people what they want to hear.
- **Trustworthiness.** Telling the truth is part of this. It's hard to trust someone who's lied to you in the past. Children need to understand that once they lose your trust, it takes a long time to regain it. The other part of keeping their word is follow-through. If they say they're going to do something, they need to do it in a timely manner. We used to call one of our boys "Will" because whenever we asked him to do something, he always said "I will" but never took any action. Offering him reminders only made him more emphatic. ("I *will!*") We finally learned to give him a deadline and impose consequences for noncompliance.
- **Helpfulness.** It always lifts our spirits when someone offers to help with a chore. Helpfulness, along with manners, makes the world a better place.
- **Consideration of others.** One of the hardest parts of growing up is learning to be other-centered instead of self-centered. Taking turns with toys is a great start but needs to be carried over into adulthood. One child may really want to try the new sushi restaurant. The other child hates sushi but realizes he can probably find something he will eat on the menu. If you do the math, you'll realize that not everyone can have his way all the time.
- **Humbleness.** No one likes a braggart.

The bonus to teaching kids to be likable is that *you* will like them more, too.

Creativity is an important component
of education—it teaches children
to think for themselves.

People are about as happy as they
make up their minds to be.
— Abraham Lincoln

Chapter 3

Education

Parents can't always model education—you can't change your background—but all parents must sell their children on the *importance* of education. In other words, model a positive, enthusiastic attitude. Start when they're young with comments like "*When* you go to college" instead of "*If* you go to college." Not every young adult goes to college, of course, but in today's world, everyone needs some postsecondary education. A high school diploma is a great start, but acquiring a specific skill set is even better. "When you go to college" includes trade schools, apprenticeships, and the like. Having more knowledge and skill translates into more options and opportunities. Knowledge is power.

Knowledge is power.

I teach computer classes at a local nonprofit that helps women get better jobs. Many of our clients are newly divorced with no marketable skills. I'm happy to teach them all I know about computers, but for some of them, bad grammar and spelling have become lifelong habits. No one encouraged them to learn and use proper English when they were younger, and now when they go to a job interview, they're facing a serious disadvantage. Any sort of office, sales, or customer service job will be out of their reach. Men and women alike need the best possible education and skill sets.

Babies are born learners. They have to be—they pop out knowing absolutely nothing. In their first three years, they learn to sit up, crawl, stand, walk, run, throw a ball, and even begin to learn a foreign (to them) language. Pretty impressive. Even more impressive is that they learned it all just by watching the people around them. Their motivation is partly extrinsic—we smile and clap when they learn something new—but is primarily intrinsic. They take pleasure in their own accomplishments.

This enthusiasm for learning continues as they enter school, but some children seem to lose that joy of learning over time. I've had many students over the years who had, it seemed, no internal motivation. They did just enough to keep Mom and Dad off their case. If the parents were happy with a D, then the student would do exactly enough work to get a D.

I admit I was an underachiever in high school, which drove my parents crazy since my father was a teacher. I just couldn't see the point in learning about something that held no interest for me. Things improved slightly in college, where I got to choose my courses, but without a tangible goal, other than graduating, my grades were still in the so-so category. After graduation I decided I wanted to be a teacher. I returned to school with a purpose and graduated with a 4.0 grade point average. I had a goal, and I knew that the school districts I applied to would be looking at my grades before they hired me. The point is that internal motivation (my desire to get a job) is much more powerful than external (pressure from my parents).

So how do parents get their children to motivate themselves? We start by:

- Overcoming their resistance to schoolwork.
- Making education meaningful to them—have them read and write about things that interest them.
- Selling them on the benefits of education.
- Giving them a safe environment emotionally, both in school and at home. Many students quit trying because they're afraid of looking stupid. Others feel that no matter how well they do, it's not good enough.

- Encouraging their efforts.
- Fostering pride in a job well done.
- Modeling continued learning.

Resistance

Resistance to schoolwork comes in a variety of standard complaints. Have your responses ready:

- **"It's hard."** Your answer: "So is digging ditches or busing tables." I had a student in a seventh-grade math class who couldn't be bothered to learn any math facts. Mike could add, but subtraction, multiplication, and division were just too much for him. It wasn't that he wasn't capable; he just didn't want to clutter his brain. Mike was a child who was raising himself. He was living with a father who was more interested in going out partying every night than checking his son's homework. I sat Mike down and explained, "If you don't learn math now, you're going to struggle all through school. If you don't learn math, the only job you'll be able to get is cleaning the elephant cages at the zoo, which is fine if you're okay with that. There's no dishonor in an honest day's work. If that's not the job you had in mind, however, then you need to buckle down.

    "Also, if you don't learn to multiply, you'll never know if your boss is cheating you, because you won't be able to figure out your pay."

    That got his attention, and his skills improved for a while. But without support at home, he fell back into his old habits.

- **"I don't like the teacher."** Your answer: "As you go through life, there will be many people in authority you don't like. Now's a good time to learn to cope." Some students seem to have the attitude, "I'll show that teacher. I'm not doing her stinkin' homework." Funny thing—teachers get paid no matter what you do. If you really want to punish a teacher, do the homework. That's one more paper she has to read, grade, record, and return. Remind your student, "Education is something you do for yourself. The only person in control of your grade is you. You don't have to like the teacher (you're never going to like all your teachers), but you owe it to yourself to learn as much as you can."

- **"I don't like the subject."** Your answer: "You're never going to like every subject, but you do need to do your best. How can we make this subject more appealing?"

  Here's a suggestion: relate the subject to something your child does like. Many classes require some sort of project or term paper. If your son likes science more than English, do a report on a famous scientist. If he likes history more than math, put together a timeline of math discoveries. If he'd rather be in art than computer class, have him do a PhotoShop or Paint Shop project; both are graphic editing programs and can be lots of fun. Talk to his teacher, who may have other ideas.

- **"I don't feel like doing homework."** Your answer: "It's a rule—you have to finish all homework and study for all tests and quizzes."

  In our house, we had a "no TV during the week" rule during the junior high and high school years, and each of my sons was required to spend a certain amount of time every day studying, based on his age. The studying could include doing homework, but if they didn't have any assignments to finish, they still had to study for tests.

  One of their favorite excuses was, "I only need to study the day before the test. If I study earlier than that I'll forget it." I'd respond with, "What's two plus three? You learned that years ago and you still remember it. Go study."

  There's a reason that many classes spend the first month or so of every school year reviewing things learned in previous years. The more often we go over something, the better it sticks in our brain.

- **"It's boring."** Your answer: "Let's find ways to connect it to something you're interested in."

SNEAKINESS

Often kids get tired of the homework/study arguments and just start telling parents that "everything is fine." Their grades are fine, and they have no homework. This works until report cards come out. Then the yelling starts. "You're getting a D in math? You said you were doing fine!"

My husband and I are very familiar with this scenario. That's when we instituted the mandatory two hours of studying rule. We also required our not-so-fine student to bring home a sheet signed by his teachers each Friday stating his current grade, test scores if any, and whether any assignments were missing. If he forgot the sheet, or his grades were unsatisfactory, he was grounded for the weekend. If there were assignments missing, he was grounded until he finished them. <u>Even if his teacher didn't accept late assignments, they still had to be completed. This helped motivate the offender to get the assignment done on time.</u> If you have to do the work anyway, you might as well get the credit.

If you start using the weekly progress report at the end of the chapter, you'll have to help your child remember the first few Fridays. Write it on the calendar, post a note by the door, or put a sticky note on his notebook(s). Ultimately, however, it has to be his responsibility. He's lost a little of your trust, and he'll have to earn it back.

HOW TO SELL THE IMPORTANCE OF EDUCATION

One of my early jobs was selling real estate. Later, when I started teaching, I realized that having a background in sales came in handy when dealing with kids. Instead of trying to *make* students do things, it's more effective to show them *why* those things will benefit them. This sometimes takes a little creativity, but it's much easier than engaging in a power struggle over behavior.

Some things for you to discuss with them:
- Where do you see yourself after high school? After college?
- What do you want to be when you grow up? How do you plan to get there?

- Homework is not busywork. In addition to helping you learn a concept, it teaches time management, research, and organizational skills.
- The reason teachers assign homework is so you don't have to stay in school an extra two or three hours each day. Wouldn't you rather come home and have a snack while you do the work?
- Grades are a reflection of not only how much you've learned, but also how motivated and ambitious you are. This is one of the major reasons colleges look closely at your grades.
- If two job applicants seem equally qualified, but one has better grades, which one will get hired?

I used to ask my students, "What if I told you I had a free cell phone for you. Would you take it?" That got their attention. "How about a free car or computer?" Now they were fully focused on me. "What if I said I have something even better: a free education. Would you take it?" This usually started a discussion about whether or not school was lame or boring, at which point I would steer them toward thinking about their future. Most kids can't plan for anything past this weekend. Getting married and supporting a family seems light-years away.

Education is something you do for yourself.

How to Motivate Students

Ideally, we want our children to be self-motivated and to believe that learning is a lifelong process. Parents can do a few things toward that goal:
- Give him choices as to how, when, or where (not *if*) he wants to study. Before or after dinner? Longest assignment first or

hardest first? When kids have some ownership in the process, they feel more empowered.
- Lead by example. Learn a new skill or take a class in something that interests you. Model lifelong learning.
- Don't distract your child. If you're watching TV during your son's study time, you can be sure he's trying to listen instead of study.
- Make sure your child doesn't have a fear of failure. Tell him, "If others can do it, you can, too. We don't expect perfection, but we do expect your best effort."
- Teach your children that mistakes are opportunities to learn and grow—not reasons to laugh, punish, or ridicule. Dwelling on the mistakes children make pretty much guarantees they'll quit trying. Much better to ask them "What did you learn?" The most famous example is Thomas Edison. It's said that he tried and failed as many as 10,000 times when working on the electric light bulb. When asked, he commented that he hadn't failed 10,000 times, rather he had learned that many different ways to *not* make a light bulb.

Internal Motivators

- Point out their past successes and how good they felt afterward. "You got a B+ on your last science project. Remember how proud you were?"
- Encourage her passions, whether it's horses, skateboarding, or drawing. Buy books and magazines on the subject to encourage her to read, or go to the library regularly. Learn about something new together. Having a common interest creates a powerful bond between you.

There's a well-known guide for teachers called *The Master Teacher*. It contains a list of motivators that work for adults as well as children:

1. **Personal gain**. (What's in it for me?) This is where you sell the benefits of a given task, which may take some thought on your part. For example, "The better your grades, the better your chances of getting a scholarship so you don't have to work during college." Or "If you study sixty minutes instead of thirty, you'll do even better on that test. Won't it feel good when you get that A?"

2. **Prestige**. (The desire to do something valued.) This is why children plan on being rock stars or basketball players when they grow up. It's not just the fortune, it's the fame. Sadly, few children aspire to be famous historians, so this motivator probably won't get your child to study for her test on ancient civilizations.

3. **Pleasure**. Doing something pleasurable releases chemicals in the brain called endorphins. When we do something pleasurable, the endorphins cause us to want to repeat that activity.

    The physiology of addiction is a similar process, so why not use that to our advantage? Let's get kids addicted to doing well. When they're successful on a test, project, or even a homework assignment, telling them you're proud is a great start, but proud parents are an external reward. Better to focus on the pleasure they get from being successful. "I bet you feel great about that. You worked hard, and it paid off. Do you think you'd do it again?" Explain that doing the work isn't as much fun, so while working we need to focus on how happy we'll be when we're done and how pleased we'll be with the result. Once they understand the process, they can use it to their own advantage.

    As a side note, if you have a child with an addiction—eating, smoking, gambling—part of the treatment is to replace the endorphin rush from the addictive behavior with some other pleasure-inducing behavior. Art, music, sports, and even reading for pleasure are all happy activities that can help rewire the brain. That's why people who quit smoking often gain weight. They've replace one endorphin source (tobacco) with another (food).

4. **Security**. For some people, especially women, this can be their strongest motivator. The better you do in school, the better your chances of getting a good job later on. Everyone—boys and girls, men and women—will need to support themselves at some point.

5. **Convenience**. When given a choice, most of us will follow the path of least resistance. That's why kids kick dirty laundry under the bed instead of gathering it up and carrying it to the hamper in the bathroom. If we can make studying convenient, it's one less excuse to avoid doing it. If possible, set up an area with paper, pens, a dictionary, etc. Hang up artwork and outstanding papers to make it a happy place. Having everything they need in one spot makes it convenient to get started.

6. **Imitation**. We all have a desire to be like others; it goes along with our desire to fit in. If your children see you taking classes or just learning something on your own, they're likely to imitate your example. Conversely, if their friends are all dropouts, they may want to take the easy road and imitate their friends.

7. **Fear avoidance**. "If I flunk this class, my parents will kill me!" It's good for children to know that certain behaviors will absolutely not be tolerated. Speeding, texting while driving, illegal activities, and failing a class because of lack of effort will all incur swift, severe penalties.

8. **New experiences**. For most of us, trying new things can be fun. Field trips, educational games, and educational toys can all motivate children.

9. **Love**. Some psychologists contend that the most basic human needs are food, water, air, and love. Rewarding kids with hugs and kisses can be more effective than toys or food, and certainly better for them.

Deborah Stipek, PhD, dean of the Stanford University School of Education, is coauthor of the book *Motivated Minds: Raising Children to Love Learning*. According to Dr. Stipek, children will pay more attention to their parents' guidance if they feel loved and respected by their parents.

Potential External Motivators

As your child is learning to motivate herself, it doesn't hurt to offer external rewards as well. The nature of the reward depends on what motivates your student. But I'd strongly recommend against using food, especially sweets, as a reward, though. It can only lead to unhealthy eating habits and potential weight problems down the road.

- Spend time with them. What child doesn't want Mom's and Dad's attention? "As soon as your paper is done, we'll go to the park or play cards." Or "Let's go to the library together."
- Encourage and praise their efforts. Offer respect. "That project took a long time. I really respect you for putting in the effort."
- Pay them for grades. Okay, this one is admittedly controversial. There's a large group of child psychologists who feel children should never be paid for grades, but I have to say it worked for two of our boys. My rationale was that school was their primary job, and if they did well they deserved a reward. If I had it to do over, however, I'd focus more on the intrinsic rewards listed above.
- Hugs and kisses, smiles and saying "I love you" are always great rewards.

Learning Styles

There are three basic learning styles—visual, auditory, and kinesthetic. While most of us use a combination of styles, we tend favor one over the others. Children frequently have a different learning style than their parents, so you can't assume that because you're an auditory learner, your child will be as well. There are several websites designed to help you determine your child's style (as well as your own). See the resources page at the end of the book. Below is a brief summary of the characteristics of each:

1. *Visual learners usually:*
- Learn by watching

- Take detailed notes
- Like to see illustrations and diagrams
- Like books with descriptive phrases so they can picture the scene
- Enjoy reading
- Look for something to watch when bored
- May have trouble focusing during a lecture

You can help your visual learner by:
- Encouraging note taking
- Using visual metaphors and analogies
- Using flash cards
- Having them draw pictures, even if they're not "artistic"

2. *Auditory learners usually:*
- Learn best by hearing the information
- Benefit from reading aloud
- Hum or talk to themselves or others when bored
- May have trouble with maps or diagrams
- Do well in classes that are primarily lecture

You can help your auditory learner by:
- Having them read their notes to you
- Encouraging reading textbooks aloud
- Having them make up songs to remember things
- Having them explain concepts to you in their own words

3. *Kinesthetic or tactile learners usually:*
- Talk with their hands
- Prefer to learn by doing rather than by lecture or reading instructions

- Need to be active and to take frequent breaks
- Like to explore
- Like to handle things to find out how they work
- May have trouble in a traditional school environment, where they are expected to sit still and listen

You can help your kinesthetic learner by:
- Encouraging movement while studying at home
- Having them act out things when possible
- Encouraging them to type their notes on the computer
- Suggesting they stand while working, say at a counter

By the time children get to middle school, their favored learning style will become apparent. Talk to them about how they remember things, using the above guide. Once you determine their style, you can use that information to help them learn more efficiently.

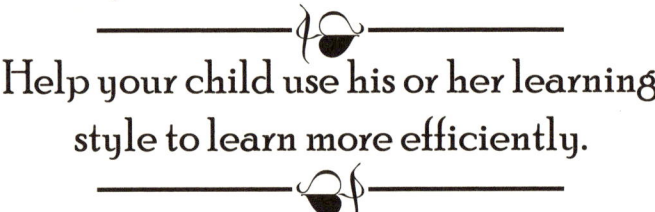

Help your child use his or her learning style to learn more efficiently.

A friend of mine was telling me about her first grader who had a mild learning disability. He just couldn't seem to remember the alphabet. I suggested she cut out letters from fine sandpaper or soft fuzzy fabric, and have him trace the letters with his finger as he said them aloud. Another method would be to write the letters in some sand or paint them on the sidewalk with water. Sometimes, especially for elementary students, combining all three styles helps concepts "stick" better.

Studies vary, but only about 20 to 30 percent of students are auditory learners, yet the majority of junior high and high school classes are delivered by lecture. When asked, most students feel they don't need to take notes because they're certain they'll remember everything that was said in class. About 70 percent of them are wrong. I always insist my students take notes, because I know the information has to pass through their brain between their ears and their fingers. Taking notes involves all three styles: listening (auditory), writing (kinesthetic), and later reading what was written (visual).

My personal style is primarily visual. If you tell me something, I'll probably forget it unless I write it down. If I forget my grocery list when I go to the store, I can still "see" most of it in my head. My boys eventually learned that it was useless to *tell* me what they needed from the store. When they'd say we were out of toothpaste, I'd just look at them and ask, "What should you do?" They'd sigh loudly and go put it on the list.

As mentioned earlier, many students benefit from combining learning styles. Students who make up songs to remember things may also dance while they sing to themselves, thereby combining the auditory and kinesthetic. Talk to your child about what seems to work best and brainstorm ideas to use that to their advantage.

How to Help Them Succeed in School

Besides taking advantage of their learning style, you can assist your little ones in other ways:

- Read to them. A love of learning starts with reading to your children. They get to spend time with you (probably snuggled on your lap), and you're stretching their imagination with every story. You're also able to teach them valuable social lessons without preaching, since many children's books offer a moral of some sort.
- When you read to them, make it more fun by substituting in their name for the main character. Instead of "Fancy Nancy," I read "Fancy Hannah" to my granddaughter. We giggled a lot.
- As they learn to read, you can have them read to you, if it doesn't put you to sleep. (Most of the stories our boys read to

me ended with "Mom! Wake up!" followed by me leaping to my feet.)

- Show enthusiasm for her interests and activities. Go to her recitals, school plays, and soccer games. Spot-check homework; help set goals and deadlines for projects. Not long ago, the motto of the National PTA was "Parents who care have children who care." In other words, if we want school to be important to our children, we must show them it's important to us.

- Encourage him to do the hardest assignment first. He'll be relatively fresh, and he'll get it out of the way.

- Encourage persistence. We can't always solve a problem on the first try. I remember when I took geometry and had to prove theorems. If I couldn't get from the premise to the conclusion, I'd work backward from the conclusion to the premise, with pretty good success. In my computer classes, I tell my clients, "Never let the inanimate object (the computer) win."

- Help them connect new facts to old. Most of us learn a new skill or factoid by relating it to something we're already familiar with. For example, when learning multiplication, tell them "times" means "groups of." In other words, 3 x 4 means three groups of four, or 4 + 4 + 4. Similarly, computer programming is like writing a recipe: you need to list all the steps in a logical order.

- Have them evaluate their own work. "How do you think you did on that math worksheet? Can you check your answers?" Or "How do you think you did on your report? Were you thorough? Can you add anything to it?"

- Get to know their teacher(s) and stay in touch. Encourage teachers to let you know early if there are any problems. In addition, you should let them know if anything unusual is happening at home—divorce, parental long-term illness, death of a pet, etc. These things affect your student's ability to concentrate and require extra compassion from the teacher.

- Help them get organized (see page 63).

- For math and science struggles, have your student explain the process to you step-by-step. Even if you have no idea how to factor polynomials or balance chemical equations, when children verbalize the steps, it helps them focus. When they get to the part that confuses them, you can help them look through the book and their notes for helpful clues. If that doesn't work, at least they will have talked about it enough to be able to ask a specific question the next day in class. Often students are too confused to even formulate a question, so this process helps to clarify things.
- Avoid doing projects for them or helping too much. Offering suggestions for improvement is fine; rewriting their term paper is not. It's natural to want to help them do better, but being overcritical or taking over the project makes them feel incompetent.

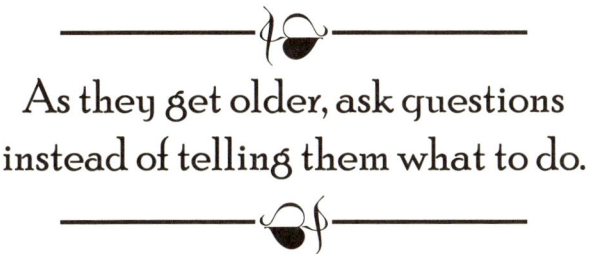

As they get older, ask questions instead of telling them what to do.

- As they get older, ask questions instead of telling them what to do. This allows you to guide their thought process while respecting their ability to solve problems. It teaches them that their opinions are valuable. Telling them what to do implies you don't think they can figure it out on their own. Even if you don't think they can, they deserve the opportunity to try. For example, your teen wants to go to Europe for a month this summer. Instead of starting—and ending—the conversation with "Don't be ridiculous," ask a few questions. "How much will it cost? Does that include food and lodging? How about transportation across Europe? Where will you stay?" Of course, you'll ask these questions in a thoughtful, helpful fashion, not in your "Don't be ridiculous" tone of voice.

This is not an easy thing for parents to learn. (I'm still learning.) We've been dictating what to do and how to do it since they were toddlers; it's hard to give that up. After all, we're older and wiser than they are. One of your parental goals, however, is to teach them to think for themselves. They will make mistakes and learn from those mistakes.

Oftentimes students have one subject that's a struggle for them. Even when they want to do well, the facts don't seem to stick in their head. Remind them that some of us have to study more than others. I might have to study something three hours while my friend only has to spend one hour. But, in the end, we both know the same material. Equally important is the fact that everyone has different talents. I may struggle with history, but I'm good at computers. Instead of dwelling on my weaknesses ("I'm so stupid—I'll never learn these dates"), I remind myself of my strengths ("I'm a whiz at computers—maybe I'll enter these dates into a spreadsheet of important events").

Study Skills

Good study habits are essential for students to succeed academically, yet learning them is usually hit or miss. Some teachers discuss study habits with their classes at the start of the year, but since most studying actually occurs at home, it's really up to the parents.

Many students believe that grades are purely a matter of luck. They think other students get good grades because they're lucky. Some believe that their classmates do well because they're smarter. The reality is that there will always be someone smarter than them. There's no point in dwelling on the fact; they need to do whatever it takes to learn the material.

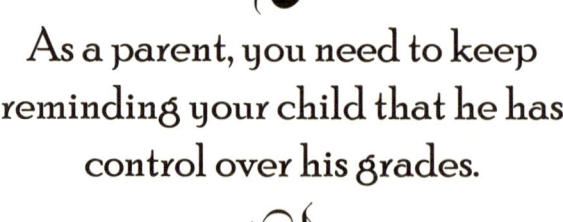

As a parent, you need to keep reminding your child that he has control over his grades.

Chapter 3: *Education*   63

As a parent, you need to keep reminding your child that he has control over his grades. You also need to provide the tools and skills to be successful. The tools he needs are:

- **A quiet place to spread out.** The kitchen table is great, especially if you're nearby for company and moral support. A desk in his room is fine as well, but you may need to peek in now and then, to be sure he stays on task. You'll also need to be sure all distractions—cell phone, TV, computer, etc.—are removed.
- **Supplies.** Pens, paper, a notebook with dividers, a calendar, highlighters, etc.

The skills he'll need to be successful in school include organization, time management, note taking in class, note taking from books, preparing for a test, and goal setting.

Organization

There are two parts to the organizational process. The first is to have a plan: a place for everything and everything in its place. The second part is taking the time to execute the plan.

Teaching organization can begin early. For small children, start with a toy box or canvas bag plus a dresser or shelves for clothing. If they can walk, they can put toys in a container. Anytime you put toys away, they can be encouraged to help. When putting clothes away, you can describe to little ones what you're doing: "Shirts go in the bottom drawer, pants go in the next drawer up." As they get older and acquire more stuff, a shelf unit and corkboard can provide display space. When those get full, it's time to downsize, which is a large part of staying organized.

As collections grow, baskets or plastic containers are useful for sorting things by type, and they make cleaning the room easier. You can start with "Put all your dinosaurs into the dinosaur box," then move on to the cars or the next large collection. The point of all this is to get children in the habit of executing the plan. Either put labels on each container or pictures of the type of toy that goes in it.

By the time students get to middle school, getting organized has become critical. Suddenly, they have six teachers, six notebooks, and a locker combination to keep track of. Some of your child's teachers may have precise requirements for how they want a notebook arranged, and your child is expected to follow those rules. Here are some organizing essentials:

- **An assignment notebook.** I prefer a small (about two-by-three-inch) notebook, but some teachers recommend a sheet inside each class notebook (see the Assignment Sheet example at the end of the chapter). At the end of each class period, your child would write down the name of the class, the homework assignment, due date, and what supplies are needed to do the homework—textbook, handout, class notebook, etc. These are the materials that would be brought home. This prevents the excuse "I can't do my homework because I forgot my book." At home, your child can write down any long-term assignments or projects on the calendar so everyone knows when they're due.

- **A notebook for each class.** Each notebook should have at least five sections: Daily Notes, Book Notes, Handouts, Homework, and Returned Tests and Quizzes.

- **A file box** (about twelve-by-twelve-by-twelve inches) containing a folder for every class. At the end of each grading period, all notes and papers can come out of the notebook and go into the file folder. Students should never throw out papers until after they receive their final (semester) grade. Teachers are human and sometimes forget to record a grade or assignment. If your son did well on a term paper, but his teacher forgot to record it, he'll either need to bring it back in to show her or rewrite the paper.

- **A color-coding system.** This one's optional, but some students find it helpful to have a separate color for each class. If your son has a green notebook and folder for history, he'll want a green pen for writing history assignments on the calendar.

- **A specific time to do homework**, usually right after school or right after dinner. This gets more complicated when there are extracurricular activities, but it's best to be as consistent as possible. Weekends are trickier—no kid wants to do homework on the weekend, and it normally gets put off until Sunday night. That's okay as long as there's adequate time allotted to complete all assignments.

Time Management

The ability to manage one's time has been linked to success later in life. A study conducted by the University of Pennsylvania concluded that self-discipline, a component of time management, is a better indicator of academic success than IQ.

> Self-discipline, a component of time management, is a better indicator of academic success than IQ.

Most students put off projects and studying for tests until the night before. Better to learn early how to set deadlines and to break large projects into manageable chunks. (See "Goal Setting" below.)

Students also need to prioritize their assignments, first by due date (what's due tomorrow?), then by difficulty. In other words, if three assignments are due tomorrow, do the hardest one first. If they get that one out of the way, they'll be glad afterward. If they get stuck, or bogged down, it's okay to do something else for a while.

Taking Notes in Class

As I mentioned earlier, many students think they'll remember everything that went on in class. If your student feels that way, have her recite everything that was said in English today. Usually by the end of the day, kids can't even remember if they *had* an English class that day.

Taking notes is an important skill because it uses all three learning styles. In addition, it gives your child something to review before a test. The topics the teacher covers in class are likely the ones she considers important and will probably show up on a test. Here's what you tell your child:

- Start each day's notes on a new sheet of paper, with the day and date prominently written at the top of the page. If the notes continue onto a second sheet, label that sheet at the top as well (i.e., Monday, March 2, continued). It also helps to include the chapter you're covering that day.
- Write key words, not entire sentences, and try to capture the main idea.
- Put everything that goes on the blackboard into your notes. If your teacher writes it down, you can be sure he wants you to write it down as well.
- Leave space in your notes to make reading easier and to add things later.
- Consider using the Cornell System of taking notes. The Cornell System is a widely used note-taking system devised in the 1950s by Walter Pauk, an education professor at Cornell University. It involves dividing the page into three sections. Leave about two inches at the bottom of each page to later summarize all the ideas on that page. The space above is divided into two columns: the left column is about 2½ inches wide and is for recording key words or main ideas; the right column is about six inches wide for the actual note taking. Skip one line between ideas and several lines between topics. After class, review the notes, jotting the key words and ideas in the left column. Then summarize in the space at the bottom of the page.

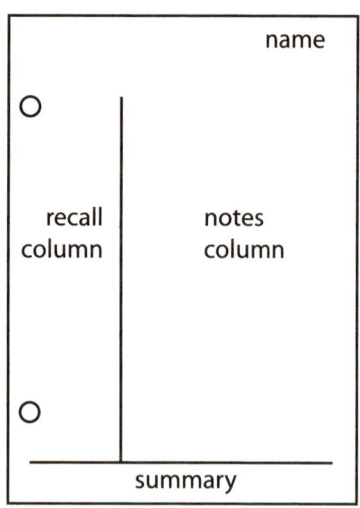

If your student doesn't use the Cornell System, he still needs to review his notes every day. He can use a marker to highlight the main ideas and potential test questions. I found it helpful to rewrite my notes every evening, since the ones I took in class were pretty sloppy and hard to read. Recopying them was just another step in the reviewing process.

All students need to learn to listen for certain "signal" words that indicate critical items to go into their notes. These words are clues that whatever comes next will probably show up again somewhere, probably on a quiz or test. Listen for:

- This is important…
- Most importantly…
- This is significant/vital/critical…
- The reasons for this are…
- Remember that…
- Don't forget…
- On the other hand…
- Similarly…
- In addition…
- All phrases with numbers or lists, such as
  - *The five steps are…*
  - *The three reasons for this are…*
  - *The first thing to consider is…*
  - *The last point is…*

Reading and Taking Notes from Textbooks

Your child should begin by skimming the chapter. Read the title and subheadings to get a feel for what the chapter's about. These form an outline of the chapter. They're also useful for studying the day before the test.

Then read the chapter fully and take notes using the section headings as the outline. Fill in with the main ideas and facts from the section. This may seem like busywork, but in reality it will make reviewing for the test much easier. If your child takes good notes here, he won't have to reread the entire chapter six times. Instead, he can reread it once or twice, then focus on his notes. Another advantage to this method is that your child will engage two learning styles, visual and kinesthetic. In addition, taking notes forces him to move forward through the chapter instead of staring at the same page for an hour.

Studying for a Test

The first test from a new teacher is always the hardest, because students don't know what the teacher will be looking for. That's one reason to keep returned tests. Over time, students can look for patterns. Did the teacher emphasize concepts or facts? Did most of the questions come from the end-of-chapter review or from the notes taken in class?

As your son is reviewing his notes—both class notes and those taken from the book—he can look for potential test questions. Have him think like the teacher. Also, have him review past homework assignments and go over the study guide questions in the chapter. If there are a lot of facts, such as math formulas or vocabulary words, flash cards can be helpful.

In upper elementary school, students need to read a chapter at least three or four times, and go over the study guide at the end of the chapter.

Encourage your child to ask questions in class. If a concept is unclear to her, it's probably unclear to others. If she can't bring herself to ask questions in class, she can always talk to the teacher at lunch or after school.

Teach your child to use mnemonics—memory tricks—to remember lists. For example, **HOMES** stands for the Great Lakes: Huron, Ontario, Michigan, Erie, and Superior. Also, **May I have a large container of coffee** will help them remember the value of π (3.1415926) to seven decimal places. The number of letters in each word represents the value of the corresponding decimal place.

Remind your child to use her learning style—auditory, visual, or kinesthetic—to her advantage.

Goal Setting

The ability to set and attain goals is useful in many areas, including school, work, finances, and life planning. It's been said that goals are just dreams with deadlines. For years I told people I was writing a book, but I didn't make much progress until I started setting deadlines for myself.

Goals need to be specific and quantifiable. If you can't measure your progress, it's hard to know if you're successful. It's not enough to say "I'm going to get better grades"; it's just too vague. "I'm going to bring my math grade up one letter grade" is clearer. "I'm going to do every homework problem and get help when I'm confused" is more specific.

The other aspect of goals is that they can be long- or short-term. For adults, long-term goals are roughly five or more years away. For children, long-term goals are more immediate since they tend to live in the moment. Their long-term goal might be a paper due next month or bringing up their final grade. Older students will be able to see farther down the road—what college they want to go to or what career field they'd like to pursue.

Once your child commits to a long-term goal, the next step is to formulate a plan. What are the intermediate steps? For a term paper, the steps might be: choose a topic, do the research, draft an outline, write the paper. Each of these steps could then be worked into a manageable timeline. If the goal is to improve a grade, the intermediate steps could be to spend an extra fifteen minutes each day on the subject. I used to tell my students that the difference between a B and an A is 10 percent. If they study chemistry for sixty minutes each day, another 10 percent effort is just six minutes. Shoot for ten to fifteen minutes per day to be safe.

English

No matter what your child's favorite subject is, English is her most important. She can be more brilliant than Einstein, but if she can't communicate her ideas, then those ideas are worthless. Even if she manages to get her ideas across, improper grammar greatly reduces her credibility. I once went to a doctor who spoke as though he had left school after fifth grade. I couldn't help but think that if he didn't learn anything in English class, what other classes did he blow off? I never went back to that doctor.

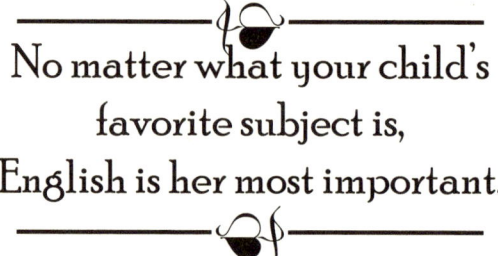

No matter what your child's favorite subject is, English is her most important.

If your grammar is less than ideal, make it clear to your munchkins that you expect them to do better. As with most skills, children will model their parents in this, so you may want to try to break your own bad habits.

One note on spelling: many schools have stopped teaching spelling since all word processors have spell-checkers. The problem is those pesky homonyms. Spell-checkers can't tell the difference between to and too, hear and here. I recently received a letter from my veterinarian that included the statement "Your pet's health should take presidents over the cost of medication." I wondered how many presidents it should take and whether the presidents should be living or dead. Encourage your student to excel at spelling.

How Do They Know When They're Successful?

The obvious answer is when they get their report card, but for those of us who hate surprises, there are ways for students to monitor their progress. Ideally, students should be able to guesstimate their grade before they turn in an assignment.

The majority of schools across the country use the traditional grading scale:

A   90–100%

B   80–89%

C   70–79%

D   60–69%

F   Less than 60%

To calculate a grade, divide the number of points received on a test or assignment by the number of points possible, and then multiply by one hundred. For example, if your child got forty points on an assignment out of a possible fifty, his grade would be 80%, or a low B.

At the start of each school year, high school and middle school teachers usually hand out a sheet with their classroom rules and expectations. It should include their grading scale for homework and tests. For example, homework problems might each be worth one point, and homework might be worth 50 percent of a student's total grade. Quizzes and tests would make up the other 50 percent. When long-term projects are announced, students should be told how many points the project is worth and what the criteria are. For example, "The paper is worth one hundred points, must be five pages long, and cite at least three sources. Include a bibliography at the end of the paper."

Math and science problems are considered objective: the problem is either right or wrong, although teachers often give partial credit on a sliding scale. True-false and multiple choice questions are also objective.

Essay questions are considered subjective: the grade depends on what the teacher is looking for. Because students need to be able to tell whether their essay is acceptable or not, educators have developed a variety of rubrics, or grading guidelines. Rubrics list the items to be evaluated, such as grammar, sentence structure, and organization. They should also describe the levels of quality for each item. For example, using a six-point scale, a six-point essay would have almost no grammar errors, while a one-point essay would have consistent grammar errors. The use of rubrics allows students to evaluate their own work by laying out exactly what's expected. It encourages students to look for and correct their errors before they turn the paper in for a grade.

Teachers usually hand out a rubric at the start of the semester. If your child didn't get one, ask the teacher for a copy. You can also search for rubrics online. The most common one is what the SAT uses—search for "SAT scoring guide." It evaluates an essay based on five criteria: point of view; organization and focus; use of language; sentence structure; and grammar, usage and mechanics.

Senioritis

This is a common "disease" that affects nearly all twelfth graders. They see graduation as their emancipation. They think their world will change; they'll be done with high school and all grown up.

As seniors look forward to the big day, they start acting as though it has already come and gone. They have no motivation to do schoolwork and are usually only interested in having fun with their friends. Some teens start talking back to parents, in an effort to break free of adult control.

Keep in mind that senioritis is God's way of helping parents to let go. At the end of the school year, it can be a relief to send them out into the world. Remembering this can help you hang on to your patience and your sanity.

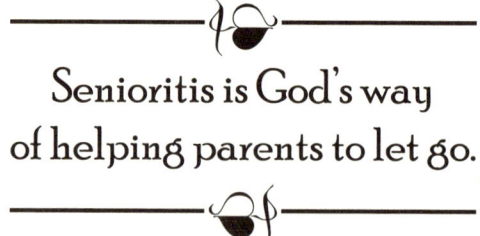

Senioritis is God's way of helping parents to let go.

Remind your senior that many colleges look at a student's end-of-year grades as an indicator of academic motivation. A sudden drop in grades may cause his college admission to be rescinded.

The bottom line is that education is important for *every* student. Not every child will get straight As, but all children can maximize their potential. Remind them that homework and project grades are completely within their control. Tests are trickier to control, but the study tips above should help.

Assignment Sheet						
Date	Class	Assignment	Need Notebook?	Need Other Book?	Supplies?	Due Date

Weekly Progress Report				
Date	Class	Missing Assignments	Estimated Grade	Initials

Teaching kids to count is fine,
but teaching them what counts is best.
– Bob Talbert

Chapter 4

Life Skills

Life skills are all the things your cherub will need to know when he or she goes out into the world, and can be divided into two categories—personal and interpersonal. You're already teaching some of them, but there may be some you haven't considered.

Personal Skills

Chores

There are compelling reasons why every child needs to do chores. First, each member of the family is part of the team and needs to be a team player. Second, when your daughter moves out on her own, she'll need to know how to do her laundry and clean her bathroom. Finally, every human has a built-in desire to feel needed. Telling your cherubs that you need their help (and showing appreciation afterward) satisfies that desire.

Toddlers can put toys away. Preschoolers can put napkins on the dinner table or help deliver folded laundry to the correct room. During their elementary school years, children can begin helping with dishes, making their own lunches, and picking up around the house. About the time they start middle school (sixth or seventh grade), they're ready to learn to do laundry, housework, and some cooking.

Remember, you'll need to explain the steps more than once as you teach each process. You'll also have to supervise closely until you're satisfied they can complete the job unassisted. Otherwise you may find greasy pots in the cupboard or discover your white clothes are now pink. I've learned these things the hard way. You can't just explain something once and expect it to stick.

Be sure you anticipate potential dangers and pitfalls so you can point them out ahead of time to your trainee. When Travis was in Civil Air Patrol, he ironed his own uniform each week. One of the other cadets told him that the best way to get sharp creases was to hold the iron in one spot "for a long time." Our son took that to mean long enough to use the bathroom while he left the hot iron sitting on the shirt. The shirt, of course, was ruined, and we were grateful that nothing caught fire. Clearly we hadn't done a great job of teaching him to iron.

As they enter high school, teens are ready for more advanced cooking duties—perhaps preparing an entire dinner, or at least creating the menu and helping with most of it. They should also be doing some ironing (safely) and car maintenance. Before they graduate, they need to be able to balance a checkbook and do their own taxes.

Chores emphasize the fact that everyone needs to contribute to the society they live in (in this case, the family). By starting chores at an early age, you catch them at a time in their development when they are still eager to please. Also, it becomes part of their mind-set: chores are something everyone has to do. If you wait until they reach middle school, when they're approaching the rebellious stage, your chances of gaining their cooperation go way down. After all, if they've spent their entire life avoiding helping around the house, they're not going to suddenly jump up and start helping. At least not cheerfully.

Some parents like to use a family meeting to assign chores, because when children are involved in the decision-making process they develop a sense of ownership and are more likely to cooperate. You can either assign tasks based on age and preferences, use a rotating system (everyone gets a new set of jobs each week), or use a "job jar." In this case, chores are written on slips of paper and kept in a jar. Every week each family member pulls one or more jobs out of the jar for their weekly assignment. This helps prevent the same person from always getting the yucky jobs, although "yuckiness" means different things to different people.

Goal Setting

I discussed goal setting in Chapter 3, but it's an important process in many areas. For children, goals can be academic, financial, social, or career-oriented, not necessarily in that order. All are important.

How many people do you know who are just drifting through life? Without goals, they feel their life has no purpose. They don't know what to do, so they do little or nothing. Fortunately, most adults at least have a goal of paying the rent and buying food, which gives them a reason to get out of bed and go to work. Other goals, such as learning a foreign language or making the world a better place, can bring joy, purpose, and direction.

Goal setting includes short-, intermediate-, and long-term goals. I always liked to ask the underachievers in my high school classes where they expected to be in five or ten years. Often, their only long-term goal was to party on the weekend. Asking them about five years into the future produced the most interesting looks, as though there was a giant question mark hanging over their head. For those who did have an answer, my next question was, "Is what you're doing now helping you toward that goal?" In other words, if they needed a high school diploma, would they actually graduate by then? If they planned on being rich and famous, would they know enough math to make sure their accountants weren't cheating them?

Some goal setting will be more immediate, such as for a term paper due next month. Goal setting can be further broken down into parts: for research, the rough draft, and the final draft. These parts can become intermediate goals, each with its own deadline. A short-term goal might be to work a certain number of minutes each day on the project or to write a page a day.

One financial long-term goal could be saving for a car. The associated intermediate goals might be to save some birthday money or do extra chores. Short-term goals could include saving part of each week's allowance.

Career goals will fluctuate wildly as children mature. Today she wants to be an astronaut; tomorrow she'll want to be a ballerina. As children get older, their passions and talents become more apparent, and career goals tend to settle into a handful of interests. Parents can help show the connection between these goals and the necessary education. Future medical professionals will need a strong science background. Writers will need to take all the English classes available. If your child plans to start his own company, he'll need some business and computer classes.

As you discuss goals, talk about how to break them down into short-term and intermediate parts. This makes the job seem less overwhelming. Now take those intermediate goals and break them down further. For some children, a checklist can be helpful. The act of checking things off a list fosters a sense of accomplishment.

Problem Solving

Not just for those pesky word problems in math and science classes, problem solving is a skill that will serve children throughout life. Choosing a college, buying a car, and picking your retirement home are only a few of the decisions that will benefit from a thoughtful, logical approach.

The widely accepted six-step process for problem solving includes the following:

1. **Identify the problem**. Your child should be as specific as possible so he can look for precise solutions. "Get an 80% in English" is better than "bring up my grades." Having a specific, quantifiable goal is important so that he'll know when he has succeeded.

2. **Brainstorm ideas**. Have him write them down, even the far-fetched ones. If he's having trouble getting started, offer a suggestion or two. You want to help, not take over the

process. Resist the urge to censor. An idea may seem silly to you but may inspire a better one later on. Let him do the thinking here; avoid the temptation to tell him what to write. If there's something you want to add, ask if you may make a suggestion. This allows him to retain ownership of the process. Once he agrees to your input, he's much more likely to listen to what you're saying.

3. **Evaluate each option**. Now's the time to throw out the unworkable ones. For the other choices, it may be helpful to list the pros and cons for each. In addition, make sure none of the options violates his (or the family's) ethics. For example, cheating on a test may raise his grade but is not an ethical choice.

4. **Choose one or more options**. If the problem is a low English grade, your student might choose to spend more time on his writing assignments, study longer, and seek help from the teacher. Remind him that avoiding a decision is actually a decision to do nothing.

5. **Develop a written plan**. Again, be as specific as possible. Do two rewrites on each writing assignment instead of one. Study twenty minutes every weekday. Ask the teacher to review the paper before it's due, to get tips for improvement. Post the plan in a prominent spot so you can both refer to it.

6. **Assess the outcome**. If the plan isn't working, he may need to tweak it. Add study time on weekends or do three rewrites instead of two. Decision making is often a dynamic process. If something isn't working, go ahead and change it. That's part of the learning process.

Perseverance and Commitment

Remember when your parents used to say things like "If at first you don't succeed, try, try again" or "Quitters never win, and winners never quit"? Personally, my favorite line is from the movie *Galaxy Quest*: "Never give up! Never surrender!" said with great enthusiasm.

What our parents didn't tell us is how important perseverance is, both in relationships and on the job. There are a number of things you can do, beyond quoting pithy sayings, to encourage perseverance:

- **Be a role model.** No surprise here. Never say "I give up" when you're stuck.
- **Encourage.** Tell them "You can do it!" Move your hands in a circle in front of you while chanting "Go, Junior! Go, Junior!" Print out a sign that says "Whether you think you can or you think you can't, you're probably right." Praise their efforts. "You really spent a long time practicing the piano today—I'm proud of you!" Read *Thomas the Train*.
- **When stuck on a problem, talk it out.** The family dinner table is a great place to brainstorm ideas and get encouragement. Make sure the discussion stays civil!
- **Keep the goal in mind.** When discouragement sets in, take a minute or two to visualize the goal. Incidentally, this is a technique used by many top trainers and athletes. Have your child picture himself winning the fifty-yard dash or printing out the term paper.
- **Break a large project into smaller tasks.** Then do the first step. My friend Julie had a goal of running a three-mile race, but when she started she could hardly run three yards. She began by walking a little farther every day until she could walk three miles. Then she started running for part of the three miles, pushing herself to run a little farther each time. It took her months, but she reached her goal of running three miles, and now she runs marathons on a regular basis.

Children need to be encouraged to stick with a task until it's completed. Learning to handle frustration allows children (and adults) to focus on solving the problem without becoming angry. It gives them the patience to keep going. Patience and perseverance are both skills essential to instilling a sense of commitment, which is one of the critical skills needed for adult life. Commitment to job, spouse, family, and God depends not only on a desire to do what's right, but also the ability to hang in when the going gets tough, as well as the willingness to put the needs of others before your own desires.

Too many young people enter into marriage and family with the attitude that if it doesn't work out, they'll just call it quits. The institution of marriage is rapidly losing value in our culture. It's not uncommon for students today to have "serial parents." They talk about their first Dad, second Dad, etc. Imagine what they're thinking. "When Mom gets tired of this 'dad,' she'll get a new one. What will happen when she gets tired of me?" Our society needs to recommit to family values and the value of a stable family.

Decision Making

You wouldn't think you'd have to teach children to make decisions, but in our society it's more important than ever that they learn to make good choices. At some point during their school years, nearly every child will be offered drugs or alcohol, and be pressured (both boys and girls) to have sex by a boyfriend or girlfriend. In addition, there are an infinite number of bad examples presented to our kids every day. School shootings, movies about drinking and sex, and all manner of reality shows inundate young people with appealing, immoral options. By age fourteen, 77 percent of youths are contacted by online predators, and 22 percent of children ages ten to thirteen are approached, according to CyberAngels.org, a group dedicated to keeping children safe from Internet predators. When kids learn at an early age to weigh the outcomes of their choices, the odds of making good decisions increase dramatically.

Choices are one of the most effective parenting tools available. Choices give children a feeling of empowerment, of being part of the decision-making process, and of having some control over their lives. Allowing them some input into things teaches them that you respect their opinions, and have confidence in their ability to choose. An important side benefit is that when faced with a difficult situation, they will have the self-confidence to make the decision they know is right.

If parents never offer choices, parents become dictators and children feel powerless. If you control everything they do with the "You'll do it because I said so" method, I guarantee you'll generate resentment instead of respect. "I said so" has its place, but should be used sparingly and mostly with very young children.

The choices you offer them can involve questions about *what*:

- What kind of cake do you want for your birthday?
- Which game do you want to play?
- Which restaurant shall we go to for lunch?
- What book do you want me to read to you?
- What color shirt do you want to wear today?

More important are the *how* questions, as in "How do you want to do this?":

- Do you want to bathe before or after your TV show?
- You must do your homework. Do you want to do it before or after dinner?
- You must pick up your toys so I can vacuum. Do you want to pick them up largest to smallest or by color?
- We need to go to the grocery store. Do you want to sit in the cart or help me push? Do you want to take a snack or a book?
- You must be in bed with the lights out by nine o'clock. You can go to bed a little early and read until nine, or you can watch TV until nine.

If they can't decide, remind them that they can make a different choice next time. At this age, you'll want to limit their options so they're not overwhelmed. Two or three choices are plenty.

When I ran a day care in my home, one of my charges was an extremely strong-willed four-year-old. Every request was met with a firm "NO" from Jenny. I quickly had to change from requests ("Please hang up your jacket") to choices ("Do you want to hang up your jacket or sit in the time-out chair for ten minutes?").

On the first day, she chose the chair, and I hung up her jacket. I did point out to her that it took me about ten seconds to hang up the jacket, and then I could play with the other children while she was still stuck in the chair. On the second day, she decided it was easier to hang up the jacket.

You can start offering choices to children as soon as they're old enough to understand the words. For very young children, decision making is about preferences and compliance. As they get older and face more complex choices, you can talk them through the options and the potential outcomes of each one:

- You want to sleep over at a friend's house tonight, but you have a Little League game tomorrow. You'll have to get up early to make the game. Do you think you'll be too tired to play well for your team? How will the coach and the team feel if you don't make it to the game?
- Mr. Smith wants to hire you to weed his garden once a week. Are you willing to commit to doing that for the next month or two? What happens if you don't feel like doing it one week?

All children will make inappropriate decisions now and then. Kids are idealists and rarely consider that something bad might happen to them. When they get caught up in something, they forget to weigh the options. Allowing them to "goof" when the stakes are small helps them learn to make better choices in the future.

When discussing any inappropriate decisions they've made, ask them why they made this particular choice. Did they consider the consequences? If they could do things over, would they choose differently? How would that change the outcome? Good kids make mistakes, and mistakes are opportunities to learn. Make it clear that you still love your child despite a bad decision.

Look for teachable moments. Watch movies and TV shows with them, and discuss the choices various characters made. Ask "What do you think about …" questions. Occasionally ask them about some hypothetical situations, such as the one on page 86.

As children demonstrate their trustworthiness, you can allow them more opportunities to make choices, within limits. They can choose their clothes as long as they conform to the school dress code, for example. Continue to discuss the outcomes of their particular choices in addition to various hypothetical situations. Talk about doing what's right versus doing what's popular. Point out that just because you *can* do something (say, tell a lie) doesn't mean you *should*. Remind them God is watching.

Just because you can do something doesn't mean you should.

Sometimes it's hard for us as parents to accept our kids' decisions, and we need to ask ourselves if what they're doing is hurtful, illegal, or just uncomfortable for us. If they're not endangering themselves or others, it may be best to accept their choice. The purple hair will grow out, and they'll probably grow into those baggy clothes. We need to choose our battles. It's more important to take a stand against drugs and drinking than the color of their hair.

Our son went through a goth phase when he was in middle school. He and his friends wore baggy black clothes, black nail polish, chains, etc. Pat and I hated it because it made him look like he was a drug dealer. We told him we'd tolerate it as long as he kept his grades up and didn't do anything illegal—but at the first sign of misbehavior, he'd be grounded and get a new wardrobe. Eventually he realized his friends were getting into some trouble that he didn't want any part of. He found new friends and cleaned up his act.

As children mature, their reasoning skills improve, only to fall victim to peer pressure. They also learn to rationalize their behavior. Teenagers especially love to debate with their parents, often arguing about something just because they can. Thus, even though they know it's wrong to steal that candy bar, they'll tell you that it isn't really hurting anyone. "It was just a small thing. The store won't even notice it's gone. Besides, everybody does it, so it can't be that terrible." Don't get sucked into the argument.

As you teach decision-making skills, there are two pitfalls to be aware of. The first is asking a child for a decision and then ignoring it. If you tell her to pick tonight's restaurant, then decide to go to a different one, what has she learned? When you ask for her input and then ignore it, you send the message that she's not smart enough to even pick a restaurant or that her opinions are unimportant and therefore *she* is unimportant.

The other pitfall is much more subtle and doesn't even involve making decisions. Its biggest danger lies in the fact that it's so insidious. It begins when they're little—we get in the habit of correcting their misperceptions about the world. "That's not a dog, silly, that's a horse." We have to be careful not to let that degenerate into constant correction:

Child	Parent
"That's a big cat."	"It's not that big."
"That's a pretty flower."	"It's a weed."
"My soup is too hot."	"No it isn't. Just eat it."
"That was a great movie."	"It was stupid."
"I drew you a picture."	"The sky's the wrong color."

Sometimes all it takes is a look or sarcastic tone to imply that your cherub is wrong:

"I made you breakfast."   "Oh great."

When we constantly correct our children, especially their opinions, we teach them to doubt themselves. They'll have trouble making choices throughout life, because in the back of their mind, they'll know that whatever they choose will be "wrong."

Correction needs to be done in a positive manner and not nearly as often as we think. Little feelings are fragile and dependent on family for validation. When we don't accept their feelings and opinions, it appears as though we don't accept the child.

Older siblings often delight in correcting the younger ones; it's part of the natural pecking order. Remind them that everyone is entitled to their opinion.

Discussion Questions: What Would You Do If...

Elementary School
- You were at the store with friends, and they wanted you to steal a candy bar.
- You were at a friend's house and accidentally broke a toy.
- At a sleepover, your friend wanted to watch a movie you're not allowed to see.
- You saw a classmate steal something, and now she wants you to lie to cover for her.
- Your friend wanted you to let her cheat off your test paper or copy your homework.

Middle School
- You were at a party and you realized the punch was spiked.
- A good friend offered you drugs.
- Your boyfriend told you everyone else is "sexting," and if you loved him, you would do it, too.

High School
- You were driving, but you realized you were late for school.
- You were at a party, and you realized your boyfriend has had too much to drink and shouldn't be driving.
- Your friend told her parents that she was spending the night at your house, but she's really going to her boyfriend's place and wants you to lie for her.

Creativity

When we watch TV or listen to music, we're listening to other people's ideas. That's fine occasionally, but kids need the feeling of satisfaction that comes from creating something of their own. In addition, children with hobbies are less likely to complain about being bored and are less likely to go looking for mischief. Creativity can take many forms:

- **Art:** drawing, painting, cartooning, working with clay
- **Writing:** short stories, poetry or songs
- **Hobbies:** jewelry making, reading, gardening, model making, juggling

Visit your local hobby store for some ideas.

Spirituality / Religion

In a 2008 national survey, 15 percent of the population selected "none" as their religious preference. If you are one of the "unchurched," I'd ask you to read this section anyway, for your children's sake.

There are many good reasons to teach religion to children. Whether you consider yourself Jewish, Christian, Muslim, or Buddhist, the common theme is that you ultimately answer to a higher power. In addition, each of these religions asks us to follow a code of ethics. The Bible has the Ten Commandments. The Qur'an and Buddhist teachings have similar wording. Parents can use these teachings to their advantage:

- Tell your kids, "These aren't just our rules, they're God's rules."
- When faced with an ethical dilemma, kids can ask themselves what God (or Jesus) would want them to do.
- Even if she feels lonely sometimes, your child will know she is never alone; God is with her.
- Religion gives children a greater sense of purpose. God has a plan for them. Jail, drugs, etc., are not part of that plan.
- When a loved one or even a pet dies, it's comforting to think of them going to heaven.

- Sunday school, vacation Bible school, and church youth groups are not only great places to reinforce religious values, they're also great places for your children to make friends.

If you're not sure how to begin when teaching religion, here are some options—for you as well as your children:

- Attend church, Sunday school, vacation Bible school, and weekly youth groups.
- Engage in rituals such as saying grace at meals or observing religious holidays.
- Say evening prayers.
- Watch DVDs like the *Veggie Tales* series or Focus on the Family's *Adventures in Odyssey* series.

One last note—many parents pray for patience. I did, too, at first, but God kept giving me so many opportunities to practice! I had better success asking Him to give me the right words whenever I was trying to reason with recalcitrant children.

Helping Others

Everyone has a moral obligation to make the world a better place and to help others when we can. Some school districts now include a minimum number of volunteer hours as a requirement for graduation, in order to teach children the importance of giving back to the community. Many participate in Random Acts of Kindness Week each February (see www.actsofkindness.org for more details).

One Saturday morning, a father told his children, "You can spend the next hour sitting in front of the TV watching a show you won't remember next week, or you can do something you'll feel good about for the rest of your lives." It had snowed heavily during the night, and he knew their elderly neighbor would have difficulty shoveling her walk. He convinced the kids to come help

Chapter 4: *Life Skills*   89

him shovel, and they were pleasantly surprised to realize that it did feel good to help someone else. They also enjoyed the cake the neighbor delivered the next day as a thank-you gift. Notice how he sold the idea to his cherubs. Instead of saying something like, "Get off that couch and get out here and help," he explained how it would benefit them. Instead of dragging them out the door, he had them join in the fun.

Children often agree that helping others is a good idea but have trouble with the follow-through. "Yes, it would be nice if I brought in Mr. Smith's trash cans, but I'm on the phone right now." Or the ever popular "I will," which usually translates to "I will think about it later." Anytime a youngster says "I will," your next question should be "When?" Then follow up. The best plan, though, is to <u>accompany them</u> on these good deed missions. If you go with them, you accomplish several things:

- You model the behavior you're trying to encourage.
- You help them do a good job instead of a mediocre one.
- You spend time interacting with your children.
- You physically get them moving. It's easier to pull someone along than push them along.

There are many things kids can do to help others. Below are some suggestions:

- Help elderly neighbors with mowing, snow shoveling, or trash cans.
- Offer to exercise someone's dog after school. It doesn't have to be every day—maybe just an occasional "play date."
- Bake cookies and take them to a nursing home.
- Volunteer at your place of worship: help in the nursery, tidy up after service, or participate in cleanup days.
- Volunteer to serve at a soup kitchen.

- Make something to donate to a charity craft sale.
- If you're a high school student, tutor younger students or siblings.

Acts of kindness can and should begin at home. Encourage everyone to help each other and be considerate of each other's feelings. Don't forget to catch kids being good—be sure to let them know you notice when they engage in positive behaviors. Praise every act of kindness.

Kindness includes thoughtfulness. Offer your seat to someone who needs it on the bus or on the subway. Open doors for others. Offer to help someone carrying a heavy load. Remember birthdays.

One Halloween, I went to the grocery store and saw one of my students working as a bagger. I tried chatting with him, but he was clearly not in the mood. He finally told me he was unhappy because he had to work that night and couldn't go trick-or-treating with his friends. I sympathized, and as I left I tossed him one of the bags of candy I had purchased. A year later, my yearbook class put out a survey to all the students that included the question, "What's the nicest thing anyone has ever done for you?" That same student wrote, "A teacher gave me a bag of candy when I had to work on Halloween." Even the smallest thoughtful acts are appreciated.

Interpersonal Skills

Communication and Listening

Effective communication is important not only in our personal relationships, but in the workplace as well. So important, in fact, that it's worth including in resumes and cover letters when applying for jobs.

There are several barriers to communication, so ask yourself if you're guilty of any of the following:

- **Having a noncommunicative family.** If your family (parents) never discussed anything, it probably doesn't occur to you to discuss things with your spouse and kids. And if you don't talk things over with your family, your kids probably won't talk things over with their (future) families. And so on. Once you start discussing problems, ideas, and plans with your family, you'll see an improvement in family trust and harmony.

- **Wanting control.** Some parents fear that if they throw things out for discussion, they'll lose control of the situation. The reality is everyone (including your child) wants to feel heard, and as the parent(s) you do have veto power. For example, your family cell phone contract is up soon, so why not ask all the cell phone users in the house what they'd like in the new plan. Of course, the teens will want it all, and you'll explain that "all" isn't in the budget, but it's an opportunity to learn their priorities.

- **Assuming.** Sometimes we're sure we know the right course of action, and we assume that everyone else feels the same way. Much better to ask for input. My own family didn't communicate much as I was growing up, so this is a skill I've had to actively work on over the years. Often it just doesn't occur to me to discuss something. I know how *I* feel, and I assume everyone else will agree. I have found that asking for inputs and opinions early on prevents a lot of conflict later.

Effective communication is a two-way street. First, one person needs to express his or her thoughts and ideas clearly, in a nonthreatening fashion. Second, the other person needs to listen attentively. Timing is an important factor: trying to get someone's attention when that person is tired or focused on something else is usually futile.

Once you've mastered the art of communicating, you can practice by communicating with the children.

Within a family, the day-to-day interactions often follow a predictable pattern.

✱ "How was your day?"

"Fine."

"What did you learn today?"

"Nothing"

It helps to ask more open-ended questions, such as "Tell me about your day while I fix you a snack" or "Tell me the most interesting thing you learned today. What's the worst thing that happened today?"

When Your Child Needs to Talk

When your youngster comes to you with a problem (it's *never* at a convenient time, by the way), they may not want you to solve the problem; they may just want a sympathetic ear. Oftentimes that's all it takes for them to solve the problem on their own. At other times, they may just want to know that you're on their side. When they're little, we kiss the "owie." As they get older, moral support and a hug are just as effective on those emotional hurts.

As they're pouring their heart out, it's important to practice a technique called active listening, which allows the speaker to know that you're fully engaged in what they're saying. The process has several parts:

- **Focus.** Give your child your full attention. No texting, watching TV, etc. Listen to both the words and the feelings, without focusing on your rebuttal. Be aware of body language. Don't interrupt—let your child talk.

- **Encourage** your child to continue. Saying "uh-huh" and nodding your head doesn't mean you agree, just that you're listening and want to hear more.

- **Provide positive feedback** when your child has finished. Summarize what you heard to make sure you understood. "So, you're mad at your boyfriend for flirting with your best friend?"
"No! I'm mad at *her* for flirting with my boyfriend!"

- **Ask questions** respectfully and in a positive manner. Instead of "You don't like your science teacher, do you?" try "Tell me about your science teacher." That way you don't put words or ideas in your child's mouth. Open-ended questions will get you farther than the yes-no variety. Avoid judging what's being said, as it will only cause your child to stop talking.

- **Empathize.** Even if you don't agree with what they're saying, children need to know you understand how they feel. Sit on the urge to correct them. Validate their feelings before you help them adjust their attitude. For example, "We understand that your friends are getting their ears pierced, and you really really really want to as well. But you're only nine, and we feel you're too young to put holes in your head. I know you're disappointed. If you were us, what age would you consider appropriate for pierced ears?"

When you're done with all that listening, it's tempting to jump in with solutions. You're thinking, "Been there, done that, got the T-shirt, so what you need to do is …" Instead of laying out a plan for your child, the first step is to ask what *they* think the solution might be. When children have a hand in constructing the solution, it gives them a sense of both ownership and empowerment, thereby increasing the odds of them following through.

Communicating with Your Children

Talking with kids usually begins with expressing your personal wants, needs, and opinions, in a calm, respectful manner. If you're angry about something, then the calm, respectful part is more difficult but doable. You can choose your attitude. You can state how you're feeling without attacking, blaming, or judging. In doing so, you greatly reduce the number of barriers your child puts up that would block the flow of communication.

Communication is important even when you're not angry. Work on expressing your ideas clearly and completely. Instead of just tossing out, "Let's go to Great-Aunt Eunice's house for our summer vacation," you might add your reasons. "She has invited us, she lives between the beach and Disneyland, and we could do lots of fun day trips."

Listening, by the way, isn't always easy. We're distracted and usually multitasking when the kids need something. That's understandable, but if someone really needs to talk to you, you need to give them your undivided attention.

Communication is especially important when there's a conflict. If your child is mad at *you*, this whole process gets much more difficult. As they're explaining what you've done wrong, it's hard to stay calm; you're thinking, "Why you ungrateful little puppy!" It's also hard to focus on what they're saying, because now you're on the defensive and thinking of all the reasons they're wrong. You can get through this. Take a deep breath and pretend they're talking about someone else, if that helps. It's vital that you hear them out. Respond to their (respectful) criticism with something like, "That was hard to hear, but I appreciate your input."

Conflict Resolution

For some of us, the mere thought of conflict sends our blood pressure through the roof and is something to be avoided at all costs. We always give in, in order to keep the peace. For others, conflict is a way of life or perhaps a way to feed an adrenaline addiction. Some people feel that the best defense is a good offense, so they try to be as offensive as possible. In a perfect, grown-up world, disagreements would be faced squarely and settled calmly, so that both parties could move on.

Everyone faces conflict at some point and needs to be able to handle it. Avoiding it is never a good idea; you just keep negative feelings inside until you either explode or develop health problems. Practice resolving conflict in an adult manner and teach your kids to do the same.

Four Steps to Resolving Conflict

1. **Identify the feelings.** When we're angry or annoyed, the first step is to figure out why. This isn't always easy. We know we're upset, but if we haven't learned to pin down exactly what we're feeling, we won't be able to verbalize it.

Anger is always a secondary emotion.

Keep in mind that anger is always a secondary emotion. It follows hot on the heels of other intense feelings, such as fear, frustration, disappointment, even physical or emotional pain. When your little one runs out into the street, for example, you may feel angry because your heart has just stopped, causing you fear and pain. Or, when you ask your teen for the third time to take out the garbage, and you see him still sitting on the couch saying "I will," your anger is likely caused by frustration and impatience.

2. **Express those feelings respectfully.** After pinpointing exactly what you're feeling, you need to explain it to the other person in a calm voice. The best way to do this is using "I" messages, such as "I feel frustrated when you promise to walk the dog right after school, and I come home to find a puddle by the door." Or "I feel angry when I find someone has left food and dirty dishes in the family room." "I" messages follow this form: "I feel _____ when _____ happens."

    By using "I" messages, you're stating your feelings instead of attacking the other person or making them feel defensive. Instead of focusing on defending themselves, they can listen to how their action affected you and hopefully offer a solution. "I" messages are a great communication tool no matter who you're in conflict with—parent, child, sibling, friend, or spouse. They allow you to express yourself in a nonthreatening way, inviting the other person to participate in finding a solution.

3. **Listen to the other side.** After the aggrieved party has explained how he feels, it's time for him to listen to the other person's side, without interrupting. Sometimes there are reasons the other person behaved a certain way. Your child may tell you, "I was starving when I got home, so I fixed a snack, then I forgot to walk the dog." Children often behave impulsively or forget to do things, without considering how their actions will affect others. Going through this process helps them understand the need to consider others.

4. **Look for a solution.** Once the participants have each had their say, it's time to find a solution that both sides can live with. Maybe he can pack a granola bar to eat on the bus ride home, so he can walk the dog right away.

Practice This

Parents can begin practicing these steps right away, no matter who the conflict is between. If yours is like most families, you won't have to wait long for an opportunity! When Pat and I first learned these steps, we kept a copy of them on the refrigerator. We would literally grab the list and go through the steps one at a time.

The added benefit of practicing these steps is that you can then teach the process to your children. When the children start shouting at each other, sit them down and explain the rules. One person goes first (toss a coin if you need to) and respectfully explains his side of the story. The other person must reflect back what she heard before giving her side of the story. When both are finished, they need to work together to find a solution. You'll have to referee this process for a while, but eventually they'll do some form of it on their own. Imagine—less shouting. It's worth it.

Conflict resolution isn't an easy process to learn. Trust me, I know. It probably won't go perfectly the first time or two, but your children will appreciate immensely the fact that you're listening to them and that you're taking their feelings seriously. It's a huge step toward building trust, elevating their self-esteem, and of course teaching them communication skills.

You'll want to practice these skills when there are minor (to you) problems, so you don't lose your temper when the major problems crop up. As in, "Mom, Dad, I'd like you to meet Donnie the Drug Dealer. We're getting married."

Sometimes a note, e-mail, or text message can take the edge off of a potentially volatile topic. It gives the recipient time to calm down and collect his thoughts before a face-to-face meeting.

You will have to do some coaching when the conflict is between children. When your son says, "Mark is a doo-doo head," you'll have to translate that into, "You're angry with Mark." As the parent, you can help your child learn to verbalize his feelings by using a technique called *reflective listening*. When he's telling you about an emotionally charged event, you can reflect back to him the emotions you're sensing. "It sounds like you're frustrated because your teacher can't find the assignment you turned in." "It sounds like you're disappointed with Monica for breaking your date." "It seems as though you're embarrassed because Chandler told others something you had asked him to keep secret." By practicing reflective listening, you help them identify what they're really feeling.

During conflict, each child will have a turn to say what's bothering him, without interruption. Your job is to pin down feelings and reasons, without necessarily offering a solution.

Johnny: "Mark is hogging all the Legos!"

Mark: "I need them to build a castle."

Johnny: "I need some to build a car."

You: "Hmmm. Two children and not enough Legos. What should we do?"

Kids can be rather creative when it comes to problem solving. If possible, let them decide the outcome, such as combining all the Legos and building one big project. If the conflict involves opposing desires, taking turns is the most common answer. Sometimes it helps to let the person who feels the strongest make the decision. "I've been dying to see this movie ever since I heard they were making it!" For small children, the loudest one is *not* the one who should get his way. All that does is teach him to be loud.

For serious differences of opinions, sometimes it's best just to agree to disagree.

If the source of the trouble is hurt feelings, an apology is in order. Children need to learn that everyone makes mistakes on occasion, and the mature thing to do is admit when you're wrong. Conversely, the "wronged" child needs to learn to forgive. Again, parents need to model this behavior for the lesson to be most effective. Don't be afraid to apologize to your spouse or child when you've made an error in judgment. Mistakes are *not* fatal errors. They're opportunities to grow.

Mistakes are <u>not</u> fatal errors.
They're opportunities to grow.

In the spirit of admitting your mistakes, it can be liberating for parents to learn to laugh at themselves when the occasion calls for it. When I started teaching, my biggest fear was that my students would laugh at me if I made a mistake. I knew they'd think I was totally incompetent and soon the entire school would know I was a failure. Talk about overreacting! After getting advice from some of the other teachers, I soon learned it was okay to admit my mistakes and even to laugh at them. It's okay to be human. My students appreciated that I was a good sport. In addition, they understood that it was safe to make mistakes in my class.

What to Look For in a Potential Spouse

This isn't a topic we usually set out to teach children, but in today's changing society I think it's important. Most of us assume that our children will fall in love with a nice guy or gal, get married, and live happily ever after. If things go wrong, and they get divorced, our hearts break for both them and their children.

Thousands of years ago, when marriage was invented, young adults usually married someone from their tribe or village—someone they'd grown up with. The families knew each other, and social standards were fairly uniform throughout the group.

Today's society is much more complex, of course. Family values vary greatly, and young people have a diverse range of expectations about what a marriage should be. Some of these expectations come from the amoral, bed-hopping culture portrayed not only on TV and in movies, but by the "cool" celebrities our teens idolize. More than one young starlet has said, "I don't know if I could commit to being married forever. I think I'd get bored." How tragic! Who's going to care for them if they get sick? Who's going to grow old with them? How many daddies will their kids have?

We need to give children a clear definition of marriage and help them find the path to achieve it. Have these discussions early. Dating is the process of auditioning potential spouses, so age sixteen-ish is a good time to start. Explain that dating is about getting to know someone prior to marriage. It's *not* about trying to see if you can "get" that hot guy or girl. In addition, marriage should last forever, for the sake of the future children. That's why the traditional marriage vow says "until death do us part," not "until I find someone better."

Marriage is meant to be a partnership: two people working toward common goals (family, finances, etc.). It's not about one person controlling the other or one doing all the giving while the other does all the taking. Marriage binds you to another person legally, financially, emotionally, and, it's hoped, spiritually. It's a process where both spouses grow and mature. It's a safe place to fall when the outside world gets harsh. It's a place for unconditional love and acceptance, for grace and forgiveness. Marriage is not fifty-fifty; it needs to be one hundred-one hundred. Each partner needs to give the marriage 100 percent effort.

Keeping all that in mind, there are some things you need to discuss with your children when they start dating. Of course you've already had the sex talk (if not, see Chapter 9). In the interest of simplifying this discussion, I'm going to assume you're talking to a daughter, although the information is just as important for boys.

When your daughter starts dating, find a quiet time and place to have a heart-to-heart talk with her. You may want to have her read this section first. Even though she's not ready to get married, discuss the kinds of characteristics she should look for in a boyfriend (besides "cute" or popular):

- **Character.** Does the world revolve around him, or does he consider the feelings of others? How does he treat her? If he treats her badly when they're dating, it's only going to get worse over time and especially after marriage. How does he treat strangers? How about family members, both his and hers? Is he polite and respectful, or rude and arrogant? Is he willing to help out when she asks, or does he ignore her requests? Can she live with rude and arrogant for fifty years?
- **Morals.** Does he pressure her to do things she's not comfortable with? Does he say things like, "If you loved me, you'd do this for me"? Does he stare at other girls when he's with her? Is he trustworthy, or has she heard rumors about him?

When your cherub starts getting serious about someone, it's time to have the discussion again. The purpose is to get her to think about her relationship, so she can decide if the guy that looks like Freddy Krueger is right for her. Tell her something like, "Remember how we talked about dating and going steady as sort of an audition for a husband? Well, now that you and Freddy seem to be dating steadily, we need to talk again. It's because we love you and want you to be happy."

Without judging, ask her questions about her values, as well as his. It's important she finds someone with values similar to her own. If, for example, she feels strongly about tithing (giving 10 percent of one's income to the church) and he feels that tithing is like flushing money down the toilet, one of them will end up feeling resentful of the other. There will always be compromise in a marriage, but compromising values tends to cause anger and resentment to bubble up. How do they both feel about:

- **Helping others.** Do they both like volunteering their time or money?
- **Ambition.** Is one of them a workaholic? Is one content to sit on the couch 24-7?
- **Finances.** Does one of them insist on saving up for all purchases while the other likes to max out the credit cards? How do they feel about saving for retirement?
- **Religion.** Can they each accept the other's beliefs? If they have children, what religion will prevail? The Bible says God wants us to be "equally yoked" with our partner. Couples with similar religious beliefs are more likely to help each other grow in their religion.
- **In-laws.** How much visiting are they comfortable with? How close to in-laws do they want to live? Next door? Different continents?
- **Education.** Is he ready to drop out of high school while she's already planning for graduate school?
- **Honesty and fidelity.** How does he really feel about these? How does she?

Other Topics to Discuss with Her

- **Household chores**. Compare attitudes on who should do what and how often. When Pat and I got engaged, I told him, "I can probably learn housework well enough to do half of it."

  He immediately replied, "I can learn to live with it half done." If one of you is a neatnik and the other a slob, you'll each have to work out what you can live with.

- **Trust**. Do you trust him emotionally, or do you always worry he'll get mad about something? Has he ever given you a reason to doubt his word? Do you trust him physically? Any physical, verbal, or emotional abuse is a sign to get out of the relationship *immediately*. It will only get worse over time. Do you ever feel like he's keeping secrets? With all of today's electronic gadgets, it's easy to text, call, chat with, or e-mail others without your knowledge. It's also easy to engage in inappropriate online behaviors. If he refuses to show you his messages, consider it a huge red flag.

- **Personality**. Is he a happy person, or is he usually cranky or moody? Do you feel you need to watch what you say and do, so you don't make him angry? Does he make jokes at your expense, or does he make you look good in front of others? How does he act when things don't go his way? Does he pout or shrug it off? Is he willing to help when you need it, or does he just give excuses?

- **Common interests**. I strongly recommend couples have at least one common interest. Pat and I knew from the beginning that we didn't have any, but figured our strong common values would be enough. We spent a lot of years living parallel lives. It wasn't until our thirtieth anniversary, when we bought a boat, that we discovered something we both love to do. Spending time together is much more rewarding than leading parallel lives.

- **Dreams and goals**. Talk about your plans for the future. If he dreams of living on a ranch in the middle of nowhere, and you love city life, someone will end up disappointed and possibly resentful.

- **Friendship**. Is he your best friend? Do you enjoy spending time with him even when you're not smooching? Can you talk to him about anything? One of my coworkers used to tell his students, "Marry someone you can talk to so that when you're too old to, um, do other things, you can still talk about stuff." Of course, some of the students would look at him in horror, saying, "I don't ever want to get *that* old," but I think they still got the point.
- **Fighting**. Do you fight often? Having frequent fights while you're dating doesn't bode well for a marriage, especially if you keep fighting over the same issues without resolving them. It will likely get worse after the wedding.

  Do you fight fairly? Do you both use your grown-up voices and work toward a peaceful resolution, or does one (or both) of you focus on winning at all costs? Does one of you always win while the other always gives in, or do you take turns winning?
- **Other perspectives.** What do your friends and family think about him? They can often see red flags better than you can, since they're not wearing your rose-colored glasses. If people you respect have concerns, you'll need to consider those concerns carefully. Ask yourself why your loved ones are worried. Do they have a valid point? Be honest with yourself. If the people you respect don't like your boyfriend, ask yourself what you see in him that they don't. Conversely, ask yourself what they see that you're overlooking.
- **Are you "settling"?** Do you think Mr. Right will never come along, so you're willing to settle for this guy? Is he pressuring you into a commitment you're not ready for?

If you suspect your daughter may be contemplating marriage, one helpful exercise is to have her make two lists. The first is a list of Freddy's faults; the second is a list of her own faults. The first list will probably be easy; the second not so much. (I once realized that one of my major character flaws was that I hated change, but of course I didn't want to change that…)

Now have her look at Freddy's character flaws to see if there are any potential deal-breakers, such as drug addiction, a history of violence, or criminal activity. Next go over the other character flaws. Is there anything there she can't live with forever? Many people think they can fix their partner over time; they're usually wrong. If something he does makes her crazy now, it will only make her crazier later on. She'll have to either change her attitude, (there are worse things he could do than leave the toilet seat up) or respectfully ask him to change his behavior. And there may be a few things he'd like her to change. Marriage is a partnership based on mutual love and respect. We all make changes in the interest of marital harmony. If there's something one person is unwilling to change, the other has to decide if they can live with it.

Which brings us to the second list: her own flaws. These will probably be things you, the parent, have mentioned to her in the past. Things like leaving a mess in the kitchen or consistently forgetting to put gas in the car. Is her future husband willing to live with these traits? Is your daughter willing to change in the interest of marital harmony?

Freddy, naturally, should be going through the same process, after which both of them will discuss potential problem areas. Better to find out where the problems are before the wedding.

If your daughter is young and idealistic, she'll probably insist that "We love each other. It will all work out." All the more reason to go through this section with her.

One final word. The goal is to get your daughter to think about whether Freddy is right for her, not to get her to stop seeing him because *you* don't like him. You'll make a lot more progress by asking questions than by demanding she stop seeing him.

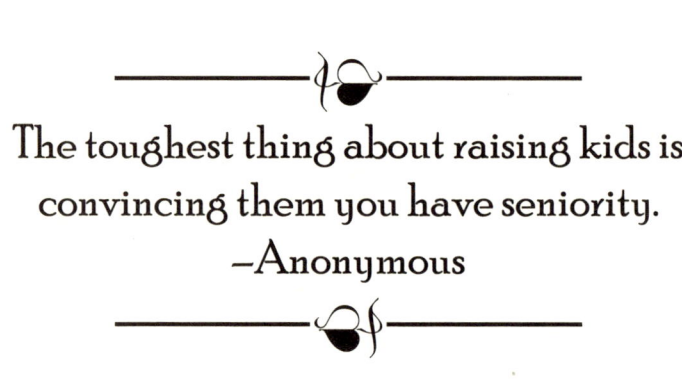

The toughest thing about raising kids is convincing them you have seniority.
—Anonymous

Chapter 5

Consequences

When I first started teaching, I naively believed that if I were a good teacher (whatever that meant), students wouldn't misbehave in class. I was mistaken. I spent a large part of class time asking the same students to please sit down, please be quiet, please get to work. I couldn't understand why my "system" wasn't working. I finally realized that most of the time, the students who were acting up in class saw it as a game. They wanted to know just how far I'd let them push the rules. For some, ignoring authority made them feel like heroes to their peers. For others, it was just a power struggle—they wanted to be in charge.

My life got a lot easier when I figured that out. In fact, it completely changed my approach to classroom discipline. After that, at the start of each semester, I'd explain the rules and the consequences for breaking the rules. I then told them the decision was theirs—if they chose to break the rules, then they automatically chose the consequences. I also explained that I'd ask nicely once or twice, but if asking nicely didn't work, I'd need to do something else to get their attention. (Asking more than twice is called nagging, and that rarely works.)

This made a world of difference in my classroom. Suddenly their misbehavior wasn't my fault. It was their choice and their responsibility to correct. Once they realized I was sticking to the rules and enforcing the consequences, they quit testing my limits.

In my computer classes, I had strict rules about where they could go on the Internet. My classroom was to be G-rated. On the first day of class, I told them if I caught them at any porn site, they'd be off the computer for a month and I would print out a copy of the site they were viewing for their parents. There are many things you can do in the privacy of your own home that you can't do at school, and inappropriate web surfing is one of those things. At first, when I caught them breaking this rule, I'd reason with them or try to make them feel guilty. I really didn't want to be the bad guy and get them into trouble. I spent a lot of time telling students "Don't do that again." Needless to say, as soon as I wasn't looking, they went right back to the porn sites. The combination of hormones and curiosity is a pretty powerful motivator. Then I started enforcing consequences.

Two weeks into the new semester, I caught a student checking out the Playboy site. I felt bad—he was a nice young man who'd merely had a lapse in judgment—but I knew I had to stick to my guns. I called him into my office and said, "So, what are the rules?"

He hung his head and mumbled, "I can't use the computer for a month."

"What else?"

His head snapped up, eyes wide. "Nooooo!"

"That was part of the deal. I need to inform your parents why you can't use the computer for a while. And Marc—I assume this won't happen again."

"Oh, no ma'am."

At this point, I was feeling guilty for being so mean. I had to remind myself more than once that it wasn't anything I had done that started the problem. I was just making sure Marc didn't have another judgment lapse at school.

The most surprising part for me was that I never had another student break that particular rule. Word got out that I would follow through, and nobody else wanted to test my resolve. It's not that they all suddenly turned into saints, but they did behave in my classroom.

When reminding kids of the rules, it's important to remember to ask nicely only once or twice. Too many people ask five or ten times, depending on their mood, then either give up and quit asking or get frustrated and start screaming. This only teaches children that they can ignore you until you lose your temper. Maybe you'll give up and quit asking (they win), or maybe you'll lose your temper and make them do whatever it is you wanted (you win). But consider the price: frazzled nerves all around. In the long run, it's much easier to calmly enforce the request early on.

Isn't that how life works? Choose to drive too fast, and you understand you could get a ticket. Choose not to get to work on time and you're choosing to have your pay docked or risk being fired.

After I started using the "Rules and Consequences" method at school, I tried it on my own children. It's very effective when used consistently, and the best part is it takes the burden of blame off the parents. Kids choose the behavior, and they therefore choose the results of that behavior. Of course, they will still test the limits occasionally and will often protest loudly when you enforce the consequences. I would tell our boys, "I'm sorry you're not happy with the results of your actions. Maybe next time you'll choose to follow the rules." Keep in mind that the more consistent you are in enforcement, the sooner they will come to accept the new plan.

 Kids choose the behavior, and they therefore choose the results of that behavior.

One of the hardest things to deal with is that when you first start administering consequences, the behavior will get worse before it gets better. Children will work hard to get back to the system they were comfortable with, especially if they were in control before. Many parents assume the plan isn't working or can't deal with the increase in conflict, and give up. Hang in there—no one ever said parenting was easy. It took years to get to the point you're at, and it will take time to see improvements. Both you and your children have to unlearn some bad habits. Explain to them that your job is to teach them to succeed in society and to grow into responsible adults.

Be patient with yourself and with them. Remind them (and yourself) that your job is to help them become responsible adults.

Identify Your Expectations

The key to this process is to let children know early on what you expect from them. Imagine handing your boss a report that has a few minor errors in it. He reads it and says nothing, so you assume it looks good to him. The next few reports also have some errors, but again he says nothing. Then one day you turn in a report, and your boss starts yelling at you in the middle of the office. "Why can't you ever get these reports right? I always have to fix your mistakes!"

How would you feel about that? Wouldn't you rather have your boss tell you up front what he or she expected? The same is true for our children. They are eager to please, but they need to know what our expectations are. Too often, we assume they know what we want or how we want things to be done. Also, we need to remember that growing up is hard work. At every stage of their development, kids are learning new skills. As with any new skill we learn, it takes repetition, reinforcement, practice, and patience.

The first step in the process is to figure out exactly what your expectations are. Too often parents have some vague idea that they just want their kids to "be good," which usually translates into "Don't argue with me, I'm tired."

When was the last time you thought about the expectations you have for your children as far as rules go? Does their homework have to be done before dinner? Before playing? Before watching TV? What chores are they expected to do and when? What do you expect in the way of manners, personal hygiene, tidiness, grades, or pet care? Are these expectations set in stone, or do they vary according to your mood? How many of these items are your children aware of? When I was in high school, my mother would yell down the hall every night somewhere around dinnertime. "Get in here and feed your poor dog! Why are you so lazy?" Every night I was yelled at for selfishly ignoring the dog. It never occurred to me to ask what time I should feed the dog; I just waited for the yelling to start. My mother probably could have saved some frustration if she had given me a time frame in which to feed the dog.

Many kids run into something similar when it comes to cleaning their room. They drift along happily, creating somewhat organized (or not so organized) piles of stuff on the floor until a parent walks in and is horrified by what they see. "How can you live like this? This place is a pigsty! You're not going anywhere until you clean this up!" Now the child needs to guess at what "clean" means to Mom or Dad. Dusted and vacuumed? Nothing on the floor (which means everything gets shoved under the bed)? Everything hung up or folded and put away? Toys sorted by color? Clean sheets on the bed (and who washes the dirty ones)? If they don't know what parents are looking for, how do kids know when they're done?

Some families find that a checklist taped inside the closet door helps children remember all the details and lets them know when they have finished the job successfully. Monitoring their own progress this way fosters independence—they don't have to rely entirely on external (parental) approval. If the job isn't done to your satisfaction, ask them what they might do to improve it. "I see you pulled the bedspread up, but it looks pretty lumpy underneath. Can you fix that?" Or simply, "How does that bed look to you?"

Remember that growing up is one very long learning process, and you are their most important teacher. No one learns a new skill on the first try, even if it's something they actually want to learn. Kids certainly don't learn how to do chores on the first try. As their teacher, your job is to guide them through each new skill and help them learn to monitor their own progress. Being clear about your expectations makes the process infinitely easier on everyone. Clearly defining your expectations in regards to chores gives your child the ability to evaluate her own performance. If you're consistent in looking over her work, and in holding her accountable, she'll quickly learn that the consequence of a sloppy job is being called back to do it over.

If yours is a two-parent household, it's important that you and your spouse come to an agreement on expectations. If one of you feels your six-year-old son's room should be spotless and the other feels that's too much to ask, the child won't know what to think. Whether or not he was successful depends on which parent he asks. If he sees his parents arguing over this matter, all he will know for sure is that he was the cause of the fight. Instead of learning how to complete a job successfully, he's learned that chores create stress and should be avoided at all costs. Probably not the outcome you were looking for.

If you're not sure whether your expectations are reasonable, your best bet is to talk to others. Teachers, friends, and extended family members can all provide input. If you and your spouse can't come to an agreement, at least try to work out a compromise.

DISCIPLINE VS. PUNISHMENT

Most people equate discipline with punishment, but there's more to it than that. Punishment is a form of reactive parenting. We get angry and spank the child, usually without much explanation. Punishment stops the undesirable behavior for the moment but doesn't offer any alternative behaviors to the child. It may involve yelling, slapping, name-calling, or blaming, all of which can damage fragile little egos.

Discipline is used by proactive parents and focuses on teaching *why* the behavior is unacceptable. It requires calm and loving communication, and may involve natural or logical consequences (see page 120) to correct the problem. "Walls are not for coloring on, and now you need to clean that up. Next time, please ask for some paper."

Parental discipline ultimately teaches children self-discipline; punishment teaches children not to get caught the next time. Punishment fosters fear; discipline fosters trust and understanding. It's normal to get angry when children misbehave, but children should not be punished out of anger. Count to ten and remind yourself that they're still learning self-control. Then demonstrate self-control. Choose your attitude.

Physical and Verbal Punishment

For thousands of years, the traditional method of punishment has been spanking, primarily because it's effective, takes very little thought on the part of the parents, and helps parents vent their frustration. Unfortunately, spanking can escalate into beating and sends the message that hitting is acceptable. Finding alternative methods of punishment requires some forethought (and restraint), but your family is worth the effort.

Another parenting pitfall is yelling. Raising your voice is not necessarily bad—it does get their attention. But all too often, yelling turns into verbal abuse. It's too easy to go from "I said clean your room right now!" to "Why are you such a lazy slob? You never do what you're told!" Those negative self-images will be internalized. Verbal abuse is still abuse. Personally, I think verbal abuse can do more damage than a quick swat on the behind. Verbal abuse can destroy children's self-esteem, sometimes to the point where they can't recover. Just ask any family therapist. Verbal abuse leaves huge scars—you just can't see them.

Verbal abuse is still abuse.

Yelling almost always arises out of anger and frustration, and when emotions are high, people tend to say hurtful things. It's true that misery loves company, and when parents are upset, it's normal to want to share that misery with the child, especially if the child is the source of the anger. Think back to a time when you were being yelled at. Were you listening carefully to the message, trying to learn from the experience? Probably not. Most likely, your focus was on defending yourself and thinking ahead to your rebuttal. Young children often focus on what they see as the underlying message: Mom or Dad thinks they're a rotten kid. Older children may, in self-defense, tell themselves that the "yeller" is a rotten person. At any rate, the end result of yelling is to cut off the lines of communication. The next time you start shouting at your daughter, stop and take a close look at her face. You'll see her shutting down emotionally. It's as if an invisible wall suddenly appeared between the two of you.

Remember that anger is a secondary emotion, arising out of frustration or fear. Try to identify why you're angry, and then explain your feelings to your child. "I'm feeling frustrated because I've asked you twice to make the salad and you're ignoring me. It's making me angry. When I ask you to do something, it's because I need it done right away, not when you're done with your game." Modeling good communication skills in this manner has the added benefit of teaching your offspring to identify and articulate their feelings.

When you feel a screaming fit coming on, remember that any two-year-old can throw a temper tantrum. As the grown-up in the relationship, you are obligated to act like one. Take a deep breath and explain that you're on the edge. "Johnny, I'm just about out of patience. I've tried asking nicely, and that's not working. I don't want to start yelling, but I will if I need to, to get your attention. What do you think I should do?" Usually this was enough to make my boys realize it was time to get moving. They didn't like being yelled at any more than I liked yelling.

How to Discipline

Effective discipline involves setting rules, consistent enforcement, positive reinforcement, and selling the benefits of the desired behavior to the child. In addition, it's essential to let the child know you care about him and are acting in his best interest.

Setting Rules

Children, especially preschoolers, need to be reminded of the rules and expectations, even when you discipline them. "Food is not for throwing on the floor. Now you'll have to clean it up." Or "Hitting is not allowed. You'll have to sit in the chair for ten minutes." Often children will say they "forgot" the rules. Explain that the object of discipline is to help them remember the rules the next time.

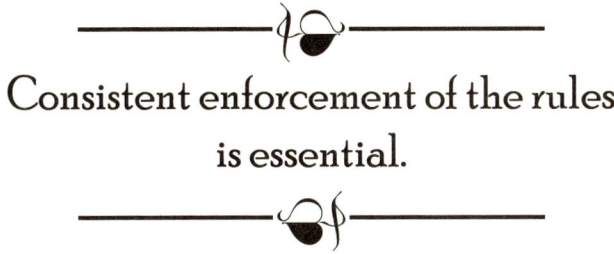

Consistent enforcement of the rules is essential.

Obviously rules must be age-appropriate. We can't expect children to follow rules they're not developmentally ready for. Toddlers can't be punished for having accidents during potty training or spilling food as they learn to feed themselves. As they grow, their needs and behaviors change, and we modify the rules along with consequences. Toddlers learn not to hit or bite others; preschoolers learn that certain words are not acceptable. By kindergarten, children know to sit quietly while the teacher is talking.

Consistent Enforcement

Consistent enforcement of the rules is essential. I can't emphasize that enough. If you enforce certain standards only part of the time, all you will get is a confused child, and I guarantee you'll hear a lot of "But you let me do it last time!" If slamming the door gets your daughter in trouble some of the time, why does it seem to be acceptable the rest of the time? When you're in the middle of cooking dinner or washing the car, it's hard to stop what you're doing to go correct her behavior—but if you don't correct the behavior, then she'll assume that it was okay this time. Will it be okay the next time? Hard for her to tell.

If you can't stop what you're doing, the next best thing is to discuss the problem with her as soon as possible. "I know you were angry earlier, but doors are not for slamming. You have a choice to make: learn right now not to slam doors, or continue slamming them in which case I'll remove your door until you're older."

It's important that both parents agree on what the consequences will be and that each parent support the other. If you disagree with the consequence your spouse has handed down, discuss it privately and then come back with a united front. "Your mother pointed out that grounding you for the next twenty years may be excessive, so we've agreed that you'll only be grounded for two weeks."

It's also important for schools and parents to cooperate when it comes to discipline. When I was teaching, one of the principals I worked for told me there are no bad kids, only kids who make bad choices. Our job as adults is to guide their decision-making process and teach them that bad choices have unpleasant consequences. You'd think parents would be happy to help schools teach that message. You'd be surprised.

Matthew, a fourth grader who happened to be tall for his age, attacked a student who had called him a name. When a teacher, who was very pregnant, stepped in to stop the fight, Matthew shoved her hard enough to knock her down and break her arm. Even though several people witnessed the entire incident, Matthew's father was outraged that the school wanted to suspend his son. In fact, he was proud of Matthew for standing up for himself. Instead of teaching Matthew self-control, he felt the teacher should have stayed out of the fight and let the boys work out their problem on their own.

Mike, a seventh grader, was going on an early morning field trip with his class. As the bus was pulling out of the parking lot, he spotted his least favorite teacher walking toward the building. Mike leaned out the window and yelled, "F-- you, Mr. Smith!" Mike's parents were called in that afternoon. As they listened to Mr. Smith and the two teachers who were on the bus at the time, the parents accused them all of lying. "Our son would never do something like that," they insisted. Put yourself in Mike's shoes for a moment. What do you suppose he learned from that exchange? Probably that he can do what he wants at school, because Mom and Dad will bail him out. What will happen when Mike gets older and gets a job? The first time he tells his boss to "f-- off," I guarantee there will be consequences. How long will Mom and Dad keep rescuing him?

Parents must enforce appropriate standards of behavior and help schools do the same.

One of the first and most important things we teach is that misbehavior and inappropriate choices have consequences. This lesson needs to begin at an early age (two-ish). Too often parents put off discipline because they're not sure what to do or because they hope it's just a phase the child will outgrow. The irony is that not only doesn't the child outgrow the behavior, he learns that his inappropriate behavior is expected. He only has to overhear "Johnny's a wild child" a few times for it to become a self-fulfilling prophecy. The more he hears this type of label, the more it becomes part of his self-image. After all, he reasons, adults know a lot more than he does, and if they think he's out of control it must be true.

For me, being consistent was extremely difficult. When my firstborn was little, I assumed that once I explained a rule to him, he would cheerfully follow the rule for the rest of his life. I'm not sure why I thought that—it certainly didn't work for my parents. Anyway, I spent a lot of time nagging, yelling, and threatening those first few years, and getting extremely frustrated because it wasn't working. That's when I started collecting parenting books, looking for a better way.

If you're just starting a discipline program, your life *will* be more difficult at first. If kids have learned to resist your efforts at correction, they will continue to resist. In fact, they'll probably resist harder. Things will get worse before they get better. You'll need to persevere and hang on to the thought that it's for their own good (and yours in the long run). A program of escalating consequences can be helpful. Something along the lines of "You need to sit quietly in the chair for ten minutes. If you scream or whine, it will be twenty minutes." Or "Go to your room. Your thirty-minute time-out starts when you quit yelling." For older children: "You're grounded for a week. If you're disrespectful about it, you'll be grounded for two weeks. I don't expect you to be happy about the consequences, but you're not allowed to make my life unpleasant."

Positive Reinforcement

Positive reinforcement involves "catching them being good," praising them when they remember things you've taught them.

When I was teaching seven-year-olds to swim, I found I got the best results when I said something positive before correcting their mistakes. Learning any new skill (swimming, cleaning the house, driving a car) involves remembering a lot of details, and positive comments about what they're doing well will do a lot to relieve some of the anxiety and/or frustration inherent in learning the skill:

- You're doing a great job of blowing bubbles. Now let's work on pointing your toes when you kick.
- I like that you put all your laundry away. Next time, you need to fold it first so your clothes will look better when you wear them. I'll show you how.
- I'm so impressed—you remembered to do the lampshades when you dusted. Now you need to remember to wipe the sides of the bookcases, because they get dusty, too.
- You're doing a great job of checking for traffic before you change lanes, but it's important to remember to signal first so other drivers will know where you're going. If someone sees that you want to get in front of them, they may back off to let you in.

Of course, positive reinforcement isn't just for correcting mistakes. We should use it as often as possible throughout the day to encourage an atmosphere of cooperation and mutual respect:

- I appreciate that you took the trash out without being asked. It makes my life easier when I don't have to be the "chore police."
- I like that you remember to say "please" and "thank you." What a polite young man you are!
- You remembered to give the dog fresh water. That was very thoughtful of you.

Since the labels children hear applied to them become part of their self-image, why not use positive ones? Comments like "I really appreciate how (helpful, thoughtful, dependable) you are" go a long way toward shaping a child into a helpful, thoughtful, dependable adult. This approach has the added benefit of creating positive interactions with your children. Instead of being the bad guy who only interacts with them when they're doing something wrong, you can remind them daily that they are loved and appreciated.

Dr. Sandahl, the first principal I worked for, was a firm believer in the "catch them being good" approach. In fact, it was one of the items he reviewed on our annual teacher evaluation. He told a story about Steve, a tenth grader who always seemed to be in trouble for something. No matter how hard he tried, Dr. Sandahl couldn't seem to catch Steve being good. Every interaction he had with Steve was to correct his behavior or administer some sort of discipline. Finally, in exasperation, he explained the problem to Steve directly. "I want to be able to give you some positive comments, but I can't ever seem to catch you being good. When are you going to be behaving yourself, so I can see a different side of you?"

Steve thought about that and replied, "How about tomorrow at lunch?" They shook hands on it, and the next day at lunch, the principal made a point of standing near the table where Steve and his friends were eating. To the principal's surprise, for the first time all year, Steve cleaned up the garbage on the table and put it in the trash can.

Immediately, Dr. Sandahl went over to the table and told Steve, "I'm so impressed! Thank you for cleaning up your trash!" Steve endured some teasing from his friends that afternoon, but after that day it gradually became easier for Dr. Sandahl to find reasons to give him "positive strokes." At graduation, Steve and Dr. Sandahl were discussing this turning point in Steve's high school career. Steve said it seemed like a pretty silly game at the time, but admitted that it did in fact feel good to finally hear someone say something nice about him, especially in front of his friends. It was enough to make him start changing his ways. Both Steve and the principal knew it was a game, but it was a game with win-win results.

Catching children being good can be difficult to remember. When things go wrong, we know we need to correct them. We expect things to go right, however, and when they do we take it for granted. It takes effort to remember to praise children for doing things right, but the results are worth it.

Not only should we catch our own kids being good, but society benefits when we catch other people's children being good and then offer them positive reinforcement. Whenever a young person holds the door for me or stops to pick up something I may have dropped, I always instruct them, "Tell your folks they're doing a great job of raising you."

I was standing outside my classroom one day when I heard two students in a heated argument. As the first one walked away, the other continued yelling obscenities at him. I walked up to this angry young man, tapped him on the shoulder, and said, "That's not the kind of language we use in mixed company, is it?"

He took a deep breath and struggled for a long moment about how to answer me. I could almost see every thought marching across his face, and I half expected him to keep yelling at the other student. He was still furious with him and working hard to keep from turning his anger on me. Finally he exhaled and replied, "No, ma'am. Sorry."

I was happy that he could pull himself together like that, and I told him so. "I can see how angry you are, and I know it wasn't easy to calm down and answer me politely. I appreciate the effort it took, and it tells me that you're a man who's working on doing the right thing."

Selling the Benefits of the Desired Behavior

When I started teaching, I realized it was a lot like being a salesperson: you need to convince the customer (student) that what you're selling is something they need or want. You'll get a much greater rate of compliance if someone can see how it directly benefits them.

One of my students in a required computer class had given up working on her assignments and was consequently failing the class. When I asked her about it, she told me straight out, "I hate computers, and I hate this class!"

"Gee, I thought this was your favorite class, because you're doing everything you can to make sure you take it again next semester." Her eyes got big as she realized I was right. "You don't have to like the class, but you do have to pass it, so why don't you make up your mind to do that much, anyway?" She did get down to work and managed to pass the class, barely. We were both happy.

Similar strategies can be employed at home. Explain how rules benefit everyone, including them:

- If you don't clean your room today, we'll have to do it together on Saturday, and I won't have time to take you to your friend's house.
- Phone calls can only be ten minutes long so everyone has access to the phone, including you.
- You can't play in the street because it's dangerous. You're the only Amy I have, and it's my job to keep you safe.
- The bathroom must be cleaned every week to get rid of germs so you don't get sick.

Show Them You Care about Them

This point seems too obvious to mention. You're thinking, "Of course they know I love them," but when was the last time you told them that they're special or that you're proud of them? In the chaos that most of us call daily life, it's easy to forget to tell them how happy you are that they're your kids.

If you're *not* happy that they're yours, the time to change this is right now. Negative feelings about a child can easily develop into a downward spiral that is difficult to pull out of. It goes something like this:

The child misbehaves, and instead of correcting the behavior, the parent says something negative such as, "You're just a spoiled rotten brat." The child internalizes this and, not having learned any consequences, continues to misbehave. The more the child acts out, the more the parents dislike being around him. In the most extreme cases, parents give up and throw the child out of the house. What a tragedy, yet it can be prevented.

Start by putting things in a positive perspective. "I love you, but I don't like the way you're acting right now." Or "I love you, and that's why I can't let you behave this way." Then follow through on the discipline. As they start complying with your expectations, you'll find more opportunities to catch them being good and to encourage their progress.

Hugs and other physical signs of love and approval are also important. A pat on the back or peck on the cheek goes a long way toward fostering self-esteem.

Natural and Logical Consequences

What happens when you get to work and find you've either forgotten your lunch or don't have enough money for lunch? What if you've forgotten to return your library book for the last two weeks? You go hungry, or pay the fine, and work harder at remembering next time. Those are the natural consequences of your actions.

As parents, we can use natural consequences to our advantage. When children forget their lunch, library book, or homework they encounter certain natural consequences. If you find yourself always running to the school to deliver some forgotten item, ask yourself what you're teaching your offspring. Are they learning to be responsible for remembering their own stuff, or are they learning that Mom will rescue them whenever they need it? How much rescuing are you willing to do? Everyone forgets things occasionally, but your job is to make them more responsible, not more dependent on you.

I'm not saying that you should never drop off the lunch that was left behind, but if it's becoming a regular event, it would be better to teach some coping skills. As soon as the homework is finished or lunch is made, it goes in the backpack. This will take some reminding by you, but eventually they'll get it. Reminders should be in the form of hints: "What two things should be in your backpack?"; or, on library day, "It's Tuesday—what does that mean?" If you ask them every morning, they'll get in the habit of asking themselves. You can help them along that path. Start out with "Stop, think. What two things do you need?" Later cut it down to just "Stop, think." Eventually just block the door and hold up your hand, allowing them to stop and think for themselves. How long you spend on each phase depends on the age of your child and how absentminded they are. Some are more resistant to training than others, but all are trainable.

Logical consequences take a little more creativity, along the lines of making the punishment fit the crime. "You're not allowed to hit your brother. Give him a hug and tell him you're sorry." My boys didn't mind apologizing, but they *hated* the hugging part. If your daughter borrows your hammer and then loses it, avoid launching into a character assassination ("You're so irresponsible—you always lose things"). Instead, ask calmly how she plans to replace it and then hold her to it. If your teenage son comes home thirty minutes after curfew, then the next time he goes out, curfew will be moved thirty minutes earlier. Other examples:

- When you're rude or disrespectful to us, we don't feel like doing favors for you, like taking you to the mall or buying you the new shirt you want.
- If you wreck your car, then you're without a car to drive until you can pay to get it fixed.
- If you lose a toy, then you do without it. We won't run out to buy you a new one.
- If you lose someone else's property (say, a library book), you must pay for it out of your allowance.
- If you don't do your chores, you're grounded until they're done.
- If we have to clean up the family room after you've eaten in there, then you don't get to eat in there for a week.
- If we ask you to help with something and you ignore us, then we may just say no the next time you need help with something.

Logical consequences take some thought, but there are several advantages. If you can anticipate potential problems (such as coming home after curfew) and can explain ahead of time what the consequence will be, then the choice is the child's. It allows you to stay calm and focus on the behavior that needs correcting.

Finding the Right Consequences

The secret to enforcing rules and expectations is to find the right motivator for each child. Several factors need to be considered, including the nature of the misbehavior, the age of the child, and the child's personality. Personal motivators vary, even among siblings. It may take a few tries to find a consequence that works, but every child can be motivated. If you try something and it doesn't appear to be working, try something else.

When my eldest son was four, he accidentally threw a baseball through a neighbor's window. Using the "you break it you fix it" theory, we made him help replace the glass. Over the next few weeks, he broke two more windows in the neighborhood, and each time we made him help repair them. After the fourth broken window, we realized something wasn't working. Clearly we were slow to catch on.

Looking at the situation from his point of view, we finally realized that instead of being a deterrent, helping replace the glass was actually a reward for him. He got to wear safety goggles just like a grown-up and help Daddy in the workshop. Pretty cool activities for a four-year-old. He was breaking windows so he could spend time with Dad doing grown-up things. We needed to find some other consequence.

Since he was our social child, we found the most effective consequence to be grounding him to his room. He was happiest when he was in the middle of a group of people, so sending him to his room was torture. Another son was more of an introvert, so he was happy to be sent to his room. He was content to read or just lay on the bed and daydream. We had to be more creative in finding effective consequences for him.

If your child is an athlete, curtailing his participation in practices or games can be an attention-getter. "If you don't get your book report done by Friday, you can't play in the game on Saturday." Schoolwork comes before sports.

Some people are reluctant to use this approach because the entire team may suffer. The reality is that peer pressure is an extremely powerful motivator; use it to your advantage. If your son's teammates are mad at him for getting grounded and missing a game, he will think twice about missing a game the next time. Keep in mind that your child's upbringing is more important than a Little League game.

Most high schools use this approach. If an athlete has a certain number of Ds or Fs, they can't participate in sports until the grades are brought up. If you feel your school's D/F policy isn't strict enough, let the principal know—or enforce a stricter policy at home. (For example, *any* Ds or Fs mean you don't play.) Be sure to talk to the coach about this so he knows why your son won't be at the game. Most coaches are totally supportive. If your coach isn't, remind him or her that your primary goal is to raise a responsible, well-educated young adult. Even students who will later become professional athletes need an education.

In junior high and high school, one of the most effective punishments a school can administer is to have a parent spend a day in school with the child. Most students would rather have a root canal than have their parents come to school with them. It just isn't cool. Ten years ago, I'd tell students, "Parents are like underwear—everyone knows you have them, but nobody wants to be seen in public with them." (Nowadays, what with sagging jeans and skimpy blouses, underwear has become more socially acceptable than parents.) If your child is getting into trouble at school, discuss this option with the principal. You may have to take a day off of work, but when you choose to become a parent, you're also choosing the responsibilities that come with the title.

Early Training Is Important

As children mature into adults, it's possible for them to overcome a lack of discipline and to learn self-discipline, but it's significantly more difficult than if they had learned it earlier. Look at all the adults with anger management issues. When things don't go the way they "should," these people explode into fits of rage. No one ever taught them self-control or that they couldn't always have things the way they want.

This is a difficult lesson at any age. Disappointment can be painful and can spark intense anger. It's better to learn the lesson early in life; having to learn it as an adult is much more painful. Kids need to know there are rules and that compliance is expected.

No one wants to see their child experience disappointment, frustration, or any other unpleasantness. Many parents, instead of acknowledging that unpleasantness is a part of life, do everything in their power to shield their children from negative experiences, including consequences.

The irony is that by allowing the child to avoid unpleasantness (consequences and discipline) at home, the parents are creating unpleasantness at school. If the training is left to the school, now the child must be reprimanded in front of his peers. Training takes longer because two different messages are being received: "do what you want" at home, and "control your outbursts" at school.

As a side note, any child who disrupts the classroom is stealing valuable education time from the entire class. Every time a teacher has to stop to correct one student's behavior, *every* student gets cheated.

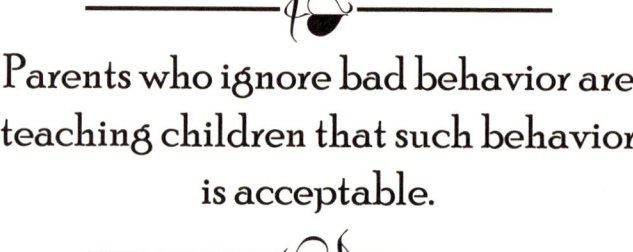

Parents who ignore bad behavior are teaching children that such behavior is acceptable.

Parents who ignore bad behavior are, in effect, teaching that such behavior is acceptable. Karen, an eighth grader, came running into class one day about two minutes before the tardy bell. "My homework is in my locker," she said. "Can I go get it without being marked tardy?" When I said yes, she ran over to her friend Jessica and told her to come with her to the locker. I told them absolutely not. There was no reason for both of them to be late for class. Jessica shrugged and sat down. Karen gave me an evil look, and as she walked away I heard her call out "Bitch!"

I knew that Karen talked to her parents that way, presumably because they allowed it, but I was certainly not going to let her get away with it in my classroom. I caught up with her at the door and told her firmly, "You may get away with that at home, but you will not talk to a teacher that way. When a teacher gives you a reasonable request, the only correct answer is 'Yes ma'am,' and if you are ever disrespectful to me again, you'll find yourself in Saturday detention. Is that clear?"

Her eyes got big, but she nodded and replied, "Yes ma'am."

I smiled, patter her shoulder, and said, "Good answer." We had other disagreements during the year, but she was never disrespectful after that.

But It's Hard!

Yes, finding appropriate consequences and being consistent *is* hard, especially in today's society, which is more isolated than long ago. Many young parents live nowhere near other family members and may have no one to turn to locally for advice or moral support. Music, movies, TV, and the Internet often create conflict by portraying undesirable role models for our children. The phrase "Everyone else is doing it" works because parents aren't close to the other parents involved and because they, too, may accept the media portrayals as normal behavior.

There are many reasons for a lack of discipline at home. Parents may be too tired to enforce consequences or may not know how. Perhaps they don't get home from work until almost bedtime and don't have time to do much more than say good night. Some people have so much on their mind that figuring out how to enforce the rules is way down on their priority list. It reminds me of the saying: "There are two things a person can produce: excuses and results." Are you getting the results you want, or are you making excuses?

Fear of Parenting

Some parents are afraid to discipline their children. They worry that their son will hate them or that their daughter will run away from home. They don't want to alienate their children for fear of losing them forever. Some parents feel guilty because they don't have time to spend with their children, and they certainly don't want to spend the little time they do have fighting with them. But parents have to realize that discipline is ultimately going to help, not hurt, their relationship with them.

Some parents actually encourage illegal activity in an effort to appear cool—buying alcohol for underage drinkers or sharing cigarettes with them. What message does that send? If it's okay to break these laws, isn't it okay to break all of them? And if it's okay to break the law, surely it's okay to break the rules—and if it's acceptable at home, it must be acceptable at school or work as well.

Some parents can't handle the conflict they know will result from efforts to discipline. They're afraid to engage in conflict because they're pretty sure they'll lose. It's much easier to hide in the kitchen or garage and let the kids do what they want.

Lack of Training

One of the downsides of women entering the workplace has been that many women have little energy left at the end of the day to deal with their children's problems. Parenting skills get replaced by survival skills. The result is that parenting skills aren't being handed down to the next generation.

I'm not saying women shouldn't work. I *am* saying that when you commit to having kids, you must commit to being the best parent you can possibly be. You are morally obligated to create a loving, nurturing environment for your little ones and to teach them to become responsible adults. If you haven't learned how to do this from your own parents, you need to get outside help. Take a parenting class, read every book you can find on child rearing, watch *Dr. Phil*. Do whatever it takes.

Encouragement

One of the functions of a family should be to bring out the best in each other and to support one another—and certainly to love one another. Parents need to start by encouraging each other in their respective endeavors and then encourage the children.

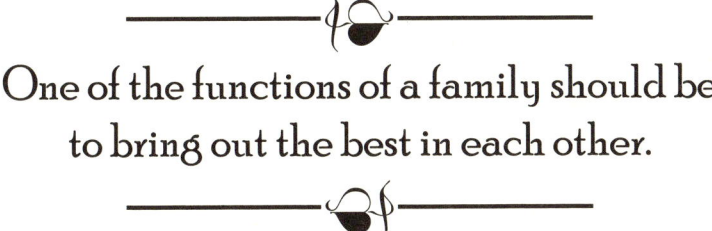

One of the functions of a family should be to bring out the best in each other.

There are many reasons we forget to do this. At the top of the list is the thought that we know better than the other person. When our spouse wants to take a skydiving class in order to fulfill a lifelong dream, we know in our hearts that it's a stupid idea and a total waste of time and money. When our five-year-old wants to grow up to be an animal psychic, our first response is often negative, in the name of being realistic. Instead of explaining why it's a dumb idea, why not allow the dream?

One of my many parental regrets is that when my son Justin wanted to take saxophone lessons, I talked him out of it. The truth was that I had no idea where to get a saxophone or how to arrange lessons (we were living in Japan at the time). I could have made some phone calls and at least tried to find a sax, but I "knew" he'd lose interest quickly. Now I'll never know if I deprived the world of a great saxophone player. Much worse, I made him feel like his idea was no good.

Sometimes when we feel stuck in our job or our marriage, we get caught up in a cycle of negative thinking. Because misery really does love company, we unconsciously bring down the others in the family. And sometimes it's just easier to say no, and end the conversation, than to listen to any reasons why we should say yes. If you find yourself being overly critical, make it a priority to break the habit.

On occasion, parents do need to be the voice of reason. If your youngster has his heart set on being a professional water-skier, you should probably talk to him about a backup plan—taking auto mechanic classes, or something—so he can support himself until the ski thing pays off.

As your family starts encouraging each other and rejoicing in one another's successes, the atmosphere in your home will change dramatically.

ENABLING

I had never heard this term until I attended a conference for teachers. I went to the seminar on enabling only because there was nothing else offered that I was interested in during one particular time slot. It turned out to be the best seminar of the conference. After five minutes, I was shocked to realize that *I* was an enabler. I was the type of person who preferred to avoid conflict, so instead of holding my boys accountable for their minor infractions, I would look the other way.

Enabling involves making excuses for someone's bad behavior and allowing it to continue. It's like the saying "If you're not part of the solution, you're part of the problem." Examples of these excuses may include:

- Boys will be boys.
- He didn't mean to hit you so hard.
- She can't help talking in class. She's always been a talker.
- The move to the new city was hard for her. She deserves to let off a little steam.
- My child would never do that.
- You didn't study for your test? I'll call the school and say you're sick.
- Your homework isn't done? Make up an excuse and I'll back you up.

- You failed your algebra test? That's okay, I'm no good at math, either.

Parents enable bad behavior in a misguided attempt to help the child or to shield him from unpleasant consequences. Instead, it helps keep the child dependent on the parent: who else will cover for them?

Jeremy was a student of mine who liked to test everyone's limits. He was disruptive in the classroom just to the point of being annoying. He was a likable kid but seemed to need the attention he got from causing trouble. (For some students, negative attention is all they know how to attract.) One day, he came to class bragging about how he got his science teacher in trouble. Apparently, Jeremy had misbehaved once too often in Mr. Stone's class and had been given detention. Jeremy was happily telling everyone, "My mom's gonna get him in all kinds of trouble for picking on me. He'll be sorry." Jeremy had learned that he could do what he wanted at school.

The most extreme case of enabling I've ever seen involved a family in Alaska. A young man had brutally raped a young girl, and instead of making him pay for his heinous crime, his parents actually faked his death, helped him change his identity, and relocated him to the East Coast. What were they thinking? Did they really want to send the message "Hurt whomever you want, sweetheart—it's okay"? How long do they think they can keep bailing him out of trouble? And why do they think they should?

Fear of unpleasant consequences is what keeps our society civilized. The threat of traffic tickets and jail sentences keep most of us on the straight and narrow. Teaching youngsters how to get around the rules of society does not make the world a better place and does not help them in any way, shape, or form.

As parents, we need to always keep our job description in mind: we're raising our children to be productive members of society. Everything we do for them and teach to them should be directed toward that goal.

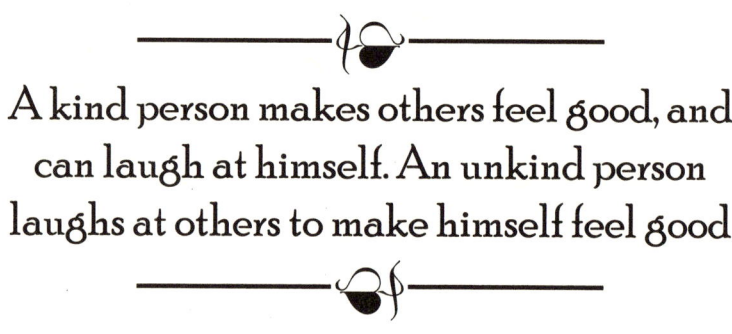

A kind person makes others feel good, and can laugh at himself. An unkind person laughs at others to make himself feel good

hapter 6

Respect

Respect for others, and especially for adults, seems to be a concept that more and more children are failing to grasp. In a school setting, the ramifications are immense. Teachers struggle to keep students from disrupting classes. There are always a handful of students who realize that if enough of them ignore the teacher or disrupt the class, they can each claim, "It wasn't me! It was the other kids!" The end result is that every student, even the motivated ones, loses valuable instructional time.

Most definitions of respect include "esteem for, or deference to, a person." Some definitions include manners, but I think respect is more of an attitude. Manners may be an expression of respect, however, such as saying "Yes, sir," "Please," and "Thank you."

We all know the signs of disrespect: talking back, a disdainful tone of voice, eye-rolling, and what used to be known as "lip" or sass. All kids will be sassy at times. Once they learn that words have power, they start experimenting to see if they can get a reaction. A calm "That's disrespectful, and it's not allowed" should be a sufficient warning. You never want to get sucked into a shouting match. You're the adult, and it's impossible to respect an adult who's screaming like a three-year-old.

I'm always amazed when I see a reality show where a husband and wife are hurling insults at each other. This is a couple who once promised to love, honor, and cherish each other. How did they go from love and tenderness to total animosity? And why doesn't someone tell them to quit acting like two-year-olds? I keep wondering if they're going to throw themselves on the ground and kick their feet during the tantrum.

Usually these are people who manage to treat friends and strangers with a fair amount of respect, so why do they treat family members so badly? Shouldn't we treat loved ones better than we treat anyone else? How can parents profess to love their children, then turn around and call them names? If you want respectful kids, you must treat them and others respectfully.

The argument could be made that all negative behavior—from talking back to adults, to disobedience, to law breaking—can be traced back to an attitude of disrespect. Teaching and modeling respect is the single most effective way to make your home more peaceful.

Teaching and modeling respect is the single most effective way to make your home more peaceful.

Why Respect Is So Important

- As I mentioned earlier, unlikable kids (and adults) have a harder time in life, and respect is a huge part of being likable.
- Kids with respect for others and themselves are less likely to engage in problem behaviors, including drug and alcohol abuse, thievery, and vandalism. They're also more receptive to doing the right thing when faced with peer pressure or difficult choices.
- It's the basis for the Golden Rule: treat others as you want to be treated. The corollary is that rudeness begets rudeness.

- It makes the world a better place. When people act respectfully to each other, everyone's day goes a little more smoothly.

You're Their Number-One Teacher

Every article I've read on teaching respect begins with the same premise: the only way to teach it is by example. If parents yell at each other, belittle one another, and engage in name-calling, then that's the behavior their kids will exhibit. Parents may be able to force their children to act respectfully at home (by threats or intimidation?), but away from home they'll be acting just like Mom and Dad. Obedience is not the same as compliance.

The only way to teach respect is by example.

I learned early in my teaching career that when you give others respect, you get respect back. I rarely had discipline problems because students knew I genuinely cared about them and that we could trust each other. I trusted them to behave like adults, and they trusted me to treat them with respect.

Younger children respond equally well to trust and respect. I was in the library one afternoon with another teacher when a group of seventh graders came in. It became clear that one of them was moving away the next day, and this was their last chance to hang out. Their exuberance was earning them disapproving stares, which they ignored. When they started photocopying their faces, a staff member ran over and told them to stop. They ignored him, too. Finally, my teacher friend stepped in. "I'm glad you guys are having fun, but you're making people nervous, so after you've each copied your face, you need to take the party outside."

They agreed, finished up at the copier, apologized to the staff member, and went on their way. It was that easy. My friend was polite but firm, and made it clear that she expected them to do the right thing.

Sit down with your spouse and take an honest look at how you speak to each other. If your exchanges are ever less than polite, fess up. This is a time for problem solving not accusations. Swallow your pride and admit that you may be a part of the problem, even if it's just a small part. Then work together on a plan to change.

Make a vow that, starting today, there will be no more disrespecting each other or the kids. When you slip up, apologize and try again. When your spouse slips and says something negative to you, respond with something like, "I'm sure you didn't mean it, but what you just said sounded hurtful to me." This allows the other person to acknowledge what he just said and apologize if necessary.

Everyone in the family can (and should) learn self-control. When you're angry with your boss, you manage to hold your tongue or at least choose your words carefully. You can do the same for the people who love you.

Every couple has disagreements and rough patches. You may be going through a period where you and your spouse aren't getting along well. You still owe it to yourself and your family to treat them civilly. Your children are watching.

When you're angry with your spouse, it's tempting to say hurtful things. It helps to think of five things about that person that you're grateful for and say them out loud. It does wonders for lowering your blood pressure. Examples:

- I'm grateful that you take care of the yard.
- I'm grateful for your job.
- I'm grateful that you help with the housework.
- I'm grateful that you're so patient with the kids.
- I'm grateful that you bring me coffee in the morning.

I use this technique when I'm mad at my husband, and he usually responds with his own list. By then we're calmer and can turn our attention to solving the problem. It's hard to stay mad at someone who's saying nice things about you, and by reminding yourself of your spouse's good points, it helps put the argument in perspective. He really is a good person overall, even if he can't remember that dirty socks go in the hamper. She does a great job of raising the kids, even if she's not as organized as you'd like.

Another helpful technique is to remember the five-year rule: will whatever you're fighting about be important five years from now? Your wife didn't run the dishwasher last night, and now you have to wash your coffee spoon by hand. Your husband didn't take the trash out this morning. Your normally responsible teenager left you with a nearly empty gas tank. Life is full of little annoyances. Don't let them ruin your day. Life is much too short to be angry all the time.

Ever heard the saying "The only exercise I get is flying off the handle and jumping to conclusions"? Pat and I have a line we use to diffuse tension that comes from this saying. When one of us explodes about something trivial, the other one will raise an eyebrow and ask, "Exercising again?" It's a subtle reminder that perhaps the angry one is overreacting.

A word of caution on using humor to lighten the mood. When the other person is truly upset about something, he'll want to know that you're taking the matter seriously. An ill-timed joke will sound as though you don't care about his concerns and may very well come across as disrespectful. Instead, use reflective listening to resolve the conflict (see Chapter 4).

Be sure to praise children when you catch them being polite and respectful:

- You were mad when Michael wouldn't share his toy. I'm glad you used your words instead of hitting him.
- Thank you for driving Grandma to the store today. I know you had other things you wanted to do, but she needed to go shopping, and she really enjoys your company.
- The things Sarah said about you online weren't very nice. I'm proud of you for not writing mean things about her to get even.

If Your Spouse Is a Yeller

Perhaps you see the benefits of a respectful household—peace, joy, and harmony—but your spouse just doesn't get it. You have two choices: you can be the one to set a good example and try to ignore your spouse's yelling as best you can, or you can work on changing his behavior. (By the way, if your spouse is not interested in changing his behavior, I highly recommend counseling, for the well-being of the children.)

There are numerous reasons to work on convincing your spouse that his behavior is harmful to his family:

Home should be a safe haven.

- Home should be a safe haven. It's the place we go to get away from the pressures of the outside world. It should not be a place where we have to walk on eggshells, always worried about angering the people we love.

- When you ignore your spouse's bad behavior (which is infinitely easier than confronting it), your children are learning that it's okay to treat you and their siblings badly. They're thinking, "If Dad can do it, why can't I?" If they're allowed to emulate the disrespectful or abusive behavior, odds are good that they'll treat their future spouses the same way. That's how the cycle of abuse is perpetuated.

- Children who live with yelling and verbal abuse have lower self-esteem because they often blame themselves for their parent's anger. "If I wasn't such a rotten kid, Dad wouldn't be mad all the time" or "Mom says I'm a miserable brat, so it must be true."

- Constant tension causes sleeping and eating problems. Some kids take solace in food, while others (primarily girls) become bulimic or anorexic. Eating (or not eating) may be the only thing they feel they can control in their out-of-control world. In addition, children who have a great deal of stress at home find it hard to concentrate at school. Often their grades suffer.

- You may understand that your spouse is just letting off steam or that his bark is worse than his bite, but your kids don't know that. They may worry about your physical safety as well as their own.
- Youngsters who live with verbal abuse often develop trust issues that stay with them throughout life. If they can't trust the people who are supposed to love them more than anything in the world, how can they trust anyone else?
- Verbal abuse can do more damage than physical abuse. There are no scars or bruises that anyone can see, but the damage is there forever.

It's a perverse fact of human nature that we internalize negative comments more readily than positive ones. If hearing "You're a moron" just once is hurtful, what happens when a child hears it every day? And it's not just name-calling that's damaging to the ego. Comments such as "Shut up and leave me alone," "I wish you'd never been born," and "Why can't you be like your sister?" imply that the world would be a better place if Junior wasn't in it.

If your spouse is a yeller, you'll need an extra measure of patience. If possible, work out a signal to let your spouse know when he's being disrespectful. Clearing your throat or putting a hand on his arm works in calmer moments. If he's in the middle of a full-on rant, you'll have to be more direct, and you may have to wait until he calms down. Try to:

- Step in front of him and ask why he's angry.
- Remind him that he's a good person and doesn't need to act this way.
- Remind him discreetly that adults don't throw temper tantrums.
- Ask discreetly that he use his grown-up voice.
- Remind him to breathe or count to ten.
- Try verbalizing the things you're grateful for.

- Empathize: "Sounds like you had a bad day."
- If possible, usher the kids out of the room, into the car, and down the street if need be.
- Make it clear that you won't allow yourself or your children to be abused.

Trying these things will help you train your children (and your spouse if necessary) to be respectful. The trick is to be respectful yourself while you do it. You and your children have the right to a peaceful home. As Dr. Phil likes to say, we teach people how to treat us.

Ways to Model Respect

- Be considerate of the feelings of your family.
- Never ever call anyone hurtful names.
- Discipline with love. Never embarrass your child in front of others or in private. In public, be discreet with discipline. Make it clear that you love him but need to correct his behavior.
- Don't allow others to be disrespectful toward you. When family members are rude, simply stand firm: "That was a disrespectful tone of voice. Please try again." You can keep repeating that phrase until you get compliance. It will sink in eventually.
- Use your grown-up voice—your calm, loving, nurturing grown-up voice. I know how hard it is to appear calm when your kids are making you crazy. Take a deep breath (counting to ten helps) and then say, "That was not okay" or "I'm very angry about this." Remember that anger is a secondary emotion. For parents, anger usually follows frustration: "I've asked you three times to take out the trash, and you still haven't done it. I'm feeling angry and frustrated right now."

With a little practice, you can learn to choose your attitude even when you're angry. You can choose between screeching or speaking calmly, between name-calling or describing the problem. You can also learn to catch yourself when you first start feeling frustrated and give the kids some warning. I used to tell my boys, "I'm running out of patience right about now. I don't want to get angry, but that's where I'm headed. Please take care of this matter RIGHT NOW." That usually worked.

Other ways to earn respect:

- **Be trustworthy.** Keep promises. Follow through on commitments.
- **Admit when you're wrong.** All parents make mistakes. An honest apology validates your little one's feelings and opens the door to a discussion on how to solve the problem.
- **Be a good listener.** Turn off the TV and ignore the phones. Give your child or spouse your undivided attention. Take his feelings and concerns seriously, even if they seem silly or trivial to you. When there's a dispute, always listen to his side of the story.
- **Be honest.**
- **Look for teachable moments.** When you see examples of disrespect, discuss them with the children. Ask why the person acted the way she did, and how she could have made her point in a more acceptable manner.

I spent several years as a substitute teacher, and I remember one eighth grader, Michelle, who would not stop talking to her friend as I was trying to teach. When I asked Michelle to please move to another seat, she flatly refused. I knew if I let her win this battle, I'd lose all credibility, so I smiled at her and said, "I'd be happy to help you." As I picked up her books and purse and carried them to her new seat, she started complaining. "Don't touch my stuff! You can't touch my stuff!"

I decided to use humor to model respect and countered with the words she should have been saying. "Thank you so much for carrying those heavy books for me, Mrs. Rhodes. You're the nicest sub in the whole school. I wish you could come home with me and help me clean my room. Then you could stay for dinner." All of this as she's telling me to leave her things alone. The point is, she did follow me (okay, she followed her stuff) to the new seat and was quiet the rest of the hour. I didn't have to yell or threaten, beg or plead.

Trust

It's hard, especially for kids, to respect someone who is untrustworthy. An important lesson, however, is that even if kids don't like or trust someone, they must still act respectfully toward that person. It costs nothing to smile and be civil.

Think of someone you trust. Do you respect that person? What about someone you don't trust? Now the hard question. Do your kids trust you? Do you keep your promises whenever possible? Do you listen attentively to their concerns, or laugh them off? Do you speak lovingly toward them, or belittle them and call them names? Remember that every interaction with your child teaches them something. If you suspect that your interactions are more negative than positive, it's not too late to change.

Respect for Others

Respect is all about considering the feelings of others, and most of the "others" your munchkins will be dealing with are their peers. Now that your family is happily modeling—and requiring—respectful behavior, your youngsters will recognize the importance of treating their friends the same way. In addition, they'll be better equipped to handle situations in which they're on the receiving end of disrespect. They can fend off teasing with questions like:

- That sounded pretty rude. Why would you say something like that?
- That wasn't very nice. Are you having a bad day today?

Children will sometimes hurt someone's feelings unintentionally. Words that sound harmless to them can often be misinterpreted. Over time, you'll help them learn to think before they speak and to choose their words carefully. When little Donny tells Marie, "Your hair looks goofy," talk to them both about how that hurts Marie's feelings. A statement of fact ("You might want to brush your hair") is much better than negative judgment calls. There's a fine line between honesty and tact.

Occasionally kids get pressured into joining a group that's teasing or bullying another student. If you suspect your child is involved, have a frank discussion about why it's not okay and look for ways he can avoid participating in the future. When pressured to join in, he could reply with:

- I don't hang out with bullies.
- Why do you want to pick on that kid?
- I hear that kid's brother has a black belt in karate.

Respect for others includes respect for the property of others. These rules are simple:

- If it's not yours, don't mess with it unless you have permission.
- If you lose it or damage it, replace it.

Respect for the Wishes of Others

When you love someone, you want to make them happy, even if you have to go out of your way. If, however, you ask family members to do something for you and they refuse, it feels unloving and disrespectful. Suppose at your house, you ask everyone to put their own dirty dishes in the dishwasher and dirty clothes in the hamper. When they don't, it implies they don't care what you want or that your wishes are unimportant. It's as if they told you, "If you want dishes in the dishwasher, *you* can put them there." Teach children that ignoring requests is a form of disrespect.

If, however, you place too many requests (demands) on family members, they may interpret those demands as you trying to control them, and may give up trying to please you. If they load the dishwasher and all you tell them is that they didn't do it right, they might figure "Why bother?" Remember to thank them for doing what you asked. Catch them being good.

Respect for Authority

Learning to treat parents, elders, and teachers respectfully will make it easy for your children to deal with bosses, clients, and possibly police officials when the time comes. I know we're all hoping to avoid the police part, but if they ever do have a brush with the law, our kids need to know that deference is important.

When we lived in Germany, our eighteen-year-old, Justin, went off base with his friends one night to see a movie. As they pulled into the parking lot, they spotted a Base Security Police car. The kid in the front passenger seat of Justin's car started taunting the officers, thinking they had no jurisdiction off base. Justin, the other kids in the car, and the police officers all told Mike to be quiet, but Mike didn't get it. He kept hurling insults at the officers. Finally, one of the officers got fed up, reached in, and hauled Mike out of the car through the open window. They took him down to the station just because he didn't understand the need for respect.

When I started teaching high school, occasionally I'd hear students in the hallways using inappropriate language. I'd walk up and say, "Excuse me?" They'd immediately clap a hand over their mouth and apologize, whether they knew me or not. They knew better than to use that type of language in school and certainly knew there'd be consequences for talking back to a teacher. During my last year of teaching, about fifteen years later, I stopped questioning students I didn't know, because half the time they'd scowl at me and ask, "Who the h-- are you?" Or worse. How are these young people ever going to hold a job? I didn't even bother sending them to the office, because bad language has become socially acceptable.

Respect for Family Members

If they want polite, respectful kids, parents must consistently exhibit that behavior themselves. Both parents. As with all child-rearing issues, a united front is the most effective. Kids often behave rudely toward Mom more often than toward Dad. Whether it's because they spend more time with Mom or because Dad is more intimidating is immaterial. Dad needs to send a clear message: "Thou shalt speak respectfully to thy mother." There's a saying that goes "The greatest thing a man can do for his children is love their mother." I'd have to add "and respect their mother."

Learning to avoid using disrespectful words and actions is a process and requires consistent teaching. It's not enough to tell your child what not to do; you need to offer acceptable alternatives. When Junior says to his brother, "Give me the remote, you moron!" step in and say, "I'm sure you meant to say, 'May I please have the remote?'" Then stand between him and the television until he repeats your words.

Siblings

You're already aware that siblings fight. It's part of the family pecking order. Parents are older and get to tell the youngsters what to do; the oldest child often interprets this to mean that she can tell the younger ones what to do. The "youngers," of course, don't see it that way. The oldest child is also offended when the younger ones get away with things that the older one can't. Baby snatches Sister's toy, so Sister pushes him down. Baby gets comforted because he bumped his head; Sister gets sent to her room. Look at it from Sister's perspective. She's being punished because the baby took her toy.

Another source of sibling rivalry is parental favoritism, whether real or imagined. When Sister was sent to her room, it looked to her like Baby is the favorite. After all, *he* didn't get punished, and he started the fight.

In our house, this perceived inequity was hard on our oldest. It just didn't seem fair to him that his little brothers didn't have to clean their room or stay at the table until dinner was over. It seemed like I was constantly reminding him that while he did, in fact, have more responsibility and higher standards than his brothers, he also had more privileges.

We finally resorted to: "We can treat you the same as your one-year-old brother, but that means we'll have to feed you and change your diapers. You won't be able to go to your friends' houses, and we'll need to take away all your 'big kid' toys. You can play with the baby toys, though." I'm not sure that was the best approach, but at least he stopped complaining while he thought it over. We probably could have made our point in a more positive manner.

If there's any chance that you do favor one child over the others, you need to ask yourself why. Mothers sometimes favor the youngest because he's her baby. It's natural for both parents to favor a child who has a disability or serious illness. Don't forget to look at the situation through the eyes of your other children. They may grow to resent the favored child, and their fighting will only add to your stress level.

Regardless of the cause of the disagreements, siblings need to learn to fight respectfully. When they're little, it starts with a reminder to "Use your words." You can help them verbalize what they're feeling. "You're angry because she won't share" or "You're sad because he doesn't want to play with you." As they get older, you can involve them in solving the problems. "Two people want the same book—what should we do?" Kids as young as four can work out solutions to simple arguments.

If the rule is that everyone practices respect for others, then what are the consequences when children break the rule? A patient reminder is best: "I didn't like the way that sounded. Please rephrase it." I realize, however, that in a heated battle, patience isn't always an option—but when the battle is over, each party should apologize for any rude or hurtful remarks. When our boys said something rude to one of their brothers, they then had to say five nice things about him. Positive things. Telling him "You're not as dumb as you look" didn't count.

Grandparents and Other Elders

In the good old days, before our society became so mobile, families usually had the good fortune to have grandparents and maybe even great-grandparents living nearby. Children learned that respect for family members included the family elders and thus all older folks.

Nowadays many of us have moved away from our hometown, and our children have little contact with the elderly. They don't learn that "old folks" are worthy of respect. In the worst case, kids may view senior citizens as a nuisance or as objects of ridicule. We need to go out of our way to model deference and respect: hold doors open, offer a seat, and listen patiently. After all, where will each of us be fifty years from now?

SELF-RESPECT

The terms *self-respect*, *self-esteem*, and *self-confidence* are sometimes used interchangeably, but there are subtle differences between them. All are important for healthy psychological development.

Self-respect is whether we like ourselves or not, and how we treat ourselves based on that assessment. *Self-esteem* is a measure of our self-worth, or value. Too much self-esteem is called arrogance. *Self-confidence* is how certain we are that we'll be successful in a given situation.

I may like myself and feel confident in my decisions (self-respect), yet feel inferior to my peers (low self-esteem). I might be certain that if I give a speech in English class, I'll look and sound like an idiot (low self-confidence in my public speaking ability), but because I'm good at math, I'm comfortable asking questions in math class or even explaining concepts to others (high self-confidence in my math abilities).

Children treated with respect develop healthy self-respect and self-esteem. They usually become nice people, and if they also learn respect for others, they're not likely to become arrogant. More importantly, they're more likely to avoid risky behaviors such as drinking, drugs, shoplifting, vandalism, and inappropriate relationships. Instead of seeking approval from their peers, they use their own judgment as to what's right for them. They're better able to sidestep peer pressure simply by saying, "I could never do that."

When my youngest was in ninth grade, some of his friends at school learned he was a drummer and invited him to join their band. He was so excited; it was all he could talk about for days. Once or twice a week, they'd get together for practice, and everything seemed to be going well. Then one day, he came home and announced that he'd quit the band. My husband and I were stunned. "Why?" we asked.

"They want to start playing songs with really raunchy lyrics, and I said I didn't want to play that kind of music. They wouldn't compromise, so I quit." Needless to say, my husband and I were very proud.

In addition, children with healthy self-esteem tend to have better grades than students with low self-esteem. A positive outlook about themselves and their abilities seems to motivate these students to try harder.

How to Be Respectful with Difficult People

Friends, relatives, salespeople, teachers, and bosses can all be disrespectful at times. Instead of responding in kind, kids can learn coping mechanisms. The rule, naturally, is to respond with respect. In addition, they can express their concern by saying:

- Is something wrong?
- You look tired.
- Has it been a long day?
- This must be a difficult job
- Why would you say that?
- Did I just offend you?

If none of these comments bring a response, they can hold their tongue and pray for the offender. When our son Daniel was going to school in Los Angeles, the rude drivers on the freeways often frustrated him. He told me one day how someone had not only deliberately cut him off, but also flipped him an obscene gesture. He told me, "I was so mad I just wanted to race after him and cut *him* off." I was horrified—people get shot in LA for less than that. I suggested instead that he ask God to make sure the other driver didn't hurt anyone. Daniel agreed praying was better than getting angry. I also reminded him not to let someone else ruin his day.

How to Sell Respect to Your Children

There are many ways to get the point across. Tell them:

- Everybody on the planet has an invisible sign around his or her neck that says, "I need to feel respected." This includes you, me, your friends, coaches, and, most importantly, your future bosses. We feel good around the people who treat us respectfully. We push away the people who don't.

- Self-confidence is a wonderful thing. However, confidence without compassion equals arrogance. Compassion is about understanding and respecting the rights and feelings of others. People admire confidence but will run away from arrogance.

- Putting the feelings of others ahead of our own desires is one of the hardest things to learn and one of the most important. Teachers, coaches, parents, and bosses all expect, if not demand, your respectful cooperation. You may not agree with the people in authority, but you need to respect their wishes. They've earned that position, and therefore they're in charge. That's just the way the world works.

- You can disagree with people without talking down to them. There's an old saying that you'll catch more flies with honey than with vinegar. Presenting your thoughts in a positive manner will go a long way toward making your case. You won't win every argument, but people will be more open to listening if they're not busy putting up defensive walls.

Our character is what we do
when we think no one is looking.
– Jackson Browne

Chapter 7

Ethics

Of all the things you teach your children, this is probably the most important. And, as with all things, it's primarily taught by example. You can tell your children that stealing is wrong, but if you come home from the store and brag about how you made ten dollars because the cashier forgot to charge you for something, which lesson will the kids remember? There can be no double standard when it comes to ethics.

Your child will face many ethical decisions over the years, but the three biggest issues are lying, stealing, and cheating. All children try their hand at these activities at least once in their formative years, usually because they don't fully understand the consequences.

Children aren't born knowing right from wrong, yet many parents believe their little darlings will always know to do the right thing. They're horrified when they discover that their daughter stole a toy from her friend's house or lied about some misbehavior. If you keep in mind that this is normal behavior for children, it will be easier to deal with the problem calmly.

Between the ages of four and five, preschoolers begin to understand the concepts of fairness, sharing, and good versus bad behavior. They also develop more self-control, and begin learning to wait their turn, share toys, and refrain from doing things they know are wrong. It's important to keep these developmental stages in mind when teaching ethics.

Lying

Preschoolers enjoy hearing stories and begin telling stories of their own. At this age, they can't really tell the difference between fantasy and reality; it's all real to them. As they approach kindergarten, they are better able to distinguish between the two. You can help them by discussing what's real and what's make-believe.

Once they start school, however, they quickly learn they can avoid, or at least postpone, unpleasantness by "rearranging" the truth. "Who left their dishes in the living room?" is often followed by a chorus of "Not me!" This poses a major dilemma for parents. How do you get them to tell the truth when it's clear you're not happy with the person who left this mess?

The first step to promoting honesty in children is to consider why they lie, then make it as easy as possible for them to tell the truth. Lying is often a symptom, and it's more important to find out why your son is lying than to simply dole out punishment. Reasons for lying include fear, convenience, and habit. Making it easier to tell the truth may involve a radical behavior change on your part. Too often parents focus on punishing the liar rather than changing the behavior.

Instead of focusing on catching them in a lie, you want to focus on solving the problem. This means not asking "gotcha" questions. Those are questions that you know the answer to but ask anyway, to see if your offspring will tell the truth. This type of question is self-defeating, since it provides too much temptation for kids to lie. If they tell the truth, that's wonderful, but you still haven't solved the original problem (the dishes in the living room). If they give in to temptation and lie, all you've done is erode the bond of trust between you. Instead of asking, "Who left these dishes in the living room?" state matter-of-factly, "When you finish eating, you need to clean up." Instead of asking, "Where were you last night?" tell them, "I know you were at Fred's party last night, even though we said you couldn't go."

When you ask "gotcha" questions, you're implying that you expect them to lie. This has the same effect as actually calling them a liar. And as I said earlier, labeling children almost always causes a self-fulfilling prophecy. Children internalize the label and act accordingly. "If my parents say I'm a liar, they must be right." The child continues to lie because, after all, she's a liar. Her parents told her so.

Some parents think that asking these types of questions promotes honesty by showing kids you always know the answer. It's been my experience that the kids just get more creative. "I only stopped by the party for a second because Shannon left her cell phone in my car, and I knew she needed it because she wanted her boyfriend to meet her at the party, and I couldn't call her to tell her I had it, so I had to go in and I knew you'd understand." By the time you get done listening to all this, you've forgotten that you heard from a reliable source that your daughter was at the party most of the night.

Lying out of Fear

Children often lie to avoid punishment, even if the punishment is only getting yelled at. They may also lie to avoid disappointing you. Suppose you find a trail of muddy footprints across your freshly washed floor. If your immediate reaction is to scream, "Who did this to my clean floor?" I'm pretty sure no one is going to come running in saying, "It was me, Mommy." It's more likely they're all busy finding hiding places. Instead of shouting, practice your Lamaze breathing for a moment and ask yourself what you're really angry about. Probably you're frustrated because now you have to wash the floor again.

Have everyone come back into the room and explain the problem to them. "Someone forgot to take their shoes off, and now the floor is all muddy. Whoever it was needs to clean it up." Now, instead of punishing the culprit, you're invoking natural consequences. (When you make a mess, you clean it up.) The child's not in trouble—he just needs to solve the problem. If everyone is still denying any involvement, appeal to their sense of fairness. "Why should someone else have to clean up the mess you made?"

Sometimes a problem is created that can't be fixed but must be accepted. The next time you come home and find that someone shaved the dog, catch yourself before you start yelling. Remember, even if you can't choose your feelings, you can choose how you act with respect to your feelings. Pat and I actually did come home one evening to discover that our two older boys had shaved the younger one's head. Fortunately (for them, at least), we were too stunned to say anything.

Gather the troops and ask as calmly as possible, "Why did you do it?" Asking "why" questions often works better than "Who did this?" The former implies that you realize there may have been a reason for the behavior, and you're willing to listen. The latter implies that whoever did it was an idiot, and if they confess, they'll never see the light of day again.

After you listen to what they have to say (see how you're modeling respectful behavior?), explain to them how their actions have created a problem. Surely they didn't realize that the now hairless dog can get sunburned.

There is a small caveat to this process. When I first decided to give up yelling, I hadn't yet realized the importance of verbalizing my feelings clearly. My kids thought that if I wasn't yelling, I must not be angry. When my eighteen-year-old came home one day with a tattoo, I figured there was nothing I could do after the fact. All I said was, "I'm not happy about it, and I think you'll regret it later."

When he came home with the second tattoo, I realized I hadn't made myself clear the first time. I spent the next twenty minutes explaining exactly how I felt and told him that if he got any others, I'd personally take him to have all of them removed. Actually, I think my exact words were "I'll scrape them off myself with a butter knife." I was still learning to come up with appropriate consequences.

If you discover your favorite vase has been broken and you know which kid did it, there's no point in asking, "Did you do this?" His automatic reaction will be to deny it. Better to ask, "How did this happen?" and explain that there's a reason he's not allowed to play baseball in the living room. Then get him involved in cleaning up (natural consequences).

The biggest challenge a parent faces is after the child tells the truth. "I'm the one who set the garage on fire while I was playing with matches." Now what? Any consequences meted out will be seen as punishment for telling the truth. This is the time for a discussion about how proud you are that he told the truth and the value of a clear conscience. Then you can explain that there must still be consequences for breaking the rules.

Pat and I had pretty good success by making a clear distinction between discipline for the wrongdoing and discipline for the lie. Usually the consequence for the lie was a lack of trust for a while. We had told them repeatedly that we would trust them until we had a reason not to. Trust is a precious thing, and once it's broken, it takes a long time to get it back. One weekend, our son wanted to sleep over at a friend's house. We would have said yes, but the previous weekend he had lied to us about where he was going. We told him we couldn't let him go because we weren't sure he was telling us the truth this time. He swore up and down that he was telling the truth. We asked him, "But how do we know that? You said you were telling the truth last time. If you were us, would you believe you?" Of course he understood what we meant, even though he wasn't happy about it.

It helps to get to know other parents in your neighborhood. It truly does take a village to raise a child. One day when Travis was six, he and his friend Josh were playing in Josh's yard. I couldn't see them from my house, but I assumed Josh's mother was keeping an eye on them. Not long after, my neighbor Ellen called to tell me she'd seen Travis and Josh playing with a can of red spray paint. She had confiscated the paint but not before Josh had painted Travis's red shirt. (I imagine raising a girl has its own set of problems, but there were days when I wished I'd had girls.)

When Travis came home, jacket zipped up to his ears, I asked him, "What did you do today that I should know about?" (I hadn't yet learned to avoid the "gotcha" questions.) After much hemming and hawing, he fessed up, which was followed by a somewhat one-sided discussion on the importance of doing the right thing (and not doing things he knew were wrong). At the end, I told him, "Do you know who else sees you when you're naughty? God does."

"*He's* the one who told you?" Travis was outraged that God had ratted on him.

If you want honest answers to your questions, remember that the first step is to make it safe to tell the truth. Instead of following their confession with "How many times have I told you…" or attacking their character, try reminding them of whatever rule they've broken. "No parties unless a responsible adult is present." "Homework must be finished before watching TV." "Shirts are not for spray painting."

Lying for Convenience

This category includes all those questions you may not like the answers to, such as:

- Have you cleaned your room/done your homework/brushed the dog?
- Where have you been?
- What time did you come home last night?
- Did you use my tools and not put them away?
- How are your grades?
- Will there be parents at the party?

Oftentimes, kids don't see these "little" lies as a problem. They tell themselves they're going to clean their room/do their homework/brush the dog when they get around to it; they just haven't gotten around to it yet. Why should they bother you with the details of the timing? Maybe they did come home a little past curfew, but it's no big deal. They know their grades aren't that great, but there's still plenty of time to improve. The problem is, if they give you an honest answer to any of these questions, you're probably going to fuss. They may even feel they're doing you a favor by sparing you from unpleasantness.

If you suspect your offspring is misrepresenting the truth, it's important to check up now and then. If they are, in fact, telling the truth, they shouldn't mind you checking. "I cleaned my room" can be followed by "Great! Let's go admire it!" If his grades are "fine," he won't mind if you contact his teacher. A friend of mine suspected that his daughter wasn't telling him the truth about where she was going. The first time it happened, she claimed she was sleeping over at a friend's house, but when my friend tried to call, his daughter's cell phone was off. Now he insists on getting the parents' phone numbers before his daughter goes on any sleepover, just in case he needs to contact her. Occasionally he calls with a question, which also allows him to see if she really is at the friend's house. Trust but verify.

Children have plenty of friends; what they really need are strong parents.

Some parents feel that checking up on their kids is an invasion of privacy. I like to think of it as helping them avoid temptation. If they know there's a good chance you'll verify what they tell you, they'll think twice about breaking the rules and about lying. If you're thinking, "My kids will hate me if I do that," keep in mind that parenting is not a popularity contest. Children have plenty of friends; what they really need are strong parents. Your job is not to make their life easier; it's to make their life better.

Lying out of Habit

Sadly, some kids get in the habit of telling you what you want to hear. If you don't consistently verify what they tell you, they have no reason to concern themselves with being honest about their activities. Yes, it's easier to accept what they say without question than to get off the couch and see if the leaves actually did get raked. Eventually, however, you'll have to deal with reality. By the time you go outside and see that the leaves are right where the tree left them, your son is long gone.

Now you have a choice to make. You can rake the leaves yourself, which will be much faster and less stressful than dealing with your teenager, but then what has he learned: if he lies pleasantly and fusses loudly when confronted, you'll probably give up and do the chore yourself. You could wait until he comes home and then ask him again to rake the leaves, and hope that this time he'll really get it done. (Do you honestly believe that will work?) Or you could call him home and deal with the issue. (That cell phone he has is as much for *your* convenience as his.) If he knows you'll stand firm and hold him accountable, he'll realize it's easier for him to get it done than try to avoid it.

If you allow your child to get into the habit of lying, you're doing him a grave disservice. You may not care, but his teachers and friends will care. More importantly, later on in life, his boss and spouse will certainly care. Take the time to help him break the habit by checking on him regularly and holding him accountable.

Some children feel that lying is the only way to deal with the demands of teachers, parents, and life in general. Eventually, this coping method becomes a habit. Help them realize that what they're really doing is acquiring a reputation as someone who is untrustworthy and frustrating to deal with. Then teach them better coping skills.

If they lie about homework being done, they may be feeling overwhelmed. Help them with time management skills. Perhaps they could do two subjects before dinner and the rest afterward. Try doing the most difficult assignment first to get it over with. Break term papers down into smaller parts: do research this week, then write a page a day until it's done.

If they're lying about chores being done, remind them that they can choose their attitude. They can fuss and scream about how unfair it is that they have chores to do, or they can turn on some music to make the job more pleasant. Either way, they still have to get the job done.

If they're lying about their whereabouts, your job is a little harder. Talk to them about how your goal is to keep them safe and help them grow up to be good people. Let them know it would be easier on you to just let them do whatever they wanted, but you love them too much to let them get into trouble. "You're the only Justin I have, and God is trusting me to take good care of you."

When Lying Is a Chronic Problem

Most of the time, once parents realize the cause of the lying, they are soon on the road to solving the problem. If, on the other hand, your child sees nothing wrong with lying to others, you may want to seek the help of a counselor. Taking advantage of others without remorse indicates a deeper problem.

Another reason children avoid the truth may be to hide a drug or alcohol problem. Children covering up an addiction will often lie about where they've been, who they were with, and where the money went. Again, you'll probably need to see a counselor for help in changing the behavior.

Let's face it—we all tell lies from time to time. Usually we believe we have a good reason for doing so and only tell "white lies." But what is a white lie exactly? Do you tell a little white lie to avoid hurting someone's feelings? ("The dinner was delicious.") Maybe for convenience? ("I'd love to keep your Great Dane while you're on vacation, but Jim's allergic to dogs.") Or to avoid confrontation? ("I can't buy you that toy right now because I don't have any money.")

The reality is that all three of these instances can be rationalized as sparing someone's feelings or keeping the peace. Your friend would be upset to know you hate her dog. Your toddler will throw a tantrum if you tell him he has enough toys and doesn't need another.

Keep in mind that kids are extremely observant, and when you get caught, it's tough to talk your way out. You also lose some credibility every time they catch you. They'll ask why it's okay for *you* to fib but not okay for them. At some point, kids learn that white lies are okay. For children, the distinction between a white lie and a self-serving lie can be difficult to grasp.

The easiest explanation is that it's never okay to lie in order to avoid the *consequences* of something you've done (or are going to do). If you have to lie about what you're doing, then you know you shouldn't be doing it. White lies to avoid conflict may seem harmless, but they can lead to a habit of bending the truth. Better to tell the truth and confront the issue.

I was watching a talk show during which a family counselor was helping people deal with difficult situations. One woman's problem was that her cousin's family would come to visit her every summer for two weeks. This year, however, the woman was remodeling her kitchen and didn't have the energy or money to entertain houseguests. She wanted to know if she was being selfish for feeling that way. When the counselor assured her it was okay to say no to guests, she asked, "But what do I tell my cousin? If I tell her we'll be out of town at that time, she'll just come later in the summer."

The counselor pointed out, "Why don't you tell her the truth? Tell her what you've told me."

"Oh," she said. Apparently this hadn't occurred to her. After a pause, she added, "But she'll be upset if I tell her not to come."

To which the counselor replied, "If she is, that's her problem, but I think she'll understand."

When we always worry about avoiding conflict, we get in the habit of making up stories. Better to stick to the facts whenever possible. If your ten-year-old daughter wants to go to the movies Friday night with a friend, and without any adults accompanying them, what do you say? You could take the easy route and tell her the theater has a policy that all children under twelve must be accompanied by an adult. Or you could explain that it's not safe for young girls to be out at night alone and you're not comfortable with the idea. This has the added advantage of teaching the importance of sticking to what you believe in. The discussion might get loud, but she will learn that you can tolerate her being mad if it means she'll be safe.

STEALING

Babies and toddlers live in a completely self-centered world. They have no concept of right and wrong; they just know what they want and when they want it (now!). You've probably seen the "Toddler Property Law":

- If I want it, it's mine.
- If I say it's mine, it's mine.

- If I give it to you and change my mind later, it's mine.
- If I can take it away from you, it's mine.
- If I had it a little while ago, it's mine.
- If it's in my hand, it's mine
- If we are building something together, all the pieces are mine.
- If it looks just like mine, it is mine.
- If I saw it first, it's mine.

By four or five, they begin learning the concept of ownership, and parents can start discussing how someone feels when their belongings are taken. The concepts are still nebulous at this age, so discipline is not very helpful. Statements such as "That's Johnny's truck, and it needs to stay at Johnny's house" or "Pretend Johnny liked your truck so much that he took it home with him. How would you feel?" go a lot farther than character assassinations such as "You little thief! I can't trust you for a minute!" At this age, you can begin explaining that when you take something without getting permission first, it's called stealing, and it's not okay.

Around the time they start school, children are aware that stealing is wrong yet sometimes find it difficult to overcome temptation.

Reasons for Stealing

- **Impulse.** He wanted it so he took it, but now he's probably feeling guilty. Explain that the reason he has a bad feeling inside is because he knows what he did was wrong. It's better to avoid temptation next time, so he doesn't have to feel that way.
- **Peer pressure.** Friends who pressure your child into illegal behavior aren't really friends. They're using your child for their own entertainment, and it's time to find some other activity for him besides hanging out with this group. Ask him why he'd want to be friends with kids who want him to get into trouble. He deserves better.

- **No money of his own.** If he's old enough to go to the store by himself, he's probably old enough to earn an allowance. When our son was in junior high, I realized one day that he had acquired a few new shirts. Since I was terrible about remembering to give my kids their allowance, I didn't think he had any money. I asked him how he paid for the shirts, and he said they'd been on sale and he'd used money left over from Christmas.

It was a reasonable answer, but I could tell by the look on his face that something wasn't quite right. He just looked guilty, so I asked to see the receipts. "Receipts? I, um, threw them out," was the reply.

"You should always keep your receipts in case you need to return something. And in the future I want to see the receipts for the things you buy."

"Why? Don't you trust me? How come you don't trust me?" Children are born knowing that the best defense is a strong offense.

I explained to him that the world is full of temptations, and one of the things parents have to do is help children avoid those temptations. I told him that since he'd never stolen anything before (that I was aware of), I would trust him this time, but in the future, I wanted to see all receipts. I also told him that if, in fact, he had stolen the shirts, I would help him do the right thing. I could go with him when he paid for the shirts, or he could do it on his own. I also immediately paid him the allowance I owed him. At that point, I had no proof that he'd shoplifted other than a guilty look on his face, so I chose to trust him. Ten years later, I asked him about the incident, and he said he really did pay for the shirts. He looked guilty because it was the first time he'd bought clothes on his own and he didn't know how I'd react.

- **Attention.** For some kids, even negative attention is better than no attention—and let's face it, stealing gets a lot of attention.

- **Because they can.** If parents don't correct bad behavior, children have no reason to change. In addition, if you ignore the behavior in the hope that it will get better on its own, your child will assume that it's okay to steal.

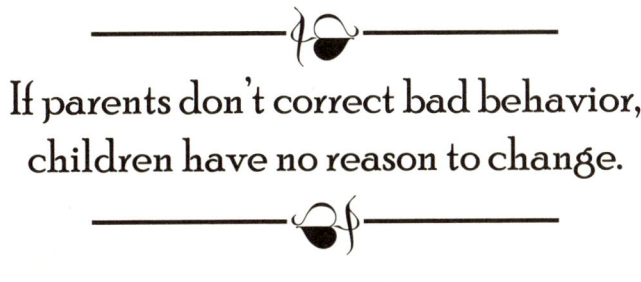

If parents don't correct bad behavior, children have no reason to change.

Prevention

Again, with preschoolers it's best to begin by teaching them about ownership. After that, you can define stealing (when you take something that's not yours without getting permission) and start talking about feelings. Clarify the difference between stealing and borrowing.

It's important to make it clear, both by words and actions, that dishonest behavior will not be tolerated. It's not enough to tell children what to do; parents must also model good behavior. You may think they don't know you've tapped into your neighbor's cable service so you don't have to pay for it, but kids see and hear much more than parents realize. Eventually, they *will* figure out where all those towels printed with hotel names came from.

Talk about alternative ways to get what they want. Offer opportunities to earn money and reinforce the good feeling they get from earning enough to pay for what they want (see Chapter 10).

Praise honest behavior. "I'm proud of you for doing the right thing" and "You must feel pretty good inside" are important phrases to remember.

Correction

If you know for a fact that your child has stolen something, you *must* impose consequences. If you let it go "just this once," the child learns that stealing is okay. On the other hand, you don't want to fly off the handle; remain calm but firm. Humiliating a child teaches the importance of not getting caught and that he can't trust you with his feelings.

Label the behavior, not the child. Succumbing to temptation does not make the child a hardened criminal. Let her know you're disappointed with her actions, but you expect it will never happen again.

The classic method of dealing with the situation is to go with them to return the item and have them apologize to the owner. If they've stolen something from a store, it helps to speak to the store manager about the situation out of earshot of the child. Make it clear that you want to teach a lesson that stealing is wrong, since well-intentioned adults might shrug off the event with "It's no big deal." That won't help your case.

If what they've stolen can't be returned (for example, an opened candy bar), then they need to pay for it. You can have them do extra chores to earn the money if they can't afford the item. (If you simply pay for it there is no lesson learned.)

Talk to your child about why she did it, why it's wrong, and how to make restitution. Tell her you know it will be uncomfortable to go back to the store or friend's house and confess, but you'll go with her. Remind her of the importance of doing the right thing. Often, young children will take small items from a store because they think no one will notice and therefore it doesn't matter. Discuss what would happen if everyone took just one small item, and how taking small things escalates into taking more expensive items. What if each of her friends took just one of her toys?

If the stealing continues, it may signal a deeper psychological issue, and you'll want to contact a mental health professional.

If you suspect stealing, but have no proof, talk to the child about ethics and your expectations for his behavior. Discuss how sad it would be if you thought you couldn't trust him or if his friends couldn't trust him. Remind him that he's a good kid and that it hurts you to suspect his actions.

Know where your child is and provide supervision when necessary.

CHEATING

Cheating in school has become rampant, and it's not just "lazy" kids. Students of all ability levels succumb to temptation and are getting quite good at rationalizing the behavior. In addition, the number of parents who just shrug off the seriousness of cheating is also on the rise.

More than once, I've given a student a zero on a test for cheating, only to get a phone call from an angry parent: "My child wouldn't do that!" The parents would rather believe that the teacher was lying about the incident than believe their child would be dishonest. Go figure.

Other parents are stunned when I explain that their child was caught cheating. "He's such a good kid! I can't imagine why he'd do such a thing."

The Josephson Institute surveys thousands of high school students nationally every two years on ethics issues. In one survey, more than one-third (35 percent) of all students polled said they had copied an Internet document for an assignment, and nearly two-thirds (65 percent) said they had cheated on a test at least once. Surprisingly, the percentage of students in private religious schools that cheated on a test (66 percent) was higher than the percentage of students in public schools (61 percent). The same was true about copying someone else's homework: 82 percent in public schools vs. 87 percent in private religious schools. Yet a whopping 92 percent of all high school students surveyed claimed to be satisfied with their own ethics and character, and almost all (97 percent) felt it's important that people trust them. Perhaps so they don't get caught cheating.

In a third survey (2001), Rutgers University's Management Education Center polled 4,500 high school students and found that 97 percent of them admitted cheating at least once. More than half had plagiarized an Internet article and three-fourths (74 percent) had engaged in "serious" cheating.

One of the reasons for the increase in cheating is that technology has made it so easy. Now students don't just peek at their neighbor's answers in class or copy someone's homework; cell phones, the Internet, and handheld computers all play a role in the cheating revolution.

Cell phones are a teacher's nightmare. Not only do students "text" each other during class (the electronic equivalent of passing notes), but they also text each other for test answers. In fact, the people they're getting answers from can be anywhere, not just in their classroom. Once they memorize the placement of the letters on the keypad, they don't even need to look at the phone while they're typing. Of course, they do have to look at it to read the reply, but the teacher only has two eyes, and she's outnumbered by about thirty to one. Many cell phones can access the Internet from anywhere. Why study if you can bring your web browser to class?

Another time-saver for students is the graphing calculator. These are required for many higher level math classes, even in high school. Most teachers allow students to use them during math and science tests, even though these too can store all sorts of information, such as test answers.

The biggest time-saver of all is the Internet. It's also the biggest mixed blessing of the twenty-first century. On the one hand, it's a godsend for anyone trying to do research. There is virtually nothing you can't look up on the Internet, from aardvarks to zygotes and everything in between. When used properly, it can be an invaluable resource, especially for students without access to a large library.

On the other hand, it has made it incredibly easy to cheat on assignments such as essays and term papers. Every seventh grader knows how to use the copy and paste features of their computer: just highlight an entire web page, copy it, and paste it into your document. Students can have their term papers done in ten minutes.

For those with more money than ambition, there are many sites that sell term papers. Perfecttermpapers.com offers custom papers starting at "just" $13.95 per page. Writework.com (formerly Cheathouse.com) offers more than 115,000 papers for $14.95 per month. Papersinn.com offers "high-quality, customized and non-plagiarized term papers" for $7.95 per page. You have to wonder how many students realize that putting their name on a paper they didn't write is the definition of plagiarism. And how many notice all the grammatical errors on the website's first page? Buyer beware.

These are just a few of the hundreds of websites selling term papers. Most have a disclaimer stating that the papers are for research only. Raise your hand if you believe that. Any student with access to a credit card number or some other method of transferring money (such as PayPal or even bank transfer) can download a paper in minutes.

The reasons for cheating are as varied as the students themselves. Here are some actual answers from various student surveys as to why they cheat:

- The class is irrelevant to what I want to do in life, so cheating doesn't matter.
- It's a shortcut.
- I have to cheat just to get by.
- I'm under excessive pressure to do well.
- Everyone looks at the grade, not how you got it.
- High school and college are a time for fun, not for studying all the time.
- It's a victimless crime.
- It's okay if you don't get caught.
- It makes up for unfair tests/teachers.

The number-one reason for cheating is "Everyone else does it." Some students are convinced that since everyone around them is cheating, they'd be at a disadvantage if they didn't cheat as well. Others are convinced that they would be foolish not to cheat when it's so easy. Some students don't want their friends to think they're dumb for not joining in.

If you're secretly of the opinion that cheating is not a big deal, how would you feel if you learned that your lawyer, accountant, or surgeon had cheated on their exams? How about the aircraft engineer who designed the plane you're about to board (or the pilot, for that matter)? When students cheat, they don't learn anything, and in the end, they're only cheating themselves.

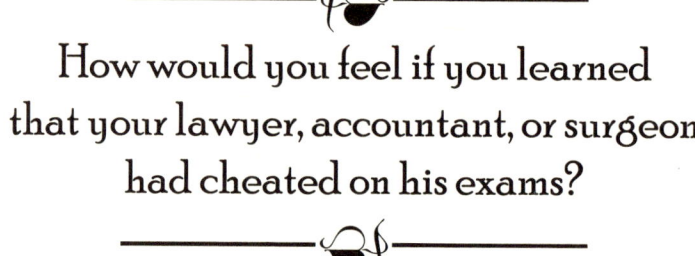

How would you feel if you learned that your lawyer, accountant, or surgeon had cheated on his exams?

Most of us assume that honesty and integrity are as important to our offspring as they are to us. As parents, we need to remember that temptation and peer pressure are powerful motivators for youngsters. We need to fight back with strong family values and positive role modeling. What can parents do?

- Explain the various forms of cheating, such as smuggling in answers to the test, copying someone else's homework, or not following the rules (such as working with other students on what was supposed to be an independent assignment). Any time they pass someone else's work off as their own, whether it's buying a book report or not citing the source of information, it's plagiarism. When in doubt, check with your student's English teacher for the preferred format for citations and when to use it. In addition, many universities offer information online on how to cite various types of work. Keywords to search for include *works cited* and *avoid plagiarism*.

- Explain why cheating is wrong—both personal cheating and helping others to cheat. Many students don't realize that giving answers to others is just as wrong as being on the receiving end. Cheating is no different from lying; in essence you're saying, "This is my work" when it really isn't. Helping others to cheat is not helping them to learn.

- Applaud their efforts, even if they don't get an A. "You really studied for that test—good job!"

- Discuss examples you may see in movies, on TV, or in books. Why did the cheater do it? How did it affect his friends and family? Will it affect his future?
- Talk to them about what they can say when someone asks to copy their homework or their test answers. "I spent two hours on that math assignment! Why should I give it away?" Or "My parents would *kill* me if I got caught cheating."
- Encourage pride in a job well done. "You did well on that project. You must feel pretty good about that."
- Praise ethical behavior. "You went all the way back to the store because you realized the cashier had given you too much change. I can't tell you how proud I am of you!"

WORK ETHIC

One of the happiest moments in any parent's life is when their children become self-sufficient. They've finished their schooling, found their own place to live, and have full-time jobs. As much as we love them, they get to be expensive little critters. It's always a relief to know they can support themselves and live within their means. (It beats having a twenty-five-year-old asking you to support him while he "finds himself.")

Teenage girls sometimes buy into the Cinderella myth—that they will meet their Prince Charming, fall in love, and be taken care of for the rest of their lives. Sadly, given today's divorce rate, our girls *must* learn how to support themselves, just in case.

Most of us don't mind occasionally helping our adult children financially. We enjoy buying presents for them, especially if there's something they need (but maybe can't afford). Be aware, however, that too much helping is a form of enabling. In other words, you'll end up sending the message "You don't have to get a better job or live on what you earn—I'll take care of you." Too much helping is also a way to keep our children dependent on us. It tells them "You can't take care of yourself—you still need me." Better to say to them, "I'm sure you'll find a way to save up for a new television/boat/car/vacation."

After your son gets that full-time job, the next thing we wonder is, can he keep the job? Will he work hard and be an asset to the company? Does he have the skills to get ahead?

If he has graduated high school or college but doesn't have a job, is he still living at home, reading the want ads every Sunday, waiting for the "perfect" job to come along? There are some problems with that plan.

For starters, what is the perfect job? One that pays one hundred dollars an hour even though he only has a high school diploma? Does he want his first job to be a professional race-car driver or pro basketball player? President of a large corporation? If so, it's time for a reality check. Those are all great jobs if he has the drive to pursue them. But if he's still living at home reading the want ads, those aren't the jobs he's going to find advertised, and it indicates a certain lack of ambition in pursuing his goals.

One common complaint about today's young people is that they seem to have a sense of entitlement, as though the world owes them a nice car, fashionable clothes, and the latest electronics. They show up for work because they want a paycheck, but spend their days texting friends or shopping online. Children must be taught that success comes from hard work and perseverance. They also need to learn that they can have it all, just not all at once.

So what is work ethic, exactly? The traditional Puritan work ethic is founded on the belief that hard work builds character and is a virtue unto itself. Later, the American work ethic included the feeling that anyone could get ahead by working harder. All you had to do was plow more acres or make more saddles.

The industrial revolution changed all that. Suddenly, instead of working for themselves, the majority of Americans were working for someone else. Because of this, attitudes about work also changed. Some people began to feel that working harder only made more money for their bosses, so why should they bother? Combined with a new "I only look out for myself" attitude, employers were faced with a growing number of apathetic workers.

Today, work ethic can be considered to have four components: dependability, initiative, interpersonal skills, and integrity.

Dependability

If your children will be depending on a paycheck, they need to understand that their boss is depending on them for certain things:

- **Be punctual.** Always aim to be five to ten minutes early. The boss may not notice, but it gives you a little leeway in case of traffic or other last-minute delays. Besides, I guarantee that the boss *will* notice anyone who's always five or ten minutes late. Being early most days probably won't offset those rare occasions of tardiness, but it will prevent the need to speed to work. It's also much nicer to start the day off with a little time to settle in instead of the stress of having to sneak past the boss.

    The five-minutes-early concept is not just for work, by the way. Anytime there is an appointment, meeting, or party to go to, you have an opportunity to remind your cherubs that it's rude to keep people waiting. If your daughter is the type of person who is always late because she hates to sit around, it's time to adjust her attitude. Being late implies that your time is more valuable than everyone else's. When you know you may have some waiting time, plan ahead. Keep a book, magazine, or Sudoku puzzle in your car for those idle moments. In the waiting room you can practice meditation. Think of all the things in your life you're grateful for. Pray for everyone you know or for the people around you. Practice these sanity savers and teach them to your kids.

- **Show up for work every day.** This sounds like a no-brainer, but it's amazing how many young people call in sick because they just don't feel like going to work. Excuses vary, but there is a common theme:

    - *I'm too tired.*
    - *My friends are going somewhere fun, and I want to go, too.*
    - *My job is boring.*
    - *I hate my boss.*
    - *I hate the people I work with.*
    - *They don't pay me enough.*

If you haven't guessed, the theme is "I don't want to go to work."

If your kids are making excuses for not going to their job, have them picture themselves as the employer. "Suppose you owned a store in the mall. Now, the mall is open seven days a week, so you need to hire someone to help out so that you can have some days off.

"Say you hire Fred to work weekends. Things go well for a while, but then Fred calls in sick one Saturday. You cancel your plans for the day and rush in to work so you can open the store on time. A couple of weeks later, Fred calls in sick once again. Again you cancel your plans and head to work. Soon it seems like Fred is sick more often than not. How are you feeling at this point? Wouldn't you rather have an employee you can count on instead of spending every Friday night wondering if you'll have to run down to the store in the morning?"

Absenteeism costs U.S. businesses up to $74 billion annually. Staying home when you're contagious or truly sick is fine. More than one mental health day a year is not.

- **Put in a full day's work for a full day's pay.** Too many young people act as though merely showing up entitles them to a paycheck. They catch up on their e-mail, shop online, and chat with their friends. If you've ever gone into a retail store and been ignored by the salesclerk, you know what I mean.

  If your child works retail, explain to her that employers expect salesclerks to stay busy, even when there are no customers. She can tidy up the clothing racks and displays, dust the counters, and make sure things are put back properly. In the food industry, there is always something that needs cleaning.

  Another concern is the employee who leaves early, getting a coworker to cover for her. Again, ask your son how he would feel if he were the boss.

- **Follow all rules and directions.** There are reasons for the rules—usually safety, efficiency, or hygiene. If you think a rule is wrong, you can discuss it with the boss, but you can't just ignore it.

I read about a young man who was hired by a transportation company to drive a van for the handicapped. His training included many classroom hours on how to properly secure passengers in a wheelchair and how to secure the wheelchair within the van. After a short time on the job, he decided for whatever reason that he could ignore those rules. Unfortunately, a passenger was seriously injured and sued him for thousands of dollars. The driver lost both the lawsuit and his job.

Most rules involving hygiene and safety are due to state and local laws, such as employees washing their hands after using the restroom or wearing gloves when handling food. Ignoring these will cost the employer in fines and possibly loss of customers.

- **Be conscientious.** Do everything to the best of your ability. Do everything you can to ensure the success of your employer and minimize potential costs. If your employer succeeds, so do you!

    A few years ago, my husband and I went to a home improvement store to buy a set of pre-hung French doors. We found someone to help us pull them off the shelf and onto the cart, but in the process the employee scraped the frame against the shelf and left a large gouge in it. My husband pointed out what had happened and told the employee we didn't want the damaged door. Setting that door aside, they began to pull another unit out when again the salesperson carelessly scraped the frame. By this time, there was only one unit left, so we sent the salesperson on his way and managed to load the other unit ourselves. As we were leaving, we passed the same salesman and mentioned that the other two doors were still sitting in the aisle. He replied, "I don't care. That's not my department." Not only did he not care about the mess he had created, he clearly didn't care that he had damaged several hundred dollars' worth of merchandise.

    It's just as important to be conscientious with money. Employees handling money are expected to balance to the penny. If they are frequently off, it implies that either they are careless or they're stealing. Not good either way.

Initiative

- **Stay busy.** A good employee will minimize idle time as much as possible. When they're not serving customers, they should be looking for things that need doing. Fill the ketchup bottles, sweep the sidewalk, wipe off the counter in the restroom, or make sure the toilets have been flushed. If you're being paid to work, you should be working. An employee who finishes a job and asks the boss, "Now what can I do?" is invaluable.

- **Be willing to help.** When I was a pool lifeguard, Sunday mornings were spent doing a thorough cleaning of the facility. My boss's philosophy was "Nobody's done until everybody's done." I had never heard the expression before, but I liked it. If one person finished his area early, he helped someone else. Everyone worked for the same amount of time, and when the work was finished everyone went to lunch. It's like the old saying "Many hands make light work."

  One of my pet peeves is when I ask someone for help and that person responds, "It's not my job" and walks away. Would it really hurt to spend a few minutes helping another human being?

- **Be persistent.** Keep at a difficult job until it's finished. If the inventory numbers are off, find the mistake. If the computer you're working on is being difficult, find a way around the problem. It's okay to ask for advice, but it's not okay to give up at the first sign of trouble.

Interpersonal Skills

- **Be polite.** In theory, our children are always polite, but it's especially important at work. I recently saw a sign near a bank teller's window that read:
  - *"Hi" is not the same as "How may I help you?"*
  - *"Uh huh" is not the same as "You're welcome."*

- ⇥ *"No problem" is not the same as "You're welcome."*
- ⇥ *"Bye" is not the same as "Thank you for banking with us."*

- **Be pleasant.** We can't always choose how we're feeling, but we can choose our actions. Everyone is entitled to a bad day now and then, but it is never okay to inflict our bad day on others. The reality is that most customers (or coworkers for that matter) don't care what kind of day you're having. They have their own problems, and just want to get the help they need and get on with their lives. Leave the drama at home.

- **Be helpful.** It is incredibly frustrating when I ask someone for help or information and all I get back is "I don't know." I know they're really thinking "I don't care." My next decision is: do I force the issue ("I'll wait while you find out") or cut my losses and leave?

    When I was younger, I made a point to never shop at a particular chain of grocery stores because, the first time I went in, the person I asked for help had that "Don't know, don't care, don't bother me" attitude. A year or two later, I happened to meet the regional manager for the chain and explained why I didn't shop there. He was shocked that I would avoid all of their stores because of one bad experience, but the reality is there are plenty of other stores to choose from.

- **Be patient, cooperative, and friendly.**

Integrity

- **Be honest.** No stealing (cash, merchandise, or supplies) and no free stuff for friends. It's hard for working teenagers to say no when friends ask for free food or an employee discount on everything they buy. Offer your young adult some possible responses:
    - ⇥ *"Sorry, but I'd really like to keep this job."*
    - ⇥ *"If you take food or merchandise without paying, that's stealing, and I don't want you to get into trouble."*

- *"It's just not right."*
- *"If you were really my friend, you wouldn't ask me to do that."*

- **If you make a mistake or break something, admit it.** The boss will respect you more than if you lie or hide the problem.

  Honesty on the job is easier if you've been teaching your youngster all along about the importance of doing the right thing. When their friends say, "No one will know," your child can reply, "*I'll* know" or "God is watching."

Job Interviews

If your child is getting ready to go to work for the first time, here's some guidance you'll want to give:

Before the Interview

- Clean up your Facebook, MySpace, or whatever other public pages you have, including the message people hear on your phone. Employers *will* check. I have a friend in the human resources department of a large company, and he tells me that his company's policy is to check the Facebook page of every applicant. Pictures of partying or compromising situations don't get them the job.
- Do a thorough assessment of all your skills and qualifications. The easiest way to do that is to list all of your achievements in what's known as a Brag Sheet (see the sample at the end of this chapter). Write down all extracurricular activities (captain of the swim team, class treasurer, 3.7 grade point average), then list the skills and attributes you used to get there (good leader, careful with money, hardworking). Ask friends and teachers to provide input, as they often see things you might not be aware of. You might not need a resume just yet, but a Brag Sheet will help pinpoint all the reasons you're qualified for the job.

- Learn what you can about the company. The Internet is a great resource, or maybe you know someone else who has worked there. Employers are always impressed when applicants, especially young people, take the time to do the research.
- Know exactly where you're going so you aren't late.
- Be fifteen minutes early. This will give you time to figure out where you're going within the building and to stop in the restroom to check your appearance (don't forget to check your teeth). If you're late, the interview is over before it starts.
- Be clean and neat. This is not the time to impress potential coworkers with your "coolness." Wear the type of clothes you'd wear if you worked there. If you're not sure, go conservative: for guys, a shirt with a collar, pants that fit, and dress shoes or clean tennis shoes; for girls, a skirt or dress that's not too short, and no bare midriff or low-cut neckline.

During the Interview

- Be aware of body language. Smile and sit up straight. Slouching implies you're bored, and fidgeting implies you're nervous. You probably *are* nervous, but try not to let it show. You don't have to be confident; you just have to act confident. Make eye contact—otherwise, you'll look like you're hiding something.
- Sell yourself. The interviewer wants to know why he should hire you instead of one of the other candidates. Now is the time to mention your skills and achievements as they pertain to the job. Be enthusiastic.
- Answer questions with statements that are short and to the point. Avoid rambling or wandering off the subject.

After the Interview

- Write a thank-you note to the person you spoke with. You're probably the only one who will, which means you'll stand out from the others. If the job is technology-based, an e-mail will do.

SAMPLE BRAG SHEET

Students should list all the extracurricular activities in which they participated from ninth through twelfth grades. Activities may include: student government, athletic teams, summer camps, clubs, church activities, internships, volunteer work, and employment. Include the name of the activity or club, years involved and achievements, awards, and titles (president, vice president, captain, MVP, etc.).

The Brag Sheet is not a substitute for a resume, but rather a tool to help create the resume.

Activities

    Church youth group, grades 9–12
    Mission trip to Poland with church, grades 9–12
    Swim team, grades 10, 11 (cocaptain in 11th grade)
    French Club, 12th grade
    Model United Nations, 11th grade
    Varsity tennis team, grades 10–12 (captain in 12th grade)
    Sophomore class president
    Volunteer reading tutor for elementary school students, 11th grade

Awards

    Good citizenship award, 9th grade and 11th grade
    Swim team: Most Improved, 10th grade
    Outstanding History Student award, 11th grade

Employment

    Babysitting, grades 9–12
    Made craft items and sold them at Christmas bazaars, 9th grade
    Pet sitting for neighbors on vacation
    Lawn mowing for parents and neighbors

Skills

    Type 60 wpm
    Word processing, spreadsheets
    Some knowledge of Spanish
    Dependable
    Self-starter
    Good leader

Sample Resume

There are many great books on resume writing at your local library, but here is a sample to get you started.

References should go on a separate sheet of paper. Always get permission before listing someone as a reference.

Your Name Your phone number
Your Street Address,   Your City, State, Zip   Your e-mail address

EDUCATION
- **Currently enrolled at** Your High School
- **Grade Point Average:** Your GPA if it's satisfactory

COMPUTER SKILLS
- **Platforms:** Windows XP, Windows 7
- **Software:** Microsoft Word 2010, Microsoft Excel 2010

EXPERIENCE

Teacher's Aide,   February 2006–June 2006
Name of Class, Your High School, City, State
- Graded assignments
- Performed some computer maintenance
- Answered questions
- Helped students with assignments

Any volunteer work

SKILLS and ATTRIBUTES
- Dependable
- Responsible
- Hardworking
- Good people skills

Chapter 8

Social Skills

The essence of social skills is the ability to make others feel at ease. This is difficult to teach since youngsters are still somewhat self-centered and need to be taught to think about the needs, wants, and feelings of others. As with any skill you're teaching, you start with a set of rules (in this case, manners), remind them often, and gradually teach them to think for themselves.

MANNERS

Just as a society needs laws to protect the rights of all individuals, it also needs a set of rules for individuals to follow to make life more pleasant. Manners are so important that many companies are now hiring experts to train employees in various social graces.

Table Manners

The purpose of table manners is to make the dining experience more enjoyable. Some people feel manners aren't important at home or when it's just family around. If children don't practice table manners on a regular basis, they probably won't remember them when out in public. Imagine how they'll feel later, when their dates are offended by their eating habits.

Julie, a friend of mine, had a neighbor whose husband traveled regularly. Thinking the neighbor and her kids might enjoy getting out of the house, Julie invited them to breakfast at a local restaurant. Things went well, until the children's pancakes arrived and Julie discovered they had never learned to use silverware. They simply poured syrup over the pancakes and dug in using their hands. Julie was horrified at the mess created by all those sticky fingers and more than a little concerned about what her car would look like after the ride home.

Clearly this is an extreme example, but the point is that most people expect a certain level of propriety from the people they're dining with. If you haven't yet taught table manners, you're not being fair to your offspring.

So what are the basics?

- **Know how to use silverware.** By age two, kids can learn to use a fork. Later you can add a child-safe knife and teach them to cut food that's about the size of the end of their thumb. The spoon comes later, when they're able to hold it level all the way to their mouth.
- **Use serving utensils, never fingers, to put food onto your plate.** The rule is always, "You touch it, you take it," meaning that if you touch it with your fingers, you're required to put it on your plate. At a buffet-style restaurant or at parties, always accompany the child until you're absolutely certain he knows this rule. No one wants to eat food someone else has been touching.
- **Close your mouth when you chew.** Chewing is part of the digestive process, and no one wants to watch that process in action.
- **Don't talk with your mouth full.** It increases your chance of accidentally spitting food at the person you're talking to, and makes it difficult to understand what you're saying.
- **Don't slurp or smack your lips.** These noises are just plain disgusting.
- **Sit up straight.** Lean forward slightly to avoid dripping on your shirt, and lift the spoon or fork to your mouth. No hunkering over your food like a hungry dog.

- **Keep your elbows off the table.** It implies you're either bored or tired.
- **Never spit anything out.** If the food is too hot, take a quick sip of your drink. If you encounter a bone or pit, discretely remove it with your fingers or fork and place it on the edge of your plate.
- **Take small bites.** Cut things to the proper size. The end of your thumb is about the right size.
- **Don't play with your food.**
- **Don't comment about what you like or don't like.** Children should be taught to taste everything. The first time my boys looked at one of my home-cooked meals and said, "That looks yukky," I told them it hurt my feelings. I explained that if they spent time working on something, and then showed it to me, their feelings would be hurt if I said it looked "yukky."
- **When finished eating, ask to be excused and thank the cook for the nice dinner.** As kids get older, they should remain in their seat until everyone is finished, especially at restaurants.
- **Don't blow your nose or pick your teeth at the table.** Excuse yourself and go to another room.
- **Use serving utensils, never fingers, to put food onto your plate.** If there are no utensils provided, only touch the item you're going to take. At a buffet style restaurant or at parties, always accompany your child until you're absolutely certain he knows this rule. No one wants to eat food someone else has been touching.

Dining out should be considered an opportunity to practice exceptional manners. When children place their order, remind them to say please. When the food arrives, say thank you. Children should remain seated until it's time to leave. Even in fast-food places, kids will need supervision. I've seen kids throw food, play tag, and even lick all the salt shakers while Mom and Dad were ordering.

Dining out should be considered an opportunity to practice exceptional manners.

Phone Manners

The house phone should be answered with "Hello" or "Smith residence." If the call is for someone else, your child should deliver the phone promptly to that person, or put the phone down and go tell the person about the call. It is not acceptable to stand there and scream, "MOM! IT'S FOR YOU!" If the person is not available, the child must be able to take a message—at the very least, the caller's name, number, and the day of the call. The message must be put where the intended recipient will receive it. Children have short memories and usually forget to tell parents (or siblings) that someone called several hours ago.

Make it easier for children to take messages by putting a pencil and paper near every phone. Some families find a dry erase board helpful—there's less chance of someone moving it away from the phone. If you're handy on the computer, you could print your own message pads, four to a sheet, then cut and staple them. Tell your children where you want messages to be posted. It should be someplace consistent, so everyone in the family knows where to look. Good places are on the refrigerator or the bathroom mirror.

Young children should not be allowed to answer the phone unless they can do it correctly. Nothing is more frustrating for callers than trying to convince a chatty toddler to go get Mommy.

A note on safety: children should be taught early to never tell callers that they're home alone. If your child is home alone and a caller asks, "Is your mother home?" the answer should always be, "I'm sorry but she's busy right now. May I take a message?"

Cell phones pose their own special etiquette problems. People tend to turn their backs to others when on their cell, as though that makes them invisible and "unhearable." Since they can't see the people nearby, they feel free to talk about personal matters as though they were alone. Some feel that it doesn't matter what they say in front of strangers. Details of your personal life should never be discussed in public. In addition, bad connections often cause people to shout into the phone, irritating everyone around them. If you feel like you have to shout, go outside. Cell phones should always be off during performances, church, and movies. They should not be answered during a meal, when you're with company, or in the restroom.

Cells should *always* be turned off and put away during school. Too many students are spending their class time texting their friends. When you get your bill, check the days and times of the phone calls. Make sure your student isn't chatting during school hours or after bedtime. Also check the pictures on the phone periodically to make sure there's nothing inappropriate. Teens should *never* answer phones or send texts while driving. Driving is hazardous enough for young people; they shouldn't divide their attention between several tasks (see Chapter 9).

Finally, teach children that phone calls (and texts) do *not* have to be answered immediately. If the call is important, the caller will leave a message.

Everyday Manners

Teaching kids to say please and thank you is a good place to start with manners. As soon as they can say the words, they should be encouraged to do so. The hard part is being consistent in the training, reminding them to use the words. As you hand toddlers things they've asked for, hang on tight until they say thanks. Be advised—this doesn't work with bread. More than once, I was left holding a crust of bread as my boys ran past.

When they say "Give me some milk" or "I want a snack," give them a puzzled look and say, "Excuse me?" At first, you'll need to remind them what it is you expect: "I'm sure you meant to say,

'May I have some milk, please?'" If you're consistent from the start, the words will quickly become a habit.

Our family was in a toy store one day when they were giving away stuffed animals. The clerk had one left and was trying to decide whom to give it to. She was surrounded by a group of small children yelling "Gimme! I want it!" when our son asked, "May I have it, please?" She looked surprised and remarked, "You're the only one all day that has said 'please.' You can have it." Children with manners should be the norm, not the exception.

Introductions

When children bring home new friends, encourage them to introduce you by simply saying, "Keenan, this is my mother, Mrs. Jones." You then offer to shake hands and reply, "Nice to meet you." The ritual may not seem necessary for kids, but they're in training for adulthood. Greet their friends the way you'd greet an adult you were being introduced to.

Similarly, when you have friends over who haven't met your cherubs, you need to introduce them. You don't need to search the neighborhood for your kids, but if they're nearby or if they answered the door, by all means make the introductions. If you have small children who are terribly shy, don't force the issue. You can practice introductions with family members first, then with people the kids already know. If they never practice, they'll never get comfortable with the process.

When my son was in fourth grade, he brought home a new friend. He started the introductions so well: "Jose, this is my mother, Mrs. Rhodes." Then he finished with, "But she prefers to be called Xena, Warrior Princess." Poor Jose wasn't quite sure what to say to that.

Hosting Guests

Good manners mean putting others at ease, so they are especially important when you have guests. When visitors arrive, take their coat, make introductions if needed, and offer them a seat. If they'll be staying awhile, offer them something to drink or eat. Often when kids bring friends home, they get themselves a snack but forget to offer anything to their friends. Remind your child "Others before self."

For sleepovers, make sure guests have everything they need: pillows, clean sheets, blankets, and a night light in the bathroom. Remind them that if they need anything else, all they have to do is ask. Clean towels should be set out if the guest plans on showering. Any special dietary needs should be accommodated as much as possible (allergies, religious restrictions, etc.)

Your child should be taught rules for being a guest at someone else's home, especially when staying overnight. If you're friends with the parents, you can have them gently remind your little one of her social responsibilities. She should help put toys away or clean up any messes created, help clear the table after dinner, and try all foods that are served; if there is something she just can't bring herself to eat, a polite "No thank you" is sufficient. In addition, wet towels should be hung up, not left on the floor or furniture, and the bathroom should be tidied up after use.

Traits of Socially Successful People

When you consider people you know who seem socially adept, ask yourself what qualities they have that make them that way. Usually these are the people who put you at ease and make you feel good about yourself. Most of them have learned the following social "tricks of the trade."

They listen to themselves when they talk.

When you're thinking about what you're going to say to someone, you must also consider how it will be received. How does what you're saying sound to the people listening?

Do you always talk about yourself? (We usually do since that's the one subject we're complete experts on.) Or do you ask questions that encourage others to talk about what interests them? Then do you listen to what they're saying, or does your mind wander?

Do you monopolize the conversation or give others a chance to jump in? Successful people let others have their share of time in a conversation. If you don't let people talk, you might notice them no longer paying attention to you or wanting to excuse themselves.

Are you always whining or complaining about everything? Even other complainers get tired of listening to whining after a while. Chronic complaining is a learned trait, by the way. If you notice your child complaining a lot, ask yourself if she learned it from you. As with any bad habit, the best way to break it is to replace it with a good habit. Whenever your child (or you) starts complaining, stop and describe something she can be grateful for. Almost anything you can complain about, you can also be grateful for:

I hate the weather.	I'm glad I wasn't born in Siberia.
My teacher is stupid.	I'm grateful it's just for nine months.
I don't get enough allowance.	I'm glad I have opportunities to earn money.
There's nothing on TV.	I'm grateful we have a TV.

They listen to others.

Listening has become a lost art. Too often, instead of listening to what is being said, we are totally focused on what we want to say next. There is also an unfortunate quirk of human nature that causes many of us to consider ourselves the only expert on any given topic. When someone offers an opinion, our first thought is often, "They're wrong." Instead of keeping an open mind and listening to their opinion, we proceed to focus on all the reasons why we feel they're wrong. Disagreeing with someone is not a bad thing unless you do it all the time. Then it's just a bad habit that needs to be broken. Some people call it playing devil's advocate; some people call it annoying.

They don't take offense when none was intended.

I once belonged to a group in which two of the women had gone to high school together, and had been bitter enemies. Twenty years later, one of them still could not let go of the anger. Kelly would smile and say, "Hi, how are you?"

Ronnie would glare at her and ask, "Why? Don't I look okay?" No matter what Kelly said, Ronnie took it as an insult.

When I was in college, I worked with a guy several years older than me. Everyone liked being around Steve, and I finally realized why: he never took offense at anything. You never had to watch what you said around him, and you could joke with him about anything. People would say things to him, either seriously or in jest, and he would just smile and agree with them. I remember vividly the day the manager yelled at Steve for being lazy. Steve just agreed with him. I would have spent the rest of the day (okay, month) sulking and telling everyone about my evil, vicious boss, but Steve accepted the truth of the statement. All he said was, "You're probably right. What do you suggest?" I was amazed.

They never ignore any act of kindness.

When someone holds the door for you or volunteers to help you in some way, of course you say thank you. People help others because it makes them feel good, and their reward is in knowing you appreciated it.

They are kind to others.

They ignore embarrassing moments that others experience. All of us, on occasion, burp or say something we wish we could take back. Maybe we trip or spill grape juice on a white tablecloth. It's all part of being human, but when it happens to us, we're grateful when others go on as though nothing happened. Instead of laughing at someone who's embarrassed, remind children the polite thing to do is ignore it.

They're patient with those who need it. Children, the elderly, people with handicaps, even people learning a new job are entitled to a little compassion and understanding.

Socially successful people consider the feelings of others when making decisions and are gracious when they don't get their way.

They look for ways to help people in need: opening doors or offering their seat to someone.

They respect the privacy of others.

They don't go through your medicine chest or closets. If they're taking care of your house while you're gone, you know they won't read your mail or go through your files. You can ask them for advice on personal matters and know that they won't share the details with others.

When they meet new people, they try to find some common interest.

Most friendships are based on one or more common interests. Your cherub won't become friends with everyone she meets, but looking for common ground is a fun game to play when meeting someone new.

Some conversation starters:

- Do you have any hobbies?
- Do you have pets?
- If you could be an animal, what would you be?
- What school do you go to?
- What classes are you taking (for older children)?
- What sports do you play?
- What do you want to be when you grow up?
- What's the best vacation you ever went on?
- What's your favorite commercial/TV show/sports team/store/type of car/movie/teacher/video game/book?

CLASS

Class is often defined as elegance, grace, and style, but I think there are many more facets to the concept. My personal icon of class is the late Princess Diana. She was the embodiment of not only elegance, grace, and style, but also manners, graciousness, and a few less obvious yet equally important traits.

Why Class Is Important

Different parts of the country—in fact, different neighborhoods in the same part of the country—have different standards for propriety. Different social circles, if you will. Wearing grubby clothes or licking your fingers at the dinner table might be fine in one social group but the subject of gossip in another. When your son goes off on his own, he may wind up in a group that has loftier standards than those he grew up with. At the very least, he should know how to rise to those standards.

I grew up in a suburb of Los Angeles. Our lifestyle was pretty casual—not much entertaining, no coming-out parties or fancy balls. As I was growing up, I had trouble understanding why my mother insisted I practice proper manners and act like a lady. "Nobody else cares!" was my favorite whine. Then I married a second lieutenant in the Air Force and suddenly found myself in somewhat more formal situations than I was used to. When Pat and I arrived at our first black tie dinner at the Officers' Club, I was incredibly grateful for Mom's nagging all those years. I still had a lot to learn about social skills (how to talk to strangers, how to put others at ease, etc.), because my family didn't socialize much, but I certainly knew which fork to use.

As Pat moved up through the ranks over the years, the amount of socializing we did increased proportionately. More entertaining, more formal dinners. When we lived in England, we regularly represented the base at ceremonies and dinner parties hosted by local British VIPs. We even went to a local mayor's reelection party, held in a 500-year-old building, where each guest's arrival was announced to the ballroom by a footman. It was just like in the movies, and I felt like Cinderella. The point is that we never know where life will take us, or our children, and it's best to be prepared.

I suspect all the royals go to some sort of finishing school to perfect their social graces. Being in the public eye is not the only reason to practice decorum, though. Look at all the celebrities in our country who behave badly. The reason that royalty practices perfect manners is pressure from family, peers, and the people they're surrounded by—their social class, if you will. They observe everyone around them adhering to the same high standards of behavior.

It's not as easy for us average folks. Our children's friends may have different standards, and many TV shows depict bad behavior. You can't control the outside world, but you can control what goes on in your house. You can also encourage young visitors to practice good manners. "In our house, we eat soup with a spoon, Timmy."

Graciousness

Everyone has an invisible sign that says "I need to feel important." We should remember this when we interact with others. Offer genuine compliments and be patient with those who need it. If you do a favor for someone, don't make him or her feel like it's a burden. Again, these behaviors must be modeled by parents.

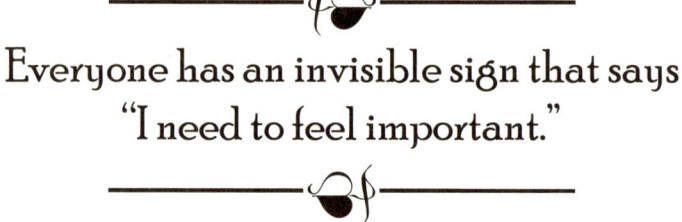

Everyone has an invisible sign that says "I need to feel important."

I once worked with a woman who was the antithesis of graciousness. We called her Dragon Lady. Sally's job was to provide technical support for the school, yet whenever teachers asked her for help, she'd make a show of how busy she was and how inconvenienced she'd be if she had to go help them. Eye rolling, big sighs, or outright hostility were her usual responses. Before long, teachers started coming to me instead. I was teaching computer classes at the time and could solve most of the day-to-day problems they encountered.

One day, Sally walked into my room in time to hear me tell another teacher, "I'd be happy to take a look at your computer.

Give me about five minutes to finish up what I'm doing here." Sally was furious. She yelled at me for undermining her position and then turned on the other teacher.

"Why the h-- are you coming to her with your problem? You're supposed to come to me! That's MY job!"

The teacher silently counted to ten, then replied, "You could answer that question yourself if you'd ever listen to yourself when you talk to people." As he left, he said to me, "I'll wait for you in my room."

Graciousness is about putting others at ease and never making them feel they're imposing. It's also about putting the wants of others before our own.

Hygiene

Once children hit puberty, their hygiene needs to change. They need to start washing their hair more often and concern themselves with shaving and deodorant. The good news is that most tweens and teens do this voluntarily to avoid teasing by peers. If your child is resisting appropriate hygiene, you'll have to set rules: shower every day, wash hair every other day, keep fingernails clean, never put on dirty clothes. Whatever works for your family.

Language

I don't mean proper English, although that's important, too. I'm talking about all those four-letter words our children learn from friends and the media. As near as I can tell, there are only a handful of words you can't say on TV or the radio, but of course anything goes in the movies and on the Internet.

Some parents don't have a problem with swearing. I've heard parents tell their kids things like "Get the h-- away from me" and even "Shut the f-- up!" I've seen parents who say nothing when their kids use the same words. These parents need to understand that there are still plenty of people who find such language offensive, disrespectful, and inappropriate. Swearing at each other at home is their prerogative; swearing in public is not acceptable. They don't have the right to teach your children those words.

Kids often think that using such language makes them appear cool or mature. In reality, it only shows that their vocabulary is limited and that they need better role models.

I was talking to an acquaintance about this recently, and he said, "You should come to one of my daughter's soccer games. The language there would make a sailor blush." I asked why the coach allowed it. Aren't kids' sporting events supposed to be family friendly? When I was coaching sports, admittedly a *long* time ago, players got benched for using foul language. It seems like nobody wants to be responsible for upholding standards anymore.

Appropriate Attire

I was in a store one day when I noticed a young man about sixteen wearing a shirt that said "What are you looking at, bitch?" I told him I found his shirt offensive. (I used to be really shy until I started teaching. Now my philosophy is that it takes a village to raise a child.) Anyway, his mother came up to me and said, "I told him I didn't like that shirt, but he wears it anyway." Three words: grow a backbone.

Our boys still talk about the time one of them insisted on wearing a ratty pair of shorts that were really more holes than fabric. I kept asking him to throw them out and even bought a new pair that was almost identical, but he kept insisting the old pair was fine. One day, he thought he'd wear the old pair to school, and I absolutely refused to allow it. After several minutes of arguing, I finally said, "You have a thread hanging down. (That was an understatement.) Let me fix that." I grabbed a pair of scissors and proceeded to cut straight up the front of one leg. I stood up, looked him in the eye, and said, "Oops. Guess you'll have to change." He really wanted to be angry with me but had trouble keeping a straight face.

At a swap meet recently, I saw a vendor selling kids' clothes with "cute" sayings on the front. One little shirt read "Playground Pimp." I asked the vendor, "Do people really buy these?"

"Oh, yes" was the answer.

"Why?" I asked. She just gave me that "you can go away now" look and turned to another (presumably paying) customer.

Another struggle for parents is the trend toward scanty dressing. This isn't really a new trend; I went through the miniskirt era in high school. Later, I saw a picture of myself and asked my mother, "How could you let me wear that?" She gave me that same "you can go away now" look.

Today, however, the scantiness of girls' clothing is even worse. Tank tops leave bra straps and more exposed. Low-cut pants can offer a view that the young lady may not be aware of. I'd frequently see girls at school sitting on the floor during lunch, unaware that the cute hot pink undies they were wearing were in plain view. We need to remind our kids that it's hard to take someone seriously when you can see their underwear. I used to ask students, "Do you want to see *my* underwear?" Their eyes would get big as they vigorously shook their head. "Well, I don't want to see yours either, so cover up."

One year, a parent came to speak at a faculty meeting at the high school. She was advocating for a stricter dress code for students. Apparently one of the girls her son knew had come to school in a rather revealing outfit, and when her son commented on it, she took offense. The girl and her friends followed the poor boy around for days, yelling "Pervert!" He was so upset he didn't want to come to school.

The mother's point was that it's hard enough for boys to deal with raging hormones; girls in skimpy outfits make it nearly impossible for boys to concentrate. The staff agreed, and a committee was formed to revamp the dress code. The other issue, of course, is that when girls wear clothing that says "Look at me, I'm sexy," they really don't get to complain when guys look at them and agree.

The argument could be made that children should have the right to wear whatever they want, but educators see it differently. In a child's life, the role of the adult is to train the child to take his or her place as a responsible member of society. School is a child's workplace, and just as most jobs have some type of dress code, so should the school. One of my favorite Dr. Phil-isms is that we're not raising children, we're raising future adults.

One last thought on attire. Our children need to learn that certain situations call for dressy clothes; jeans are not always appropriate. These events include ceremonies such as weddings and baptisms, job interviews as well as many jobs, and church. I know God doesn't care what you wear to church—He'd rather have you there in jeans than not there at all. Dressing up is a sign of respect, however, for God and His house. That's where the phrase "Sunday best" came from.

Propriety

Propriety can be defined as seemliness or modesty, both in appearance and behavior. The behavior part implies you should try not to offend the people around you. I've talked about kids swearing in public, but older children (and adults) need to remember that certain adult topics and personal tidbits don't need to be discussed in public, either.

My husband went to lunch recently with some coworkers. The restaurant was fairly noisy, yet the two young women at the next table were speaking loudly enough to be overheard. One of them had a yeast infection and was describing the symptoms. The other was offering helpful hints. Finally, one of his male coworkers leaned over and said, "Excuse me, but we can hear every word."

The women just looked at him as if to say "So?" These women clearly had no sense of propriety.

Where Have All Our Standards Gone?

Most people blame the entertainment industry for the decline in moral standards, and there's a lot of truth to that. Movies, TV, and music are all competing for our children's entertainment dollars, and will do what it takes to get their attention. Ultimately, though, parents are responsible for holding their youngsters to higher standards.

TV

There's an unbelievable amount of money at stake in the primetime ratings wars, and it's long been understood that sex sells. Chastity and monogamy are boring. Lap dances and pillow talk are much more compelling, especially to children and young adults. While the actual physical act may be off-limits on TV, story lines often revolve around who's sleeping with whom. Bed-hopping and extramarital affairs are commonplace, and young viewers quickly get the impression that these are normal behaviors. By the way, daytime soaps are just as bad—something to keep in mind if your little one happens to be sick and stays home from school. In an effort to get ahead, some shows continually push the limits of propriety. Words that were censored last year are suddenly acceptable this year. Topics that used to be off-limits are now commonplace. Where will it end?

Cable TV has become a place where anything goes. Not only do they run those R-rated movies you didn't let your kidlets see, there's an abundance of porn channels. Even if you don't watch the pay-per-view programs, are you sure your kids don't? Check your bill carefully. See Chapter 9 to find out how to lock out certain channels on your TV.

Movies

While most movies are rated by the Motion Picture Association of America's Rating Board, too many parents ignore the recommendations. Either they give in to the pleading ("Please please PLEASE can I go? Everybody has seen it but me!"), or they convince themselves that their child is mature for her age and can handle the R-rated movie. Some parents don't want their kids to suffer the pain of disappointment; some can't be bothered to get a sitter, so they take the kids with them to an adult movie.

We all know how important it is for kids to feel like they fit in. No child wants to be the only one in school who hasn't seen the latest movie. If you're convinced, as I am, that your twelve-year-old shouldn't see an R-rated movie, sit down with him and explain why. There will be other movies that you'll be happy to take him to, and he can rent this one when he's older. You love him too much to give in on this issue. Part of growing up is learning to deal with disappointment.

In addition to the entertainment industry, parents need to worry about:

- **The Internet,** which is totally unrated and uncensored. Here you can find all manner of wild, out-of-control behavior that kids see as cool and therefore desirable (see Chapter 9).
- **Celebrities who will do anything for attention.** We've all seen the news stories about the singer who had a "wardrobe malfunction" (raise your hand if you believe it was an accident) and celebrities who "forget" they're not wearing panties as they climb out of the car in front of cameras. These are just more examples of people for whom negative attention is better than none. Our celebrity-worshipping culture elevates these people to hero status, at least in the eyes of impressionable tweens and teens.
- **Society's declining moral standards.** As values slip in the entertainment industry, so do they slip in our society. Shows about so-called average families who behave badly make us think that it's okay to behave badly. It takes the "everyone else is doing it" argument to an entirely new level.

It seems as though there are no longer any repercussions for bad behavior. You can say anything you want in public and no one raises an eyebrow, but try to lead a public prayer and you could be in trouble. Why is that? Students have been expelled for handing out invitations to their church youth group. Others have been refused permission to conduct the annual "See you at the pole" event, where Christian students gather around the flagpole before school to pray.

During the 2010 Super Bowl, the Focus on the Family commercial about Pam Tebow's miracle baby, Tom, generated a firestorm of controversy because it advocated against abortion. The commercial showing men at the office in their underwear? Not a peep. Not too long ago you'd get arrested for indecent exposure if you walked around in your underwear. Now you can watch a one-hour TV special devoted entirely to models wearing nothing but revealing lingerie.

In a perfect world, we'd bring back shows like *Leave It to Beaver* and *Andy Griffith*, and boycott programs that oppose family values. In the meantime, we need to know what our kids are watching and talk to them about those shows and movies. Look for teachable moments. Let them know why certain behaviors are unacceptable or even dangerous.

The whole *Girls Gone Wild* phenomenon baffles me. What are these girls thinking? They allow strangers to make a movie about them taking their clothes off. Someday their boss is going to say, "You look familiar." Even worse, ten to fifteen years from now their children may say, "Doesn't that look like Mom?" Talk to your daughters. This behavior *will* come back to haunt them someday.

How to Sell Propriety (Classiness) to Your Children

Manners and Hygiene:

- It's a rule.
- That's what ladies and gentlemen do.
- You'd be embarrassed if someone said you were "gross."

Behavior and Attitude:

- First impressions and bad impressions last forever. You can't unring a bell.

- Anything you post on the Internet is there forever. Even if you "unpost" it, people may have already copied it, forwarded it, or saved it for future use.
- The same goes for digital pictures and videos. Thousands of girls have sent naked pictures of themselves to their boyfriends, only to learn they've been passed on to his friends, who have passed them on to more friends, etc.
- Nobody regrets displaying good behavior; most people eventually regret bad behavior.

Chapter 9

Safety

It's no secret that our children are nowhere near as safe as they were a decade ago. Internet predators, online pornography, school shootings and all manner of adult programs on TV are relatively new threats. Stranger danger, underage drinking, and drug abuse are on the rise. In addition to teen pregnancy, parents worry about STDs and AIDS. Middle school children see nothing wrong with oral sex because, they argue, "it isn't really sex."

The biggest obstacles for parents are the kids themselves. Children almost always consider themselves invincible. Their mindset is that "nothing bad is going to happen" and "I'll be careful, I promise." They're too young to have experienced tragedy firsthand and too optimistic to consider that anything could happen to them.

The best defense for parents is setting strict safety rules for younger kids and talking to older children about examples from the media. You'll need to find a balance between getting them to be realistic about potential dangers and scaring them so badly they'll never leave the house.

Infants and toddlers have their own safety needs, which seem to change daily. One day, you turn around and suddenly the baby has learned to crawl well enough to get to the lamp cord—and chew on it.

Let's start with the basics.

Physical Safety for Small Children

According to babycenter.com, children between the ages of one and four are more likely to be killed by fire, burns, drowning, choking, poisoning, or falls than by a stranger's violence. It's important to babyproof the bottom four feet of your home before your little angel learns to crawl. Babies are curious creatures and can get themselves into trouble in the blink of an eye. Be sure to:

- Put plug covers on *all* electrical outlets.
- Know your state's law about seat belts. Every state requires car seats for infants, and most hospitals won't release the baby until they see the car seat. Remember that the minimum requirement is just that: minimum. Your angel deserves the best you can afford.
- Never ever leave a small child unattended on a changing table or bed, or in a tub or pool. Even though your little one has never rolled over, today could be the day she learns. Toddlers can drown in an inch of water in less than four minutes. Permanent brain damage occurs even sooner. If the phone or doorbell rings, ignore it, or wrap baby up and take her with you.
- Consider lid locks for the toilets, and empty any containers of water around the house, including wading pools, when not in use. Toddlers are top-heavy, and can easily fall into a toilet or bucket of water and drown.
- Don't use flotation devices as a substitute for constant supervision around water. Flotation devices are fine but not foolproof, and tend to give parents a false sense of security.
- Install latches on cupboard doors to keep little hands away from poisons. But keep the phone number for the national poison control center close to the phone: (800) 222-1222.
- Put houseplants out of reach—many are poisonous.
- Use playpens when you have to leave the room for a minute or two and need a safe area to put the baby.

- Pick up any small objects that baby could choke on, such as loose change, paper clips, or small toys belonging to older siblings.
- Put gates at the top and bottom of stairs. Teach baby how to crawl down safely (feet first, on her belly).
- Beware of cords on window blinds. They pose a strangulation hazard. Place a hook up high to hang the cords on, and keep cribs away from cords and any window treatments with ribbons. When buying new shades or blinds, look for cordless models.
- Avoid the temptation to set your child on a railing with his feet hanging over the side. Kids often complain that they can't see something because they're too short, but is the view worth the risk? Michael Jackson made headlines when he held his baby over the side of a fourth-story balcony so fans could get a better look. Less well-known is the father who perched his son on the wall of an alligator enclosure at a Florida zoo. The son slipped, fell in, and was killed before anyone could react. On a ferry boat several years ago, I watched as a woman sat her five-year-old daughter on the two-inch metal railing of the upper deck, three stories above the water. Fortunately, a crew member ran over and pulled the child to safety. Accidents happen. Don't let them happen to your children.
- Put a trigger lock on any gun you own and keep the bullets in a separate location. Keep the keys with you and take a gun safety course. You may think the gun is well hidden, but I guarantee that if the kids know you have a gun, they'll find it.
- Test the temperature of the bath before placing a child in the tub. Scalding water is a major source of injury for children under five. Turn the water heater down to between 120 and 130 degrees.
- Keep hot liquids, curling irons, portable heaters, etc., well out of reach of curious fingers, and don't set hot things on a tablecloth, as they can easily be pulled down by a toddler. Keep appliance cords out of reach for the same reason.

- Keep medicine out of reach. Child-resistant packages are not childproof. My one-year-old was able to open a prescription container of pills by throwing it against the wall.
- Use the back burners of the stove and turn pot handles inward so they can't be pulled over.
- Secure any window that your child can reach so it opens no more than four inches.
- Secure your furniture. Every year, thousands of people, many of them children, are injured when furniture falls on them. Dressers, TV stands, and bookcases become potential hazards once baby learns to climb. Load dressers and bookcases with heavier items on the bottom, and strap them to the wall if possible, especially if you live in earthquake country. Make sure TV stands are stable—children have died from a TV falling on their head.
- Provide constant supervision outside. It's a must until they're old enough to ask permission to leave the yard.
- Don't let babies under six months old spend time in direct sunlight. Those older than six months should always have sunscreen applied.

Other important rules for children (around age four and up)

- If someone tries to touch you in a way that makes you feel uncomfortable, say "NO!" loudly and run away.
- If someone makes you feel scared, uncomfortable, or confused, get away as soon as you can. Again, tell a parent or trusted adult.
- Always get permission from a parent or trusted adult before going anywhere, especially in a car, or before taking something from strangers.
- Never ever run into the street—not after a sibling, friend, ball, or animal. Remind your children that it would break your heart if something happened to them.

- Have your children memorize their address and phone number early. It's probably best if they learn your cell phone number instead of the house phone. That way, if you get separated while you're out, they can call your cell. Memorizing numbers is easier if set to a song they already know, such as "The Alphabet Song" or "Jesus Loves Me."

- Most states have a law requiring seat belts for all passengers. Enforce it. Tell your kids the car won't go unless everyone's seat belt is fastened.

- Don't talk to strangers, men or women. Children don't have to be rude, but a simple "I'm not allowed to talk to strangers" as they back away will suffice. Explain to kids that sometimes bad people use the lines "Help me find my puppy" and "Come see the kittens in my car" as a way of tricking children.

- Have a secret word or phrase for your family in case you ever have to ask a friend to pick up your children from school or the sitter. In theory, your kids should know your friends, but in case they don't, or if you've recently moved, the secret phrase gives everyone peace of mind. In our house, the phrase was, "Aunt Lisa said it's okay if you come with me." We reasoned that strangers wouldn't know the name of their aunt.

- Never go into a stranger's car or house. Of course, when we lived in Alaska, we had to modify that a little: "Don't talk to strangers, don't pet the moose, and if you see a bear, go into the nearest house—I don't care if you know the people or not." Fortunately, we never had to use that rule.

- If they like to wear dark clothing, as teens and tweens are wont to do, explain to them that at night they're invisible. It helps to demonstrate this by having a friend or family member put on dark clothes and stand in the shadows. As I was driving through base housing one early morning, I nearly ran over a woman wearing camouflage as she stepped off the curb. She was angry until I pointed out that she was dressed like a bush and that there's a reason they call it camouflage. She looked down at herself and said, "Oh yeah." We both apologized and went on our way.

- Fire drills save lives—practice these with the entire family. If there's a fire, get out and go to the designated meeting place. Leave the door open, if possible, so pets can get out. This discourages children from running back into the house after Fluffy. If there are bedrooms on the second floor, have emergency ladders available. They cost around twenty-five to fifty dollars and hook over a windowsill. Don't forget to test your smoke alarms and carbon monoxide detectors monthly.
- Check the rooms of older children periodically for contraband (drugs, alcohol, weapons, and porn). Their safety is more important than their privacy.

As your child gets older, his world expands, as does his exposure to potential dangers. Proactive parenting involves communicating with your kids about what to do if a problem arises, as well as making sure they know they can talk to you about their fears. That means taking their fear seriously, no matter how silly it sounds. If you laugh at them or ignore their fear, you greatly reduce the chances of them coming to you with bigger problems.

Bullies

Most children have a run-in with a bully at some point. It seems as though every school has at least one bully, so it's important to give your kids tips on how to handle an encounter:

- **Ignore the bully.** Bullies are looking for a reaction to their teasing and meanness. Pretending you don't notice them takes away their power. Act brave and walk away.
- **Use your words.** Kids can stand up for themselves by telling the bully to stop it and then walking away.
- **Don't start a fight or get physical.** It's dangerous, and most schools suspend any student involved in a fight.
- **Use the buddy system.** Walk with a friend or two if you're going somewhere you might run into the bully. If your friends are being bullied, offer to walk with them.

- **Tell an adult.** Teachers, principals, parents, and lunchroom helpers at school can all help to stop bullying, and it's important to tell someone. If you're being bullied, then probably other kids are, too.

Anytime your child exhibits school avoidance behaviors or seems fearful, talk to them about the reason. If you suspect your child is being bullied, speak to the teacher or principal immediately. If you're getting reports that it's *your* cherub doing the bullying, talk to the school counselor or seek professional help. According to KeepKidshealthy.com, some bullies may engage in bullying behavior because of low self-esteem, but some may have a need to control others. They usually have little self-control and are more likely to engage in criminal activities as adults.

Clearly it's in everyone's best interest to get help for both the bully and the victim. Bullying has been linked to school shootings, beatings, and even teen suicides.

DRIVING

Teaching a teen to drive is one of the scariest jobs a parent has to face. You're putting your life in the hands of a person who thinks driving a car is the same as playing a video game: when you hit something, you bounce off of it and yell, "Yahoo! Here we go!" Teens just don't understand how dangerous cars are. Most young adults believe they're invincible because so far nothing bad *has* happened.

It's up to parents to make it clear that driving is serious business. Consider all the things a driver has to think about: stay between the lines; watch the other cars because those drivers might be distracted; change lanes without hitting anyone; watch out for pedestrians, children, dogs, and cats; read street signs; read warning signs; look for signals, speed limit signs, and stop signs; watch the speedometer.

That's just the driving part. When you add in all the other things kids do while driving (putting on makeup, changing the music, programming the GPS, eating, talking on the phone, and, heaven forbid, texting), it's a wonder that any teens survive the driving experience.

Driving Rules

- Before their child starts driving, proactive parents will lay out the rules (and, of course, the consequences). Pat and I always told our boys that the first ten rules of driving are:

1. **Don't hit anything.**
2. **Don't hit anything.**
3. **Don't hit anything.**
4. **Don't hit anything.**
5. **Don't hit anything.**
6. **Don't hit anything.**
7. **Don't hit anything.**
8. **Don't hit anything.**
9. **Don't hit anything.**
10. **Don't hit anything.**

- Rules 11–20 are don't speed.
- No friends in the car for the first year unless an adult is present. Some states have enacted this into law, but since it's not practical for officers to stop every car full of young people, it's up to parents to enforce this.

    Friends in the car are a distraction at the very least. In the worst case, friends may pressure the driver to take risks, usually speeding. I've heard students tell stories of throwing food at or tickling the driver. One told of being a passenger in the backseat and releasing the driver's seat latch, so the driver fell backward while driving down the freeway.
- No nighttime driving for a few months. Glare from headlights, limited visibility, and fatigue all make driving more difficult, especially for a new driver.
- No driving in extreme weather for the first few months, either.

- Absolutely no phone calls or texting. Drivers who break this rule should lose both their driving privileges and their phone privileges for a few weeks.
- No driving while impaired. Whether they're tired, sick, or have been drinking, they should call for a ride home.
- A new driver who gets a ticket loses driving privileges. Getting a ticket indicates a flagrant disregard for the law.
- Any complaints from the neighbors about the new driver will also result in a loss of driving privileges.
- Everyone in the car will wear a seat belt at all times.

Note: Ford is developing a car key for teens that will allow parents to set limits on the car's speed and stereo volume, and will enforce seat belt use. I hope other carmakers follow suit.

A Note on Texting

Recent studies have shown that texting while driving may be much more dangerous than driving while drunk. Too many young people have gone to jail for injuring or killing pedestrians because they were texting behind the wheel.

The problem is that today's teens have grown up with cell phones and computers, and are used to getting immediate responses. They feel they have to answer every phone call and every text right away. Make it clear that whatever the message is, it's not to die for. If they think the message is urgent, they need to find a safe place to park the car; otherwise, they'll have to wait until they get to their destination. Their safety and the safety of others are paramount. Both the phone and car are conveniences, not rights, and will be taken away if the rules are broken.

Many states have enacted laws prohibiting texting and/or handheld phone use while driving. There is an application called OTTER available for some phones, which prevents incoming texts and calls while the car is moving (www.otterapp.com). It can also be programmed to silence the phone during a specific time, say during school hours. It was developed by a father whose daughter was nearly run over by a woman who was texting.

Things for all drivers to consider:

- Why don't football players text or answer their phone while on the field?
- How would you feel if your surgeon was texting during your operation?
- How would you feel if you hit a child who ran out in front of you in that brief second you looked at your phone?

Driving Practice

After a few months of practice in good weather, you'll need to start them driving at night and in inclement weather. If you happen to live in a cold climate it's a good idea to find an empty parking lot and practice skids in the snow.

Empty parking lots are also handy for practicing parallel parking and other maneuvers. One father wanted to teach his daughter how easy it is to be distracted when driving. He set a box in an empty lot and told her to pull up to the box and stop in front of it. As they approached the box, he deliberately dropped his cell phone at her feet. She was so busy fishing around for the phone that she ran right over the box. The father said he tried this with all three of his children; all three hit the box.

Driving While Intoxicated

This is a tricky topic. Of course you don't want your kids to ever do drugs or alcohol. More important, however, is that if they have a lapse in judgment and try illegal substances, you absolutely do not want them to get behind the wheel of a car. Get them home safely and then deal with the substance issue.

Remind teens often that they should call you for a ride if they have doubts about their ability to drive. The same is true if they're a passenger in a car being driven by someone who starts drinking or doing drugs. You'll likely have to choose your attitude. Instead of yelling at them for waking you up in the middle of the night, give thanks that they're safe and let them know you're glad they called.

Some teens claim they're not intoxicated, just "buzzed." Buzzed driving is still impaired driving!

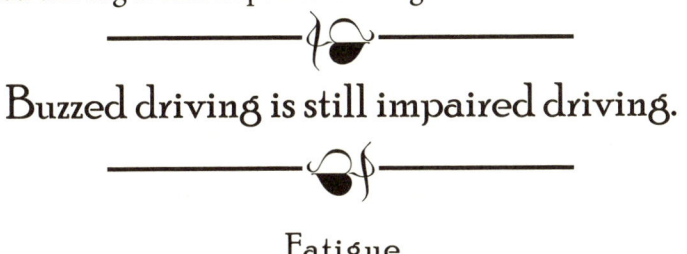

Buzzed driving is still impaired driving.

Fatigue

Driving drowsy is as bad as driving drunk. Hundreds of people have been killed because another driver fell asleep at the wheel. If your child is sleepy, he should find a safe place to pull over and take a nap, or call you to come get him.

A note of caution: tell your child to *never* leave the car running if he's going to nap in it. There is a chance of succumbing to carbon monoxide poisoning. If it's too cold to sleep in the car, call for a ride.

The Driving Contract

Many parents find it helpful to have their new driver sign a contract that spells out all expectations and the consequences for breaking the rules. When you present it for their signature, you may hear some moaning. Remind them that driving is a privilege, not a right. If they want the privilege of driving, they'll have to agree to follow the rules.

You can create your own contract or download one from your insurance company's website. Almost every insurance company has a contract, so you might want to compare a few. The one at USAA (http://www.lawlab.com/driving/drivcont.htm) is especially thorough.

If your contract doesn't address the issue of repairs, talk to your spouse and teen about who will pay for maintenance and repairs, and what happens if the car is out of commission for a while due to unforeseen circumstances (accidents).

What to Say to Your New Driver

- Now that you're driving, you have more freedom and independence than ever before. You must realize that what you're driving can be a deadly weapon. Used improperly, cars can kill the driver, passengers, or strangers. Unfortunately, teens often overestimate their driving skills and underestimate the dangers involved. Our job is to keep you and others safe while you're working on all the necessary driving skills.

- We know you think you're a safe driver, and we hope you're right, but you still have a lot of learning and practicing to do before we're convinced. Any violation of your driving contract will result in the loss of not only driving privileges, but of our trust.

- We want you to have fun and enjoy driving. Just don't break your parents' hearts.

EMOTIONAL AND MORAL SAFETY

Media

Decency standards for all forms of media have steadily declined over the last few decades. TV, movies, music, and even magazines have all changed their standards in order to remain commercially competitive.

One of the best sermons I ever heard was entitled "Sin Is Like a Pig Farm." The chaplain was explaining how, as a child, his family would go visit his grandparents' pig farm. He could tell when they were approaching the farm—the odor got steadily stronger until he thought he would be ill. When they arrived, he'd think to himself, "How can anyone possibly put up with this?" By the second day, however, the stench didn't seem as bad, and by the third day, he hardly noticed the smell.

His point was that this is exactly how sin—also known as declining moral values—works. At first, we're appalled by a certain behavior, but pretty soon we get used to it and even accept it as normal.

Television is a perfect example. In the early days, TV was about family entertainment. We enjoyed shows such as *I Love Lucy, Leave It to Beaver, Andy Griffith*, and *The Wonderful World of Disney*. If you have ever watched *I Love Lucy*, you'll remember that Ricky and Lucy slept in separate beds even though they portrayed a married couple and were married in real life.

When the Federal Communications Commission (FCC) eased broadcasting restrictions in the early 1970s, the first pay TV was born in the form of HBO. The new station had more leeway in the types of programming it could offer and also had more lenient censors. Thus began the downhill slide, as the network stations quickly followed suit. Today, the story lines for most afternoon soap operas include who's sleeping with whom, married or not. While they don't show the actual act, they come pretty close. Many prime-time shows have one or more characters whose primary goal is to sleep with as many partners as possible. Think about *Friends, How I Met Your Mother, Will and Grace, Scrubs*, and, of course, *Sex and the City*. Rarely do these shows discuss the dangers involved with having multiple partners. One reality show allows a single man to date twenty-five women, with the assumption he will propose to one at the end. He even has overnight dates with several of the women. Think about that—the studio arranges for him to presumably have sex, and the studio profits financially from the event. Isn't there a word for that type of activity?

In addition, there are stations such as MTV and the Comedy Channel that pride themselves on pushing the boundaries. Raunchy music videos and stand-up comedy acts are now available in your house and in your kids' rooms.

More alarming are shows like *Pants Off Dance Off* (a stripper competition with strategically placed black bars) and the ads for phone dating, with their implications of phone sex. One show I ran across in the middle of the day was called *Blind Date*. Actual statements from the participants include, "My definition of love is good sex. How can you love someone if the sex isn't good?" and "My biggest turn-on is anything kinky."

Teens watching these shows and ads assume that indiscriminate sex is normal behavior or at least what the "hot" people are doing. Many are inspired to join in the fun. The message is that sex is no big deal, even expected, and being hot is synonymous with being popular.

Watching these shows deprives children of their innocence and implies that the behavior is acceptable. When parents allow kids access to these types of programs, they're sending the message that they, the parents, condone the behavior. Parents need to actively explain why they're opposed to such behavior and use prime-time shows as teachable moments. Explain that people with any sort of self-respect and moral decency don't behave that way.

A recent study by the American Academy of Pediatrics found that young people who watch sex on television are likely to engage in sexual activities earlier than those who have less exposure to such programming.

The good news is that most adult content is on late at night. The bad news is that teenagers are nocturnal. Fortunately, there are plenty of family shows our kids can watch. Note, however, that the shows on some so-called family channels are not always family friendly. Know what your kids are watching.

As parents, we need to take back control of what our kids are viewing. We need to stand firm in the face of their protests. We have to be able to say no and mean it, for their own good.

As you are limiting their viewing options, explain why they're not allowed to see certain shows:

- That show is for grown-ups. You can watch it when you're twenty-one (or fifty).
- My job is to protect you from bad influences, and there are lots of TV shows that teach things kids shouldn't learn.
- This show goes against our family's values and principles, and we won't have it on in our house.
- Watching trashy TV is like eating out of the garbage can. One is harmful to your body, the other to your mind.

There are several ways to take control:

- **V-chip:** The FCC requires that all TVs manufactured after the year 2000 and larger than thirteen inches must have a V-chip. If your TV doesn't have one, you can purchase a separate V-chip box to attach to your TV. According to the FCC, most programs are now assigned a rating according to a system established by the broadcasting industry. The rating is encoded with the program so that, using the remote control, parents can program the V-chip to block shows with certain ratings.
- In 1996, Congress asked the broadcasting industry to establish a voluntary ratings system for TV programs. The industry did so by creating the "TV Parental Guidelines." Ratings appear in the corner of your television screen during the first fifteen seconds of each program. The ratings are also included in many magazines and newspapers that provide TV listings. Ratings are given to all television programming except news, sports, and unedited movies on premium cable channels. There are six possible ratings:

    - **TV-Y** *(All Children), found only in children's shows, means that the show is appropriate for all children.*
    - **TV-7** *(Directed to Older Children), found only in children's shows, means that the show is most appropriate for children age seven and up.*
    - **TV-G** *(General Audience) means that the show is suitable for all ages but is not necessarily a children's show.*
    - **TV-PG** *(Parental Guidance Suggested) means that the show may be unsuitable for younger children. This rating may also include a V for violence, S for sexual situations, L for language, or D for suggestive dialogue.*
    - **TV-14** *(Parents Strongly Cautioned) means that the show may be unsuitable for children under fourteen. V, S, L, or D may accompany a rating of TV-14.*
    - **TV-MA** *(Mature Audience Only) means that the show may be unsuitable for children under seventeen. V, S, L, or D may accompany a rating of TV-MA.*

The V-chip can easily be activated by using the MENU button on your TV's remote. You'll be asked to create a numeric password, and you'll probably want to record it somewhere the kids won't find it. Then use the remote to block the channels or shows you don't want kids to see.[1]

- Cable or satellite: Blocking channels or specific shows using the cable remote is similar to using the V-chip. Use the MENU button on the remote, then follow the on-screen guide. For more information, go to TheTVBoss.org.

It does take time to block inappropriate channels and programs, and of course the more channels you receive, the longer it will take, but after it's done you'll only have to tweak it now and then. Once you have each of your TVs set the way you want, encourage other parents to do the same.

When your daughter goes over to a friend's house, you'll want to speak to the parents about what she's not allowed to watch. Maybe send along a safe movie from your collection. Better yet, have the kids play outside.

Music

Music is another form of entertainment that has deteriorated into an "anything goes" mentality. CDs with especially offensive or adult language will have a warning label on the front of the package. These warning labels are helpful if you're in a store with your kids, but most music can be downloaded easily, either legally or otherwise. Even if your kids don't pay for music downloads, they can acquire songs from their friends. Talk to your kids about what's not acceptable and why. Let them know you'll be listening to their tunes now and then.

When our son was in the sixth grade, he borrowed a CD from a friend. We were shocked by some of the lyrics, including, "Do

---

[1] United States. Federal Communications Commission. V-Chip - Putting Restrictions on What Your Children Watch. http://www.fcc.gov/guides/v-chip-putting-restrictions-what-your-children-watch

you like it when I go down on you?" Not the sort of thing we wanted him hearing.

It's often unpleasant listening to your teen's music—at least it was for me, and I admit I didn't do it often enough—but with so many negative influences coming at our young people, parents need to keep their guard up. If your kids don't want you to listen to their music, there's probably a reason.

One day, my kids and I visited a friend whose young daughters were listening to a song with rather adult lyrics. I asked my friend to turn it off because my kids weren't allowed to listen to it. She looked sheepish and said, "It's the music for their dance recital. What can I do?" I pointed out that she was paying for these dance lessons. She needed to insist that the instructor choose kid-friendly music and get the other parents to do the same.

Stand up for family values. One person with a passion is worth ninety-nine with an interest. Be passionate about your children's moral safety. Too many parents are afraid to speak up because they won't look "cool." Our job is not to be our kid's friend, but to protect them when they're too young or naïve to know they need protecting.

Internet

The Internet is undeniably one of the most significant creations of the twentieth century. Sometimes I wonder how we ever got along without it. We can communicate with people anywhere in the world, get information on virtually any subject, and (my personal favorite) shop for anything 24/7.

As with any invention, there are unintended consequences and, in this case, some serious disadvantages. Since no one actually owns the Internet, no one person or organization is responsible for the content that can be posted. And because the Internet is worldwide, it's virtually impossible to police.

Two of the biggest problems are:

- **No editors or censors.** Anyone can say whatever they want or post whatever pictures they want. Because absolutely anyone can publish a website, the amount of adult material, perverse imagery, and hateful rhetoric is beyond appalling. Girls think it's fun to post suggestive or racy photos, and they know it's all too easy to hide these sites from parents. Even if you monitor their personal website, they can have other sites they're not telling you about.

- **A false sense of anonymity.** Because they use screen names, many children feel they can say anything without repercussions. This can lead to cyberbullying or all manner of inappropriate postings by anyone from any part of the world—or even your own child.

Internet dangers can fall into four categories: predators, inappropriate material, things the kids themselves post, and cyberbullying. I'm using the word *post* to mean anything uploaded to, or transmitted across, the web, including photos, websites, blogs, and messages.

Predators

Children are too young and naïve to understand that there are evil people out there who may want to harm them. In addition, most people believe what they want to believe, and this is especially true for kids. (The idealism of youth often extends into the college years, by the way.) If they find someone online that seems to care about them, it's difficult for anyone to shake that faith.

One of my tenth-grade students ran up to me one day and said, "Mrs. Rhodes, I'm in love! I met a movie producer online. He's twenty-five, and he loves me too!"

"Michelle," I explained, "he's probably eighty-five and toothless. *Everyone* says they're a twenty-five-year-old movie producer."

"Oh, no, I know he's telling the truth."

I changed tactics, trying to get her to see reality. "So, how old did you tell him *you* were?"

"Twenty-one."

There was a pause before the lightbulb came on over her head. You just can't believe much of what you read in chat rooms.

As kids approach puberty, they find it exciting to say things online that they wouldn't have the courage to say in person, especially to strangers. They may seek out chat rooms, pretending to be an adult, or may be approached by a predator in what seems to be a child-safe chat.

Predators often spend weeks, even months, chatting with a potential target, gathering personal information and gaining their trust. The predator's goal is to build an emotional bond with the child, offering flattery and fostering animosity toward parents or other adults. Over time, the conversations become more personal and explicit. Some predators will send photos of child pornography to prove that such behavior is "normal." Eventually, the predator will suggest a face-to-face meeting.

If your children seem secretive about their computer activities, or you suspect they're engaging in inappropriate activities online, it's important to talk to them calmly and without judgment. You want to keep the lines of communication open, yet still communicate your concern about the dangers involved.

If a predator does contact your child by phone or in person, contact your local police or the FBI *immediately*.

Inappropriate Material

The more time children spend online, the more garbage (such as predators) they're going to encounter. Make it easy for them to stay safe. *Keep the computer in a public place* and keep the Internet locked down when you're not in the room. If you're not sure how, click on your browser's help button and look for security or filtering content. As with the V-chip in your TV, you'll set a password that must be entered before anyone can use the browser. Windows Messenger and other instant messaging applications have similar methods for locking down the program. There are also software programs you can purchase to prevent inappropriate web surfing.

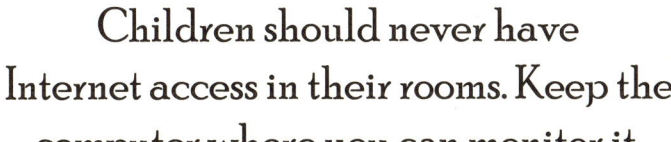

Children should never have Internet access in their rooms. Keep the computer where you can monitor it.

Having a computer in their room makes it too easy for children to get lost on the information highway, either accidentally or intentionally. I was searching for local quilt stores one day and ran across a white supremacy website! Social media sites such as YouTube, Facebook, and MySpace have links to plenty of adult content which, in turn, have links to even less desirable sites.

In addition, when kids learn a new word at school, they don't come to their parents anymore to find out what it means. They just enter it into a search engine, which often takes them to places you don't want them to go. Finally, you want to keep an eye on their computer activities to make sure they don't engage in any type of online harassment of other students.

When you take the computer out of their room, you'll probably hear, "You don't trust me!" Counter with, "It's my job to keep you safe, and it's not fair for me to put temptation in front of you."

A study by the University of New Hampshire found that much of the pornography that children come across accidentally is extremely graphic and includes images of both violence and deviant sexual behavior. The more often children see these images, the more "normal" this will seem to them. In addition, they will meet other people who also consider deviant behavior to be the norm. If that's not enough to convince you to keep the computer in a public place, be advised that many states now consider the act of allowing children to view pornography as child abuse.

Besides being subjected to unwanted pornography, many teens and even preteens deliberately seek out adult sites. Children this age are naturally curious, and the information age has made it incredibly easy to learn more than they need to know. A recent Canadian study by the University of Alberta found that over a third of the thirteen-year-old boys in the study frequently view Internet porn, and very few parents are aware of the activity.

Other studies indicate that many teens admit to actually doing some of the things they had viewed online.

Things Children Post

Some parents don't realize that what kids post can be just as problematic as what they might see on the Internet. Other parents choose to look the other way, hoping their kids will stay safe. Hoping for the best is not a great strategy.

For young children, the greatest danger is giving out too much information. Names, phone numbers, addresses, or school names should never be given out over the Internet. Predators have been known to piece together a first name, school, and sports team roster in order to meet students face-to-face. Even knowing only a phone number, predators can use a reverse directory (similar to a phone book, but the information is sorted by phone number) to get your address.

Keep in mind that *nothing* you post on the Internet is private. With the right equipment, strangers can hijack your transmissions, especially from nonsecure wireless connections. (By the way, that's why you should never e-mail account information, passwords, or Social Security numbers.)

You should also be careful about how much information you post on any family website. If a predator can figure out your location and the child's name, it'll be easy for that person to convince the child that he's a friend of the family. Something like, "Hey Johnny! You're Johnny Smith, right? Your Mom is running late and said I should give you a ride home." Or "Hey Johnny, I think I found that little brown dog of yours. Can you come over to my car and get him?"

I know the chances of these things happening are slim, but when it comes to safety, it's best to take a huge step toward caution. Look over each of your family websites, social network pages, and blogs for personal information.

Cyberbullying

One rapidly growing problem for children is cyberbullying. Kids who would never threaten another person face-to-face somehow feel safe doing it online. The problem is so severe that there are numerous organizations devoted to preventing it. More than a few young people have committed suicide because of online bullying and harassment.

Cyberbullying is typically defined as the harassment of a minor by another minor by means of electronic transmission. The harassment can be in the form of embarrassment or threats, and can be anywhere from mild to life-threatening. Often children don't see this behavior as a problem; they think of it as venting their frustrations. They may tell adults, "Everyone knows I was just kidding."

- **Texting:** Threatening messages to the victim's phone, computer, or personal web page are all considered harassment. Occasionally several students gang up on another by sending dozens or even hundreds of text messages to the victim's cell phone. Since some phone plans charge extra for each message, this sort of harassment can result in an enormous phone bill.

- **Blogs and personal web pages:** Say Sally is having a bad day. Her boyfriend dumped her for that you-know-what Lucy, and now Sally is sure everyone at school is calling her a loser. She'll get even, though. She'll update her website with all sorts of nasty lies about Lucy. Maybe tomorrow Sally can use her cell phone to get a picture of Lucy in the locker room and put it on the web page.

   These types of sites make it easy to post nastygrams because only someone with the password can remove the postings. Needless to say, any form of hurtful rhetoric must be removed immediately.

- **Password stealing:** This is a more malicious form of bullying. Someone who knows your child's password has the ability to do all sorts of damage. A stolen school password can be used to delete all of the victim's assignments or to put damaging material in the directory where electronic documents are stored. When someone steals a personal password that person can log in to the victim's messaging service and send out all kinds of messages while pretending to be the victim, upload things to the victim's website or even change the password, thereby locking your child out of her own site.

   A variation on password stealing is when someone sets up a blog or web page in the victim's name. Sometimes the bully creates an account using a screen name that is one letter off from the victim's screen name. Friends of the victim may think they're chatting with the victim instead of the imposter. Again, the bully can post anything while impersonating the victim. Several states have enacted laws making this type of impersonation illegal.

If you suspect your child is being bullied, it's critical that you talk to her about it. This type of harassment is just as damaging as face-to-face bullying and needs to be stopped immediately.

Rules for safe computer usage:

- Put the computer in a public area, where you can keep an eye on the activity. In my classroom, all the computer monitors faced my desk, and I kept a pair of binoculars nearby so I could monitor my students' activities. Students thought the binoculars were funny, but they knew I was serious about watching what was going on.
- Don't buy your child an iPhone, Smartphone, Blackberry, or any other portable device with Internet access.
- Never give out *any* personal information over the Internet, especially in a chat room. Even if you know the person you're chatting with, others in the chat room may be able to read what you're typing.
- Don't chat with strangers online, just as you don't talk to strangers in person.
- Treat people online the same way you'd treat them in person: kindly and politely. There is, after all, a real person on the other end of the conversation.
- Insist on access to your child's website or blog. You should be able to see his site and have his password. If he refuses, he doesn't get to use the computer. Check his profile to make sure no personal information is included. The settings on Facebook are especially tricky to navigate and seem to change often. Check them regularly.

- *Never* open unsolicited e-mail. Some contain viruses, while others may contain pornography or phishing scams (attempts to gain your personal financial information).
- Never respond to online harassment. It will only escalate and never solves the problem.
- Make it safe for your children to talk to you about anything that makes them uncomfortable. Be sure they know to report potential problems to you.
- Install Internet activity monitoring software. Most record all keystrokes in a log, which you can read later. Some record all instant messages sent and received, and may allow you to view the record log from another computer (your work computer, for example).
- Make sure your kids know to get permission from you to meet face-to-face with someone they've met online, including someone their own age.

Dating

It's not unreasonable to insist on meeting your daughter's date. Your job is to keep her safe, and that includes meeting the young man she's seeing. Invite him in and ask what their plans are for the evening. Be sure to set a curfew and stick to it; nothing good happens after 1 a.m. If she accuses you of being old-fashioned, smile and thank her.

Remind your boys that when a girl says no, it means NO. It does not mean maybe or that she wants to be talked into something. He *must* be a gentleman and respect her wishes. Also point out that if he gets a girl pregnant, he'll be a daddy for the rest of his life. Is he ready to be a daddy?

Remind your girls that their future and self-respect are more important than having sex to be popular. No birth control is 100 percent effective. In addition, talk to your girls about date abuse. If a boyfriend is controlling or verbally or physically abusive, she should tell you *immediately*. She will need help getting out of the relationship.

Sex

Talking to children about sex can be one of the more uncomfortable jobs we have as parents, yet one of the most important. Experts agree that parents should answer questions from young children truthfully but simply. Very young children don't need to know everything at once. Somewhere around the age of eleven or twelve, or even earlier, children become curious about the changes beginning in their bodies, and that's a good time to have a talk about the mechanics of sex. If you're too uncomfortable, there are many good books available on the subject. In addition, most schools teach the basics, and have a parents' information night so you can look over the materials and ask questions about the program. It's important to go to this meeting, by the way, so you know what material will be presented. Will they advocate abortion? Condone homosexuality? Promote abstinence? You want to know if the values presented are in line with your family's.

It's important to maintain an ongoing dialogue about values and the myriad reasons to not have sex outside of marriage. Sit down with your teen and go over these reasons, and continue to talk about them as your teen matures.

Physical reasons for abstinence:

- **Pregnancy.** I always told my boys that if they produced a child, they were morally obligated to help raise it. The only 100 percent safe birth control is abstinence.
- **Sexually transmitted diseases** (STDs), which can range from annoying to extremely painful to life-threatening.
  - **Chlamydia:** *symptoms include painful urination, unusual discharge from the penis or vagina, testicular pain in men, possible abdominal pain in women.*
  - **Pelvic Inflammatory Disease** *(in women): causes severe abdominal pain and can lead to infertility.*

- **Herpes:** *begins as small blisters which burst, leaving painful lesions. The disease can be controlled somewhat, but there is no known cure. Once you get herpes, you have it for life. It's possible to contract the disease from a partner even when the partner has no visible symptoms.*
- **HPV** (Human Papillomavirus): *causes genital warts and has been shown to cause cervical cancer.*
- **Syphilis:** *if left untreated, can cause heart failure, insanity, or even death.*
- **Gonorrhea:** *may cause painful urination, abdominal pain, and a yellowish discharge from the penis or vagina.*
- **Hepatitis B:** *can cause liver damage including cirrhosis, liver failure, or even liver cancer.*
- **Pubic lice:** *cause intense itching in the genital area. Occasionally the lice bites will become inflamed or infected.*
- **HIV/AIDS:** *symptoms include extreme fatigue, rapid weight loss, persistent diarrhea, and swollen glands. The virus invades the body's immune system, destroying the ability to fight infection. The progress of the disease can be slowed, but there is no cure. Remind your children that sex is not worth dying for and that a partner may have a disease but no symptoms.*

Religious reasons

Most religions advocate abstinence before marriage. God created sex as an expression of love between a husband and a wife. What young people don't understand is that sex often creates a bond between partners. Outside of marriage, they may find themselves emotionally attached to the wrong person and may have difficulty breaking that tie.

Educational reasons

Less than half of teen mothers finish high school. Boys, too, may struggle in school if they take a job to help support their partner and baby.

Emotional reasons

Sexually active teens have a host of new worries, beyond the normal adolescent concerns. These include:

- **Pregnancy, STDs, and AIDS.** Many teens spend a great deal of time worrying that they may be pregnant or that they've contracted a serious illness. These teens are often distracted and have trouble concentrating.

- **Guilt.** They're afraid their parents will find out and be disappointed in them. They feel guilty for violating their family's values. They may also feel guilty for using another person as a sex object, especially if they pressured that person into having sex.

- **Loss of self-respect.** This goes along with feeling guilty. They may tell themselves they're weak or that they're a bad person. They may feel unclean, especially if they've contracted an STD.

- **Relationship issues.** Young people who get pressured into having sex, then get dumped by their partner, may feel betrayed, and develop trust and commitment issues that continue into adulthood.

- **Depression and suicide.** Studies have determined that teens who are sexually active are twice as likely to be seriously depressed and much more likely to contemplate suicide. Three times as many sexually active girls reported considering suicide, and a surprising nine times as many sexually active boys had considered it.

    An important study by the American Psychological Association looked at how the sexualization of girls is linked to common mental health problems in girls and women. According to the association, sexualization occurs when a person's self-esteem or perceived worth is completely dependent on their sexual appeal, or when a person is merely an object for the sexual use of others rather than an independent person.

What Parents Can Do

- Talk to your child regularly about sex, contraception, relationships, love, and values. Make sure he or she knows how to properly use the various forms of contraception. I know it's an uncomfortable topic, but improper use of contraceptive devices accounts for a large number of teen pregnancies.
- Emphasize that having sex just once puts them at risk for both pregnancy and STDs.
- Tell them you don't want them to have sex until they're married, but if they feel they must, use good birth control. Parents don't have to condone a sexual relationship, but they must be realistic. Ignorance only puts teens at risk.
- Look for teachable moments on TV. Discuss risky behavior and potential outcomes.
- Don't put temptation in their way. Set a reasonable curfew and don't allow the boyfriend or girlfriend over when your child is home alone. Similarly, don't allow boyfriends or girlfriends to spend time together behind closed doors.
- Talk to them about their goals and plans for the future. Having a baby now could completely destroy those plans.
- Explain that:
  - *Having a baby should be a blessing, not a burden.*
  - *Babies deserve a loving, two-parent family; that's one of the major reasons for not having sex before marriage.*
  - *When you have sex with someone, it's like having sex with all the people they've slept with in the past. If just one of those partners had an STD, you could get it, too.*
  - *Oral sex carries the same risks of disease as intercourse.*

- Give them ideas on what to say if someone is pressuring them to have sex.
    - *I'm waiting for marriage. (Yes, some people still do wait for marriage.)*
    - *My life is too busy to have to worry about pregnancy and AIDS.*
    - *I couldn't possibly have sex with everyone who asks me.*
    - *If you love me, you'll respect my feelings.*
    - *I'm too young to be a mommy (or daddy). Aren't you? No birth control is 100 percent effective.*

Smiles are free—give lots away

Chapter 10

Finances

Most of us agree that kids need to learn to manage money, but not enough of us actually have a concrete plan to teach them how. The biggest reason is that when parents struggle with their own finances, they don't feel qualified to teach their children how to be successful. Some parents feel that there's no need to discuss money until kids leave home or that it's all just common sense: spend less than you earn. Others of us find it hard to be consistent about handing out an allowance and find it easier just to hand out money on an as-needed basis. In addition, it can be difficult to decide how much allowance to give and what it should cover. Should they pay for their own lunches or clothes? What should they do with Christmas and birthday money?

There are many reasons to avoid teaching financial skills, but the reality is that money management is critical in today's world and, like all skills, must be practiced. Mistakes will be made and lessons learned. Better to make mistakes with an allowance than with their first paycheck when the rent is due. Dave Ramsey, syndicated radio host and author of several books on financial advice, contends that kids who can't manage money by the age of eighteen are disabled. I'd have to agree. By the way, Ramsey's books should be required reading for anyone over the age of eighteen. His advice is invaluable for anyone wrestling with financial decisions.

In his Financial Peace seminars, Ramsey points out that our attitude toward debt in this country has reversed over the years. In

1962, the average family had one car and about 900 square feet of house. In 2001, the average family had 1.9 cars, and in 2004, the average single family home was 2,349 square feet. According to MSN Money, revolving debt—mostly credit cards—has doubled in the last decade, and 43 percent of American families spend more than they earn. What a disturbing trend, and it's caused in part by parents not emphasizing the pitfalls of living beyond one's means. As important as this topic is, it's rarely taught in schools, which means it's entirely up to you, Mom and Dad, to drive the message home.

WHY SHOULD WE TEACH MONEY SKILLS?

For parents, the biggest perk that comes from teaching children money management skills is that you won't have to constantly listen to the whining about why they need more money. After you decide on an allowance and explain how the plan works, what they do with their spendable money is up to them. They'll nag at first about needing more, but once they realize you won't give in, the nagging will stop. The trick, as with all parenting endeavors, is to be consistent. As hard as it is to add one more thing to your to-do list, the benefits to both you and your children will be worth it.

The benefits to your kids, of course, are huge. Eventually, they'll be able to retire comfortably, and in the meantime they won't suffer the stress of not being able to pay their bills or save for their own children's college educations. They'll have the peace of knowing that should they lose their job, they'll still have money in the emergency fund to tide them over so they don't have to move back in with Mom and Dad.

Learning about money does more than allow children to become financially independent. It also helps you, the parents, save money in the long run and, most surprisingly, helps them do better in school according to financial expert Clark Howard. In addition, putting part of their money into savings each week teaches the important concept of delayed gratification. If they don't learn that when they're little, they may never learn it. There's too much input from the media to buy whatever you want and buy it right now.

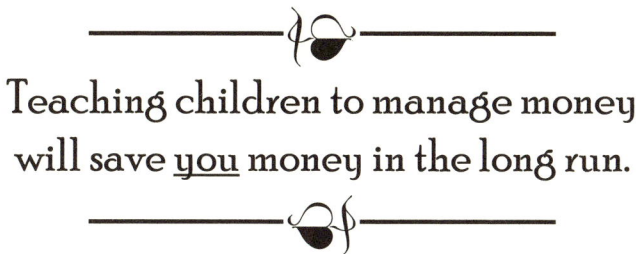

Teaching children to manage money will save <u>you</u> money in the long run.

Delayed gratification is another term for willpower and is important in several areas, most notably eating, money, and sex. In his Total Money Makeover Live event, Ramsey points out that our society has forgotten how to delay pleasure. We want it all, and we want it now. Obesity, bankruptcy, and the *Girls Gone Wild* behavior now permeate our culture. We *must* teach our kids that waiting for things won't kill them. My friend Kathy used to tell her kids, "Wanting is half the fun of having." In other words, the thrill of the hunt is as much fun as the acquisition itself. How many times have you bought something you thought you *had* to have, only to feel slightly let down afterward? Talking to your children about your experiences may help them avoid the same mistake.

We all know that you'll be about as successful at convincing a kid to save for retirement as you would be teaching him to fly—which is why, in the beginning at least, the savings plan is non-negotiable. The goal is to foster good habits to carry him through his lifetime. Over time, you'll continue to explain the reasons, and when he gets to high school, you'll start teaching him about the adult financial plan:

1. Have $1,000 in an emergency fund.
2. Continue adding to your retirement savings every month, and don't touch it until you've actually retired.
3. Don't use credit cards; pay cash for everything.

If your son goes away to college, he'll be bombarded with credit card offers, often accompanied by incentives such as free

T-shirts. Many college freshmen think it's smart to sign up for the card just to get the free gift. It doesn't take long for them to start using the card for so-called essentials, ranging from books and supplies to pizza. Students who max out their assortment of cards can hardly pay the interest each month, much less the principal, and soon find themselves in a downward spiral trying to maintain a lifestyle they can't pay for. The same is true for student loans. When students get that loan check they feel like they've won the lottery. They forget that they have to pay it back. By the way, credit card companies count on parents to bail out their students by paying off the balance on the card. Parents beware.

Studies have shown that severe debt can lead to depression and even suicide in adults, and is a leading cause of marital problems. Marriage may be a long way off for your child, but again, start those good habits early. They'll thank you later.

At this point, I have to admit I did a terrible job of teaching my boys about financial matters. It was a classic example of skills not being passed down to the kids; I had no skills to pass down. As I was growing up, there were no stores near our house, so I didn't need much money. When I did need a few dollars, I'd usually badger my father until he gave it to me.

After I got my first apartment, I managed to pay my bills, but saving was an unknown concept. Any leftover money at the end of the month was promptly liberated at the mall. I knew that if I had a financial crisis, my parents would bail me out, so I had no compelling reason to save. I'm pretty sure that's not the lesson my parents wanted me to learn.

Sadly, that's also the lesson I passed on to my children, and after they left home they had to struggle to learn to be financially independent. Their lives would have been so much easier if they'd learned money management when they were younger. The life lessons that stick are usually the ones learned early.

Getting Started

One thing most experts agree on is that money is an emotional topic, and before you can talk to kids about it, you need to identify how you and your spouse feel about money. Are you afraid of not having enough? Do you go shopping to cheer yourself up? Are you a compulsive saver or spender? What are your goals for the future? Do you stick to a budget, or spend until the money runs out? Do you and your spouse have an unspoken competition to see who can spend the money first?

Even if you and your spouse have trouble agreeing on money matters, you need to agree on a plan for training the kids. Of course, the lessons will be much more effective if you set a good example. Learning financial management is a process, not an event, and the sooner you begin the process with your kidlets, the better.

In order to learn about money, children need to have actual money to practice with. Some experts recommend a dollar per week for each year of age, while others advise a dollar per grade level per week. You'll need to take into consideration your family's finances and what your child's friends are getting. If your five-year-old's friends are getting ten dollars a week, you'll have trouble convincing him he only needs a dollar. This doesn't mean he needs ten dollars, but perhaps something in between.

Many financial advisors—including Joline Godfrey, author of *Raising Financially Fit Kids*—advise using a three-pot system for dividing money received: one pot for spending, one for saving for short-term goals, and one for long-term saving/investing. Jayne A. Pearl, author of *Kids and Money: Giving Them the Savvy to Succeed Financially*, recommends that parents determine what percentage should go into each pot, while Clark Howard, author of *Clark Smart Parents, Clark Smart Kids* suggests that the allowance be divided into thirds.

It may seem too early for them to start investing, but what you're really doing is creating a state of mind. The sooner they develop the habit of saving part of each "paycheck," the better. Many experts point out that if a teen can save $2,000 a year from ages fifteen to twenty-two, he'll have more than $1 million by age sixty-five. That's the power of compound interest over time. I sure wish I'd known that when I was fifteen! And imagine how well off your child will be if she continues saving *after* age twenty-two (see Figure 10.1).

The Power of Compound Interest

Betty saved $2,000 each year at an interest rate of 12% from age nineteen through age twenty-six, and nothing after that. She left it untouched until age sixty-five, at which time she had $2,288, 996.

Veronica didn't start investing until age twenty-seven, then saved $2,000 each year until age sixty-five, at which time she had $1,532,183.

Betty invested a total of $16,000, whereas Veronica invested a total of $78,000. Yet Betty retired with over $750,000 more than Veronica.

This works because each year, you earn interest on the interest you received the previous year.

Age	Betty Invests:	Value at end of the year	Age	Veronica Invests:	Value at end of the year
19	$2,000	$2,240	19	$0	$0
20	$2,000	$4,749	20	$0	$0
21	$2,000	$7,559	21	$0	$0
22	$2,000	$10,706	22	$0	$0
23	$2,000	$14,230	23	$0	$0
24	$2,000	$18,178	24	$0	$0
25	$2,000	$22,599	25	$0	$0
26	$2,000	$27,551	26	$0	$0
27	$0	$30,857	27	$2,000	$2,240
28	$0	$34,560	28	$2,000	$4,749
29	$0	$38,708	29	$2,000	$7,559
30	$0	$43,353	30	$2,000	$10,706
61	$0	$1,454,699	61	$2,000	$966,926
62	$0	$1,629,263	62	$2,000	$1,085,197
63	$0	$1,824,774	63	$2,000	$1,217,661
64	$0	$2,043,747	64	$2,000	$1,366,020
65	$0	$2,288,997	65	$2,000	$1,532,183

Figure 10.1 – The Power of Compound Interest

The Plan

First, decide on how much allowance each child should receive, then decide on a specific day and time to hand it out. Saturday morning is a good time, because if you've forgotten to set aside cash for them, you still have time to run to the bank or ATM. Consistency is key here; you have to hold up your end of the bargain. If you keep forgetting to enforce the plan, as I did, all they will learn is that managing money really isn't that important.

Second, remind them that this is all the money they're going to get until next week at this time. They can spend it on whatever they want, but when it's gone, they will do without for the rest of the week. You're not going to give them money for candy, toys, or movies. If they want fun stuff when you take them to the grocery store, they can buy it *if they have the money with them*. It's critical that you stand firm on this—Money Lesson Number One is that when the money is gone (either because they've spent it all or because they've forgotten to bring it with them to the store), they're done spending. The object is to teach them that money is a finite resource and that they must learn to prioritize. Mom and Dad aren't going to keep handing out the cash. Remember, you're training them for adulthood, and you can't keep handing them money forever. You're not going to live forever.

My biggest problem was remembering to bring their money when they accompanied me to the store. In retrospect, that should have been their responsibility. If your son forgets his wallet, he doesn't get to buy anything. One of my boys was an expert at forgetting his money. He'd find something he wanted and promise to pay me back when we got home. Of course, he knew that by the time we got home, I'd have forgotten that he owed me money. All he was learning was to manipulate the system (also known as his mother). He now laughingly admits that he probably owes me a few thousand dollars. Make the children be responsible for remembering the money.

The third step is to have a convenient place for their money. It doesn't matter if you use three jars, three envelopes, or three wallets, but they at least need access to their spending money. If you control when they can spend it and what they spend it on, they won't learn anything. It's often difficult for parents to let go of control over what the kids are buying, but that's what parenting is all about: letting go little by little.

The final step—keeping track—is just as important as the others. You can't manage your finances if you don't know how much you have or where it goes. As you start the plan, purchase a journal or notebook for each child. It should look similar to an accounting spreadsheet, with at least five columns: Date, Type of Transaction (i.e., type of income or what it was spent on), Income, Outgo, and Balance (see figure 10.2).

Daily Journal for Tracking Finances							
Date	Type of Transaction	Income	Outgo	Balance	Short-Term Savings	Long-Term Savings
Jan. 1	Allowance	9.00		9.00		
Jan. 2	Savings		6.00	3.00	3.00	3.00
Jan. 2	Candy		1.00	2.00		
Jan. 3	Toy		2.00	0		

Fig. 10.2

You can add columns for short-term and long-term savings, or use separate notebooks for those. Older kids will be tech-savvy enough to do all of this on a computer spreadsheet. The only drawback is that not all transactions will get entered right away if they have to boot the computer first. Even if your kid prefers tracking his finances electronically, it's still a good idea to keep a written record as backup. Electronics always seem to die at the most inopportune moments. With a written record, they can't claim that their computer deleted the information

You'll want to keep the notebook in a convenient place so they can enter their expenses regularly. If their notebook is in their room, post a reminder where everyone can see it and help each other remember. You could pull the notebooks out after dinner each night, which has the added benefit of tying the habit to a daily ritual. If your family eats out often, then bedtime or homework time would be better. If you think they'll be dipping into the savings stashes, you might want to move the money to higher ground. Periodically you'll need to take their long-term savings to the bank or put it into some type of investment program.

Many parents find it easier to give in to demands for money than to stand firm in the face of an angry child. If you give in, what have they learned? (Answer: that being angry literally has a payoff.) Remember, your job is to guide them into adulthood. Explain that you give them an allowance so they'll learn to handle it wisely. If they demonstrate responsibility, you'll consider increasing the allowance. If they squander it, and keep pestering you for more, you'll consider taking away the allowance completely until they're older and better able to handle the responsibility.

In the meantime, they can earn more money by doing extra chores. Even if you're wealthy enough to have a personal maid for your offspring, it won't hurt him to clean the refrigerator or pull some weeds. When kids earn the money to buy something they want, it builds their self-esteem. In addition, they value the item more than if it was just handed to them. The added bonus here is that they'll take better care of the item if they had to pay for at least part of it. Of course, don't forget to have them save the receipts in case they need to return something.

Right now, you may be thinking that this is all *way* too much work. You can hardly get them to do their homework, much less find the time and energy to look at their finances every week. Trust me, I know the feeling. But understanding money and building good money habits are every bit as important as understanding algebra and English and much more useful in the long run than many of the extracurricular activities we involve them in.

When to Begin

As soon as your child learns to ask for things in the store—around the age of four—you can simply explain, "We don't have money for a new toy today." At this age, it seems as though Mom's wallet contains an infinite supply of cash. If the cash runs out, there's always that magic plastic card. This is a good age to start explaining that money is a finite quantity and that you have to pay for necessities before fun stuff. "Mom and Dad get paid every other week, and if we spend all our money the first week, we don't eat the second week. We have to save some of the money for next week." It's an easy way to introduce the concept of saving.

You can start your child on a small allowance at the age of five. Explain the plan and how the money will be divided. She won't understand much about investing, so for now just tell her, "It's a rule. You have to put part of the money you get into the bank."

You know the next question will be, "Do you do that?" I hope you'll be able to say yes.

If your child is older, it's not too late to start a money management plan. It may be harder for her to get into the habit, but she'll be better able to understand the concepts of saving and investing. Explain how this will benefit her in the long run: car, house, travel, retirement. For kids, the thought of buying a house or retiring comfortably is so far away it seems like fiction. The idea of having a million dollars may be more appealing.

Since early training is essential to the formation of good habits, you need to start the process as soon as possible. This isn't something you can keep putting off; the time to start good habits is now.

The Three Pots

Spending

The one-third set aside for spending should be totally theirs to do what they want with, within reason; of course they can't buy anything illegal or something that violates your family's values. If they spend the entire amount in the first ten minutes, they'll have to do without until the following week. Your most important job is to not interfere, so they learn from natural consequences. The dialogue will go something like, "Sounds like you really want that toy. How long do you think it will take to save the money to buy it? Are you sorry that you spent all your money on candy yesterday?" (Try to make that last part sound like a sincere concern and not an "I told you so.")

One of the hardest parts of the plan is letting them spend their money on what seems to be frivolous things. As long as they're fulfilling the saving part of the plan, the spending decision is theirs. Yes, they will make mistakes—that's part of the learning process. It's important not to pass judgment, as tempting as that might be. Sympathize but don't criticize. Dialogue, don't dictate. Keep in mind that what makes them happy is not the same as what makes you happy. That twenty-dollar accessory for the phone may seem like a total waste of money to you, but it might make him the happiest kid on the planet. One day at the mall, I saw a young man wearing the most horrid pair of hot pink high-top tennis shoes. I was thinking to myself that someone should tell him how awful they were, when a few of his friends walked up and said, "Those are the coolest shoes!" There's no accounting for taste, especially with kids.

If your children do buy something that they never use/wear/play with, they'll learn to think more carefully in the future. Talk to them about your own mistakes with impulse buying (we've all made our share of those), and remind them that wanting something—the anticipation itself—is half the fun of having it.

Short-term saving

This pile of money is for short-term goals, like that new video game they want. It's important to enforce this category because there will always be something they want that costs more than one week's allowance. If they have a specific purchase in mind, you can help them do some comparison shopping and remind them to add a little to the total for taxes.

Even if they don't have a purchase in mind, they need to keep putting that one-third into the short-term pot so they have the cash when they do find something they can't live without. If they get in the habit of putting money into savings, they'll be much less likely to run up huge credit card bills when they get older. The best way to stay out of debt is to put off purchases until you have the cash. *Never never never* buy "toys" on credit, no matter how old you are. If you don't have the cash, you don't need the toy.

When you first introduce the financial plan, have them choose something small to save for—about two or three weeks' worth of saving. This helps build their delayed gratification muscles while offering an intermediate reward of buying something in the not-too-distant future. As they get older, their "wants" get more expensive, but they'll be better able to wait for the reward.

By requiring your children to put a fixed amount of money into savings, you're creating the habit of paying themselves first instead of putting whatever is left at the end of the week into savings. For the average American, that's not much. As the song goes, "I have too much month left at the end of my money."

Long-term Saving and Investing

In today's world, this category is more important than ever. The future of Social Security is in question, and corporate retirement plans can no longer be counted on to provide a guaranteed retirement income (think Enron). By the time today's five-year-old retires, he'll need to have several million dollars in his own investment portfolio in order to retire comfortably.

The biggest problem will be when he turns twenty-one and realizes he's now in control of all that money he's been saving. The appeal of a new sports car is infinitely more compelling than some vague notion of a comfortable retirement that's decades away. That's why it's so important to start the saving habit early. As they start asking "Why do I have to save?" you can explain that grown-ups usually work until they're about sixty-five, then they like to quit working and take it easy. What retirees don't want is to worry about paying the bills, which is why they need to have plenty of money in their investment portfolio. As your child gets older, you can explain how investing works to grow their money.

Finally you'll want to explain the Rate of Return chart (see Figure 10.3). For example if, when they retire, they have a $2 million investment earning 5 percent annually, the interest would be $100,000 annually, or $8,333 per month. That's what they get to live on each month. This sounds like a fortune, until you account for inflation and taxes. Use the inflation chart (Figure 10.4) to determine how much money will be needed fifty years from now, based on a given inflation rate. For example, if $3,000 would provide an adequate monthly income today (assume he'll be supporting a family in the not-too-distant future), he'll need over $13,000 fifty years from now, based on an inflation rate of 3 percent. Using the Rate of Return chart, he'll need to have more than $3 million in the bank by then to bring in $13,000 each month. Keep in mind that the inflation rate varies greatly from year to year, so it's best not to underestimate.

Some parents feel strongly enough about this category that they add a set amount to the pot every week. Some offer to match whatever their child puts into the long-term account. A few worry that when Junior turns twenty-one, he'll fritter away all the money on lottery tickets, so they set up a trust that can only be accessed when he's older. How old is up to you.

SHOULD ALLOWANCE BE TIED TO CHORES?

There are two schools of thought on this and compelling reasons for both. Financial experts and child psychologists alike have strong opinions about whether children should be paid for doing chores. You'll need to decide what works for your family.

Pros

Tying allowance to chores prepares children for working in the real world: if you don't work, you don't get paid. Some experts recommend prorating the allowance based on the percentage of work that was completed to your satisfaction. If they did half their chores, they get half their allowance. The potential downside here is that kids will argue about what the percentage was. You may think two out of four jobs equals half, but they'll argue that they did an hour's worth and left a half-hour's worth undone, so they should get two-thirds of their allowance. One way to avoid that argument is an all-or-nothing approach. If even one chore doesn't get done, no allowance is paid. This is difficult if you're an enabler, as I was. I found myself making excuses for my kids: "He had too much homework last night and couldn't do the dishes." Or "He had a tournament all day Saturday and was too tired Sunday to do his work." My kids ended up getting their allowance whether they finished chores or not.

Cons

Many financial experts feel that chores and finances should be two separate life lessons. Chores should be done because everyone in the family needs to contribute. Mom and Dad don't get paid to clean, so why should children? Good citizenship dictates that everyone should pitch in. In addition, paying kids every time they do things for you may teach them not to do anything for free. As in, "I'll help bring in the groceries if you pay me." (Of course your answer to this is, "I'll take you to soccer practice if you pay me.")

Allowance, on the other hand, is a tool to teach the important lessons of money management. If they don't have the money, they can't learn to manage it. Since both citizenship (chores) and financial skills (allowance) are difficult concepts, it's best, the argument goes, to keep these lessons separate.

Another downside to paying for chores is that kids will only get their work done if there's something they want to buy. This can be frustrating for parents who feel that dishes should be done more often than twice a month.

With our boys, we tried to go with the "no work no pay" method, but since I couldn't bring myself to enforce the rules, it didn't work very well. I wish I had realized that I was teaching them the opposite of what they needed to learn. The message I was sending was, "Don't worry about money right now. You'll have the rest of your life for that." I guess I was right—they may spend the rest of their lives worrying.

If I had it to do over, I'd separate the two concepts and spend considerably more time and effort on their financial education.

STRATEGIES FOR CONTROLLING OVERSPENDING

Discuss marketing ploys. Commercials are carefully designed to make toys and junk food as appealing as possible, while glossing over any negatives. The commercial may run a disclaimer across the bottom of the screen, such as "Action figure does not actually fly," but your four-year-old will never see that.

When they see a commercial for something they "must have," ask what they like about it and whether they think it will live up to the claims of the commercial. They'll get better at this the more you practice. Ask them how often they think they'll play with it.

Before going to the toy store, mention that being surrounded by thousands of toys can be overwhelming and might make you want all of them. That's why stores are designed the way they are—to get you to spend more money. Decide ahead of time what you want to buy or at least how much money you have to spend.

Discuss "needs" versus "wants." New jeans may be needed, but $200 designer jeans are a "want." If you're planning on buying your daughter a pair of jeans, tell her she can have the designer pair if she pays the difference. If she's been saving regularly, she may decide she's willing to do that.

Parents can reinforce this lesson by paying attention to their own needs and wants. When you hear yourself saying, "I need some new shoes," stop and ask yourself if you need them or you want them. Some families make a game of asking each other, "Do you need it or want it?" Wanting something isn't bad; we all have plenty of stuff we want. The key is to balance needs, wants, and available funds, and to make informed decisions.

At the grocery store, teach about shelf tags and unit pricing. (The unit price is the cost of the item divided by the number of units. If a fifteen-ounce jar of peanut butter costs three dollars, then the unit price is 3.00/15, or 20 cents an ounce.) Talk about why you choose particular brands, especially if they're not the cheapest ones.

Help them learn to comparison shop. Have them compare items between the high-end mall stores and discount stores. When shopping for a specific item, say jeans, start at the discount stores. Keep in mind that buying something at a discount store is only a bargain if they'll actually wear it. Remember to compare the quality as well as the price.

When you're considering a major purchase such as a new refrigerator, include your older children in the discussion. You may not need their input, but it's good for them to listen to the decision process. They can also help with online research.

Talk to them about the concept of "living within your means." Explain how, as an adult, you must make sure that your bills are paid on time, you put money into savings every month, and if you do use credit cards, you pay them off at the end of every month to avoid interest charges. The reason you do all these things is for your own peace of mind, now and in the future. It's much too stressful when you have to worry about whether you can make the house payment every month.

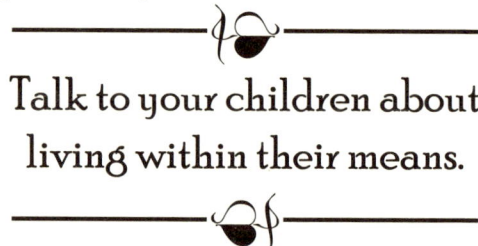

Talk to your children about living within their means.

Some parents find it helpful to sit their older children down and show them the household budget. The first reaction is usually "We're rich!" when they see the income, followed by amazement when they see what the bills amount to. It's a great reality check. If you're not comfortable revealing your income, at least consider showing them the bills.

BUDGETING

Just talking about a budget can cause some of us to panic. I'm reminded of the episode of *I Love Lucy* where Ricky hires an iron-fisted financial manager to rein in Lucy's out-of-control spending. Lucy ends up with something like five dollars to get her through the month, and no amount of begging and pleading can change Ricky's mind.

A budget, of course, is just a piece of paper; it doesn't care if you follow it or not. If it's not working for you, it's easily modified. It does have two very useful functions though.

First, it allows you to see what you're really spending your money on. It's easy to spend without thinking, until you suddenly realize you're broke. By creating a budget and setting limits on each category, you're forced to think about your spending patterns and problem areas. If you find you're exceeding your limit in a certain category, you can either adjust the budget—raise the limit for this category by lowering one or more others—or make more of an effort to change your spending habits.

Second, a budget helps you reach your savings goals. For younger children without any fixed expenses, saving (short-term and long-term) *becomes* the fixed expenses. After those portions are put into their respective pots, what's left over can be further divided into categories, such as church offering and haircuts. As your child gets older and incurs fixed expenses, such as car maintenance, the budget changes to reflect those needs.

How to set up a budget

1. Have your child make a list of both her income sources and what she pays for. In order for this to be a learning experience, she needs to do this on her own, although you may offer suggestions if she's forgotten something. The time period for the budget can be weekly for younger children (say, middle school age), but may need to be monthly for teens with monthly expenses such as a phone bill or a car payment. Another option is to use a weekly budget that includes one-fourth of fixed monthly payments. Some categories, such as car maintenance, will vary greatly from one month to the next. Help her decide on a reasonable estimate. In the months that she doesn't pay for maintenance, that amount should go into savings, and in her savings notebook she should have a column that keeps track of these funds so she doesn't accidentally spend them. There *will* be months when maintenance will exceed the monthly allotment.

2. Compare income to total expenses. Ideally, her income will be greater than her expenses. If not, she can either find places to trim her spending or consider ways to earn extra money.

3. At this point, she can use the envelope system to divide her allowance or paycheck into categories such as clothes and

phone, so she'll know exactly how much is available at any given moment. Remind her that if she doesn't spend all her clothes money this month, she'll be able to use the remainder next month, or put it towards whatever she's saving up for. If she's using a checkbook, she can track the budget in a notebook or in a computer program such as Quicken.

4. At first, she will want to review and revise the budget every month to make sure she's keeping her spending in line. Over time, she can tweak it to reflect her changing income, needs, and wants.

Online Banking

Go over the rules for keeping her information and her money safe:

- Use a secure password: more than eight characters, at least one number or special character, and a capital letter somewhere in the middle of the password. Never use your name, middle name, birth date, or pet's name.
- Don't do your banking on a public computer. Sometimes they save your information.
- Always log off when you finish your banking session. If someone hacks into your computer, at least they won't be able to get into your bank account.

Online Spending

E-commerce is undeniably a growing trend, especially among tech-savvy youngsters. You'll want to discuss the pros and cons with your kids when they get old enough to realize they can shop online.

Pros

- You'll find a much greater selection, especially if you live in a small town or rural community.
- It's easy to comparison shop without running all over town.

- Online stores may offer better prices than brick-and-mortar shops.
- You can shop in your pajamas at 2 a.m. if you want.

Cons

- Always consider shipping costs. You may find a great deal on an item, only to discover that the shipping costs are higher than the price of the actual item.
- Read the fine print. Not all merchandise is guaranteed, and not all vendors will allow returns. If you do return something, the buyer usually pays the cost of return postage, and you may be charged a restocking fee.
- Not all sites are secure, meaning if you send a credit card number or other personal information, others (bad guys) may be able to see it.
- Some sites charge different prices for the same item, depending on how you arrived at the site. Use two or three search engines to comparison shop.
- It can be hard to tell the exact color or fit of an item online. See if the merchant has a local brick-and-mortar store for returns.

In my opinion, children should *never* use the Internet unsupervised, and that includes for shopping. They should always get permission before going online, and you'll want to review all purchases before they're ordered. Check your credit card and PayPal statements each month for any irregularities. Students have been known to borrow credit card numbers from Mom and Dad.

How to Sell Money Management to Your Children

- For very young children, the simplest answer is "It's a rule." Every time you get money, some of it goes into savings.

- That's what grown-ups do, so it's important for you to get in the habit now. Everybody has to be able to control their spending, and everyone must have money in savings.
- Your stuff doesn't define who you are. Being able to pay your bills and save for your future says more about who you are than the type of car you drive or clothes you wear.

Again, money management may be one of the hardest skills to teach, because most of us have our own issues with spending and saving. Keep reminding yourself how important this skill is. Stick with it, be consistent, and not only will your kids learn to live within their means, but your own financial skills will probably improve as well.

Rate of Return on Savings/Investments				
	Monthly Interest Earned At:			
Amount in Savings at Retirement	3%	5%	7.50%	10%
$100,000	$250	$417	$625	$833
$500,000	$1,250	$2,083	$3,125	$4,167
$1,000,000	$2,500	$4,167	$6,250	$8,333
$5,000,000	$12,500	$20,833	$31,250	$41,667

Figure 10.3

The Rate of Return chart above is usually read backward. If your child is earning an average of 5% on his investments when he retires, and feels he will need $4,167 per month, he'll need to have about $1,000,000 in total investments. If he will need $8,334 per month (2 x $4,167), he'll need to have $2,000,000 in investments.

Inflation Chart: Future value of $2,000							
Inflation Rate	Equivalent Amount Needed in:						
	Today	10 years	20 years	30 years	40 years	50 years	60 years
3%	$2,000	$2,688	$3,612	$4,855	$6,524	$8,768	$11,783
4%	$2,000	$2,960	$4,382	$6,487	$9,602	$14,213	$21,039
5%	$2,000	$3,258	$5,307	$8,644	$14,080	$22,935	$37,358

Figure 10.4

If your child needs about $2,000 a month now to support himself and his family comfortably, and the inflation rate averages 3% per year for the next fifty years, he'll need $8,768 per month to maintain that standard of living when he retires in fifty years.

―――――※―――――
Every human being is the author
of his own health or disease
– Hindu Prince Gautama Siddharta, the
founder of Buddhism, 563-483 B.C
―――――※―――――

hapter 11

A Healthy Lifestyle

My goal in this chapter is to change the way you think about food, so you can teach your children healthy attitudes. It's time to form new habits for their sake. If you're eating badly, they will follow suit. As with everything we teach our kids, it's up to us to set a good example.

Our children would gladly live on sugared cereal, snacks, and junk food if we let them, but none of that is good for growing bodies. You're the parent, and you need to buy what's healthy for the family, not what they think they must have because the commercial was cool.

Here's the disclaimer: I'm not a nutritionist, so all the data in this section is obtained from one or more of the highly reliable sources listed at the end of the chapter. What I found interesting is that while many of the experts approached the issue of nutrition from different perspectives (cancer treatment, heart disease, diabetes), they say the same thing: plant-based foods *fight* disease, and animal-based foods (beef, poultry, pork, lamb, fish, and dairy) tend to *promote* disease.

In the process of improving my family's health, I've learned just how insufficient my own diet has been. My personal four food groups were always chocolate, coffee, sugar, and salt. I'd tell myself I was eating "healthy" because I'd have a few veggies with dinner. That's just not good enough.

People (including me) believe what they want to believe, and most of us believe that our diet is okay because we're not sick. The reality is that we're not sick *yet*. Worse, we may be sick and not know it. How many people get an initial diagnosis of cancer or heart disease from their doctor and think, "Yeah, I knew that"?

Most of us believe that our diet is okay because we're not sick. The reality is that we're not sick <u>yet</u>.

Some frightening statistics:

- By the age of twelve, *70 percent* of American children have developed the beginnings of hardening of the arteries (heart disease).
- The number of overweight children in America has doubled in the last twenty years.
- Forty million children in the United States have high cholesterol levels.
- If the current rate continues, *half* of all children born today will develop heart disease.
- More than *one in three* Americans will be diagnosed with cancer.
- *Half* of all children born after the year 2000 will be diagnosed with type 2 diabetes before they turn thirty.
- A full two-thirds of American adults and one-third of American children are considered overweight or obese.
- It's been estimated that as many as 80 percent of all the people in hospitals are there for a lifestyle-related illness: smoking, drinking, or poor nutritional choices. These are *preventable* illnesses.

- Children born after the year 2000 are the *first generation to have a shorter life expectancy than their parents.*
- Dozens of diseases and illnesses can be linked to an unhealthy diet, including allergies, heart disease, high blood pressure, acne, autoimmune diseases, eczema, gout, obesity, stroke, and most forms of cancer.

THE STANDARD AMERICAN DIET

The Standard American Diet is also known as SAD. How ironic. It includes a predominance of animal and other unhealthy fats (saturated and hydrogenated), processed foods, fried foods, and a whole lot of sugar. It's low in fiber and plant-based foods. Most of us think we're eating well if we have a banana for breakfast or a salad with dinner. As if a serving of veggies will cancel out the french fries and soda we had for lunch or the bowl of ice cream we'll be having before bed.

The statistics boggle the mind. As a country we spend *billions* of dollars each year on lousy food ($110 billion on fast food alone, plus more on the junk food we get at the supermarket). Then we turn around and spend *billions* more on diet and fitness programs, and *trillions* on health care. We're one of the richest countries in the world, yet one of the least healthy. We're poisoning ourselves and our children.

Back when God invented people, He also invented all the nutritious food they needed to thrive. Animals, yes, but also fruits, vegetables, nuts, grains, and seeds. He did not toss down any deep-fat fryers, soda dispensers, refined sugars, or chemical preservatives. *Thousands* of studies in recent years have shown that the healthiest diet is one made up of about 80 percent plant-based foods, 20 percent (or less) animal products, and no sugar. Only 15 to 20 percent of our daily calories should come from fats as opposed to the 40 to 50 percent most Americans take in.

I never thought about how much processed food we consume until our family moved to Germany. We rented a house in a village near base, and when we moved in, our landlord dropped off a roll of plastic bags that were specifically for disposing of recyclables.

We quickly learned that if we walked through the village on trash day, we could tell exactly where the Americans lived. The German families would put out about half a bag of recyclables, whereas the Americans put out as many as five or six bags. Soda cans, remnants of TV dinners, fast-food containers, and processed food packages all filled the bags as a testimony to American dependence on convenience foods.

My cousin, who lives in Sweden, came to visit us one Christmas. As we were preparing a dinner of prebasted turkey, packaged stuffing mix, refrigerator dinner rolls, frozen vegetables, and a frozen "pie in a box," Eva was laughing at our so-called home-cooked dinner.

Plant-Based Foods vs. Animal Foods

In a nutshell: eat plants. Plant-based foods are good for you; animal foods not so much. Plants are the only foods that strengthen the immune system; animal foods feed cancer and increase the risk of heart disease. Most fruits and vegetables are naturally low in sodium and contain no cholesterol.

In a nutshell: eat plants.

Around one hundred years ago, the American diet was about 90 percent plants; today, it's about 7 percent. Compare that trend with the dramatic rise in death by cancer and heart disease over the last century.

More than **4,500** studies in several countries (including the United States) have shown that fruits and vegetables prevent cancer. In contrast, most cancers are caused by the Standard American Diet and can be reversed and even cured by proper nutrition. According to T. Colin Campbell, author of *The China Study*, animal protein promotes cancer, and plant protein will reverse it, even if cancer growth has already begun.

Raw fruits and vegetables contain all the enzymes needed for their digestion, which eases the strain on our digestive system. Conversely, the more we cook our vegetables, the more enzymes we destroy.

Other benefits of eating fruits, vegetables, nuts, and seeds (which are all excellent sources of fiber):

- Most Americans eat about 5 to 15 grams of fiber a day; we need 20-40 grams or more depending on age and gender. Every 14 grams of fiber we add to our diet *decreases* our calorie intake by about 10 percent by tricking the brain into feeling fuller.
- Fiber improves the passage of food through the intestines, reducing the chance of colon cancer and diverticulitis.
- Fruits and vegetables generally have a low glycemic index, meaning they take longer to digest than bread, sugar, and other simple carbohydrates. Thus, they don't cause blood sugar spikes and won't contribute to diabetes.
- Most plants contain little to no saturated fats and won't contribute to heart disease.
- Beans and lentils are high in fiber, protein, and many other nutrients. When combined with grains, they form complete protein. Think red beans and rice.

Some Advice about Medical Advice

To be honest, I don't know how anyone survives medical school. There's so much to learn, and the competition is incredible. Sadly, though, most doctors receive very little nutritional training—their focus is on treating symptoms once disease has presented itself. If your doctor tells you nutrition isn't important, walk out the door and never return. Find a new doctor.

The other problems facing doctors are the patients themselves (that's us). It's infinitely easier to get a patient to take a pill than to change their lifestyle. Part of the reason is due to the mass-marketing of pharmaceuticals. How many commercials end with "Ask your doctor about [insert name of drug]"? There's a lot of money to be made treating disease and *no* money to be made preventing it.

Why did the American Diet Change?

As I mentioned earlier, Americans have gone from a diet of 90 percent plants to about 7 percent. The change has been gradual but steady: more convenience, more flavor (read fat and sugar), and more chemicals and processing to improve shelf life, taste, and price. Add to that mass-marketing and the rise in food lobbies, and you can see how and why our tastes have been changed over the years. We're at the point where many children refuse to drink water or milk unless it's flavored, or eat cereal that isn't sugared. Other kids honestly believe that french fries with ketchup equals two servings of vegetables—three if you "supersize" them.

We really need to take back control of what we're eating. We need to start retraining our taste buds and, more importantly, our children's taste buds. We don't need sugar and salt on everything, we don't need dessert every night, and we can learn to like veggies. We need convenience occasionally but certainly not every day. If our lives are so busy that we can't find time to cook or chop some vegetables, then we need to rethink our priorities. We must learn to make thoughtful choices based on nutritional needs, not on the commercials we watch. Nothing is more important than the health of our loved ones.

As you read through this chapter, you may start to feel overwhelmed. Take heart—there's a summary at the end.

A Healthy Weight

Food can be a touchy subject and can sometimes be as emotionally charged as the subject of money. Many parents use food as a reward: "Your team won the game! Let's celebrate—how about some ice cream?" Or it's used to comfort a child: "Your team lost today? Let's go out for ice cream to cheer you up." No wonder so many of us eat when we're happy as well as when we're sad, stressed, or upset.

Body mass index, or BMI, is an estimate of your height to weight ratio. It allows physicians to gauge whether or not you're overweight. Generally speaking, if your BMI is over twenty-five, you're considered overweight; over thirty means you're obese. One note: just because a child's BMI is in the normal range doesn't mean that child is healthy. Many teens are living on empty calories—all those foods that taste good but have absolutely no nutritional value.

There are quite a few BMI calculators online, or you can use the formula:

$$BMI = \frac{(\text{weight in pounds}) \times 703}{(\text{height in inches})^2}$$

The formula was originally created using metric units, so 703 is a conversion factor.

Obesity in American children and adolescents has almost tripled in the last thirty years. Obese children are at risk for myriad health problems now and into adulthood, such as type 2 diabetes, high blood pressure, high cholesterol, heart disease, sleep disorders, and asthma. They're more likely to be obese as adults and likely to be the target of teasing and discrimination. Their self-esteem suffers, and they tend to feel powerless to change. Don't do this to your kids. I've said it elsewhere in this book: allowing a child to become overweight is tantamount to child abuse for all the reasons listed above.

Obesity in American children and adolescents has almost tripled in the last thirty years.

I was always overweight as a child and am well aware of how horrible it feels. I tried hard to spare our kids from the same fate. The more research I do on nutrition, the more I realize how worthless the Standard American Diet is.

If anyone in your family has a tendency to be "fluffy," you owe it to them to remove temptation as much as possible. Don't buy junk food or empty calories—chips, soda, cookies, candy. Keep plenty of fruits and vegetables on hand. Instead of just being the food police, teach them *why* healthy eating is critical.

Calorie requirements for children vary greatly and depend on age, gender, and activity level. Instead of counting calories for your kids, take an honest look at how they compare to other children their age and height. If any of your offspring are struggling with their weight, gently help them cut back on how much, and what, they eat. In addition, help them find fun alternatives to eating out of boredom or habit.

It's important, of course, not to ridicule children who are overweight. They've already been comparing themselves to their peers. What they need are parents who are on their side. Tell them you love them and want them to learn healthy habits, so there will be some changes to the shopping list. When they start reaching for snack foods, help them find a distraction: play a game, go for a walk, listen to music, or drink a glass of water or a cup of decaffeinated tea. Help them limit their portion sizes, eat slowly, and chew thoroughly. Too many of us race through dinner, hardly tasting what we eat. (An added bonus of chewing thoroughly is that the enzymes in saliva get the digestive process off to a good start.) If you've ever tried to lose a few pounds you'll be able to empathize with your child.

Conversely, some children, especially young girls, tend to see themselves as fat when their weight is fine. There's probably no need to worry as long as you see them eating healthy foods and don't suspect that they're throwing up after meals. If, however, you do suspect an eating disorder, it's important to get professional help immediately.

DISEASE FACTS

Research on disease is evolving daily. This is especially true of cancer, heart disease, and diabetes. While eating right cannot guarantee you'll never get sick, it *will* go a long way towards preventing disease.

Cancer can be *treated* through a variety of invasive means—surgery, radiation, chemotherapy—but the only *cure* is a healthy immune system. Our bodies produce cancer cells all the time, but a healthy immune system hunts these cells down and destroys them; a weakened immune system can't. When that happens, the cancer cells multiply unchecked. A proper diet can prevent its growth.

More than one hundred studies have shown that people who eat the most vegetables have a 50 percent lower rate of cancer. Cruciferous vegetables (cabbage, broccoli, cauliflower, kale, bok choy, collard greens, Brussels sprouts) support liver enzymes that neutralize cancers. Cancer's favorite foods are sugar and fat. In addition, Bovine Growth Hormone (BGH), found in milk, has been shown to promote breast and prostate cancer, as well as facilitating the spread of cancer throughout the body.

Heart disease is a by-product of a poor diet. Animal foods, including dairy products, contain saturated fat, which can clog arteries. The abundance of salt found in most processed foods can lead to or worsen high blood pressure. Up to 80 percent of our daily salt intake comes from processed food. Smoking, obesity, and lack of exercise can all contribute to heart disease.

Type 2 diabetes often arises in people who are overweight and have a poor diet. An excess amount of fat in our cells blocks insulin efficiency. Low glycemic index carbohydrates are good for our bodies in that they produce only small changes in our blood glucose levels and help prevent diabetes. These foods include brown rice, bulgur, quinoa, pasta, fruit, salads, most vegetables, bran cereal, yams and sweet potatoes, oatmeal, rye bread, and pumpernickel bread. High glycemic foods include sugar, white and wheat bread, white potatoes, and cold cereal.

Three Types of Nutrients

Food can be sorted into three broad categories: proteins, fats, and carbohydrates. All are necessary for optimal health, which is why it's important to eat a variety of foods.

Proteins

Proteins are used by adults for repairs throughout the body, but are used by children for growth. People think of protein as synonymous with meat: beef, pork, fish, chicken, and lamb. It's true that meat provides a concentrated source of protein, but almost all plants contain some protein as well. The difference is that animal products contain complete proteins (all of the essential amino acids), while most plants do not. By eating a variety of plants, including nuts and seeds, or eating a small amount of animal protein with plant-based foods, it's possible to get enough complete protein.

People tend to eat a lot of meat because they think they need more protein than they really do. The reality is that adults only need 50 grams per day—just 2 ounces of pure protein. Since we get a good deal of it from plant-based foods, we really only need a small amount of meat each day, if at all.

Fats

A certain amount of fat is needed in the diet because some nutrients are fat-soluble (dissolve in fat or oil), and because our nerves have a coating of fat around them that helps them to work properly. Also, we all need essential fatty acids to maintain optimum health. Both animal and plant-based foods can contain fats (oils, by the way are fats that are liquid at room temperature). But overconsumption of fats is one of the leading causes of obesity, both in children and adults. Note, however, that children under the age of two should not be on a fat-restricted diet because fats and essential fatty acids are, well, essential for their brain development.

According to Dr. Susan Silberman, founder of the Center for Advancement in Cancer Education, our intake of fats should be limited to 15 to 20 percent of our total calories. (The Standard American Diet is usually around 40 to 50 percent.) She adds that when oils start to go rancid, they produce free radicals (molecules that float around in the body harming healthy tissue). Oil should always be stored in the refrigerator so it doesn't go bad before you can use it up. She also points out that fat is cancer's second-favorite food after sugar.

Here are the types of fats:

Saturated fats are found in animal products including meat, cheese, eggs, butter, ice cream, and some vegetable oils. Most stay solid at room temperature. Eating too much saturated fat is one of the leading causes of high cholesterol levels. Cholesterol is needed for cell development, but our body generally produces all the cholesterol we need.

Unsaturated fats include monounsaturated (olive and canola oils) and polyunsaturated fats (safflower, corn, and soybean oils). Both types help lower cholesterol levels and should replace some of the saturated fat in the diet (but not be used in addition to the saturated fat).

Trans fats are unsaturated fats that have been hydrogenated and can raise LDL ("bad") cholesterol and lower HDL ("good") cholesterol levels. The process adds hydrogen to unsaturated fats to make them solid at room temperature. They're usually found in processed foods: baked goods, popcorn, margarines, chips, and french fries. Trans fats are bad. That's why the FDA now requires the amount of trans fat to be listed on the nutrition label. (Also look for the words "partially hydrogenated oil.") Avoid them.

Carbohydrates

These include sugars and starches, and are only found in plants. This category can be further broken down into simple and complex carbohydrates. Simple carbs are things like sugar and white flour. Complex carbs—fruits, vegetables, and whole grains—take longer to digest and don't cause the spikes in blood sugar levels associated with simple carbs.

Problem Foods

Sugar

It's been known for some time that sugar has dozens of negative effects on the body, yet sugar consumption in the United States has increased from about five pounds per person per year in the late 1800s to **135** pounds per person in 1999, according to the U.S. Department of Agriculture.

Sugar suppresses the immune system: ten teaspoons, the amount in a single can of regular soda, causes a 50 percent reduction in immune response, which can last up to five hours. Sugar raises the blood-glucose level, which raises the insulin level, which encourages the storage of fat. It can lead to diabetes as well as hypoglycemia; can lead to deficiencies in minerals; increases the fermentation of bacteria in the colon; is addictive; and can cause behavior changes in children. According to Dr. Susan Silberman, sugar is cancer's favorite food.

Most of our sugar intake comes from processed foods: soft drinks and juices, desserts and sweets, peanut butter, ketchup, even canned fruits and vegetables. Low-fat foods often add sugar to make up for the decrease in flavor when the fat is removed. Read the labels, and look for sugar, sucrose, dextrose, and high-fructose corn syrup.

> Low-fat foods often add sugar to make up for the decrease in flavor when the fat is removed.

Artificial sweeteners sucralose (Splenda) and aspartame (NutraSweet, Equal) are not the answer; they are chemicals, not food. Honey, while chemically different from sugar, is still a simple carbohydrate. Raw honey contains small amounts of some nutrients, which is why some proponents claim it's more nutritious than sugar. But use it sparingly, since our goal as parents is to reduce our kids' collective sweet tooth—and never give it to infants under one year of age, because of the risk of infant botulism and because babies don't need sweets!

White flour

White flour is one of the worst things children can eat. During processing almost all of the nutrients are removed and a few inexpensive vitamins are added back in, giving us "enriched" flour. All this processing is designed to give us whiter, fluffier bread with a longer shelf life.

Its high glycemic index (around 70 on a scale of 1 – 100) means it rapidly increases blood sugar levels. This causes large amounts of insulin to be released and causes excess sugar in the blood to be stored as fat.

Milk and Dairy

All milk contains Bovine Growth Hormone (BGH) because cows produce it naturally. Most meat and dairy cows are given extra BGH to help them mature faster. BGH has been implicated as a possible carcinogen. If your kids drink milk, buy the organic fat-free kind. "Organic" means no added BGH. Milk is also one of the most common sources of food allergies, and about 25 percent of Americans are lactose intolerant (they can't digest milk sugar).

Milk is not the only (or the best) source of calcium. According to the Physicians Committee for Responsible Medicine, green leafy vegetables such as kale and broccoli are better sources of calcium than milk, contain no fat, and are excellent sources of iron. Milk contains virtually no iron. Flavored milk, by the way, has almost as much sugar as a can of soda. If you must allow it, save it for special occasions such as their high school graduation.

Other excellent sources of calcium are soy and almond milks, as well as calcium-fortified orange and apple juices. Organic kefir and organic low-fat yogurt are better than milk because they contain the good bacteria that aids in digestion. Greek yogurt has twice as much protein as regular yogurt.

Processed Foods

Some processing helps extend the shelf life of certain foods, and adding various chemicals improves taste and texture. The problem is there are thousands of chemicals approved as food additives, and the long-term effects of combining all of them haven't been studied. Some of these have caused serious reactions in sensitive individuals even though the FDA has deemed them safe. The other problem is the abundance of added sugars, salt, and fats, which is why they taste so good.

Our liver does a great job of filtering out toxins, but as more and more chemicals are added to our food supply, can our liver keep up? Eating more fresh organic foods reduces our exposure to these potential toxins. The general consensus, by the way, is that there are twelve foods you should buy organic: peaches, apples, sweet bell peppers, celery, nectarines, strawberries, cherries, pears, grapes (imported), spinach, lettuce, and potatoes.

Junk Food

Junk food is just that—junk. Empty calories that may fill you up, but do more harm to your body than you think. Remind your children that if they're not hungry enough to eat a healthy snack, they're not really hungry.

Easy Changes to Make

Plan on changing one thing every week or two. If you try to change everything at once, your family will mutiny, and you'll quickly go back to bad habits. Here are some ideas for making healthy food choices:

- Serve fresh fruit or veggies with a healthy dip for snacks. My grandchildren love raw vegetables with hummus or guacamole.
- Serve a variety of fruits and vegetables. Try new ones every week or so. Have the kids search the Internet for a recipe using the new ingredient.
- Eat more fresh foods as opposed to packaged products.
- Buy organic whenever possible. Organic food is more expensive, but if you cut back on meat, you may come out ahead in the long run. Organic produce not only has significantly

fewer pesticides and chemical fertilizers, but may have more total nutrients. This is because organic farms use crop rotation and the time-honored practice of allowing a field to lie fallow every seven years to reduce depletion of nutrients in the soil.

- Limit sweets and desserts to special occasions only.
- Instead of white bread, switch to a good quality multi-grain bread.
- Have a handful of nuts instead of a handful of candy. Not too many nuts, as they are high in fat.
- Limit fast food to once a week. Then cut back to every other week or less.
- Insist that your children eat a nutritious breakfast. They just can't concentrate when their brain is undernourished. Teachers can tell when a student hasn't had breakfast.
- Cut back on fats and oils.
- Give up sugar. Okay, cut way back on sugar. Save it for special occasions.
- Keep cutting back on the amount of soft drinks you buy. I started by allowing each kid six sodas per week and then started reducing it to five, etc. When their sodas were gone, they drank water or juice.
- Monitor what your kids take for lunch; otherwise they'll be taking chips and candy.
- Keep mealtimes calm and pleasant. Stress greatly hinders digestion.
- Drink more water. Most nutrition experts recommend half your weight in ounces daily. For example, if you weigh 100 pounds, drink 50 ounces of water daily. (The average drinking glass holds 12 ounces without ice.) Start by drinking an extra glass a day and keep increasing the amount. Water is needed for many biological functions, including digestion, healthy brain functioning, and body temperature regulation. Drinking adequate amounts of water helps us feel full, preventing overeating. Water helps the blood carry nutrients to

the cells and aids metabolism. And the big one: Water is so important that without it, we'd die in just a few days.
- Get the kids involved in cooking and meal planning. You'll get extra help in the kitchen while teaching valuable lessons. In addition, children are more likely to actually eat something they have a say in choosing and preparing.
- Limit meat to one meal per day. Try other sources of protein.
- Water down your salad dressings so you're getting more veggies and less fat in your salads.
- Put lots of extras in your salads: carrots, snap peas, radishes, cucumbers, tomatoes, olives, avocado, and soybeans. You can also try adding other green leafy vegetables a little at a time. By the way, iceberg lettuce is almost all water and has very little in the way of nutrients. Try other lettuces instead. Even better, add some kale to the other lettuces.
- Read the labels on all packaged foods. Look at total fat, saturated fat, and cholesterol. Read the ingredient list. The ingredients are required to be listed in order by quantity. (If sugar is the first ingredient, put it back!)
- Insist that your children at least taste everything that's being served. It not only helps train their taste buds, but it's just good manners. And no one is allowed to say "yuk."
- Sneak pureed vegetables into spaghetti or other sauces.
- When baking, you can substitute applesauce for all or most of the oil in most recipes.
- Avoid processed foods and fast food as much as possible.
- Throw out the deep-fat fryer. Nobody needs fried food.
- Try edamame (soybeans). They're high in complete protein and delicious with a little low-sodium soy sauce or added to salads. Look for them in the freezer section.
- Try quinoa (pronounced keen-wa) as a side dish or as an entrée with lots of other vegetables added. It's one of the few plant-based complete proteins, along with soy and hemp. And

since I brought it up, food-grade hemp is a different strain of plant than the one you're not supposed to smoke.

- Don't buy junk food, especially if anyone in the family is overweight. Why pay money to ruin their health? Why put temptation in front of them?

A note on vegetarianism

Vegans eat no animal or dairy products. They have 30 percent less fat in their cells, and their diets have been shown to lower blood sugar, as well as blood pressure and cholesterol. I don't recommend vegetarianism, because most of us aren't ready to make such a drastic change. Once you start eating more plants, however, you'll realize you feel better and may decide to go meatless occasionally. If you're interested in becoming a vegetarian, it's critical to do the research. For example, you'll need to know how to combine certain foods to get adequate complete proteins, and what nutrients you'll need to supplement.

EXERCISE

Growing children need about an hour of physical activity each day, according to many pediatricians. Elementary-age students have recess at school, of course, but toddlers and older children need exercise as well. In our electronic society, too many children are coming home from school and "plugging in." They're becoming couch potatoes in training.

Obvious solutions are after-school sports or classes at local fitness centers. Family activities are ideal: walking the dog, biking, playing tag at the park. Chores are also a good way to get moving. Look for ways to make them fun. "Who'll be the first to put away ten things in their room?"

Parents are often afraid to tell kids to run outside and play because of the potential danger of child abduction. In larger cities, there may not be a safe place nearby. In addition, in many parts of the country there's the problem of inclement weather.

Some ideas for indoor games include:

- Play balloon volleyball. Use several balloons. See how long you can keep them all in the air.
- Get a kid-size jump rope (and an adult-size one so you can jump together).
- Have a push-up or pull-up contest, and give a prize for the most improved.
- Put on some fun music and dance.
- Invest in a Wii game console or some exercise DVDs.

Sleep

It goes without saying that kids need sleep. School-age children need nine to ten hours of sleep or more each night. Insist that they go to bed on time. If they can't fall asleep, consider letting them read for a short while.

Be sure to remove all electronics from bedrooms, especially cell phones. Many kids leave their phone on all night and often are up for hours, texting their friends. Similarly, with a computer in their room they could be up half the night on the Internet. Designate a spot in the kitchen or living room to keep cell phones when the children go to bed.

Breakfast Ideas

Food	Calories	Protein grams	Fat grams	Calcium mg
1 cup oatmeal + 1/4 cup low-fat soy milk + 2 Tbsp. ground flax	260	11	8	90
1 extra-large egg + 1 Tbsp. butter	160+	7+	14.5	20
1 vegetable patty	150	18	5	100
8 oz. fat-free Greek yogurt +1/2 cup berries (fresh or frozen)	165	24	1	310
¾ cup organic granola + ¼ cup soy milk	290	7	11.5	70
2 Tbsp. organic peanut butter on 1 slice whole grain toast	300	12	16.5	-
3/4 cup cooked quinoa with ½ cup fruit	220	7	3	0

Milk Alternatives	Calories	Protein grams	Fat grams	Calcium mg
Soy milk, low-fat, 8 oz.	20	4	1.5	200
Coconut milk, 8 oz.	80	1	5	100
Rice milk, low-fat, 8 oz.	120	1	2.5	300

Lunch and Snack Ideas				
Food	Calories	Protein grams	Fat grams	Calcium mg
1 slice whole wheat bread + 2 Tbsp. natural peanut butter + ½ banana, sliced	360	13	17	10
½ cup raw carrots + ¼ cup hummus	180	5	12	20
¾ cup cooked quinoa with added vegetables and spices to taste	170+	6+	3	0
½ cup soybeans (edamame), shelled	150	15	7.5	180
¼ cup raw or toasted almonds	170	6	14	80

Other Ideas

- Low-fat, low-sodium soup
- Raw veggies with dip: ranch dressing, guacamole, peanut dip
- Apples with peanut butter
- Roll-ups made with whole wheat tortillas and plenty of vegetables
- Salads with a variety of ingredients: carrots, snow peas, corn, toasted nuts, tomatoes, avocado, raisins, olives, cheese, onions, broccoli, any leftover meat or vegetables

Chapter 11: *A Healthy Lifestyle*   271

Resources for Healthy Living:

Books:
- Emekak Mauris L. 2008. *Cancer's Best Medicine, a Self Help and Wellness Guide*. Port Orchard, Washington: Apollo Publishing International.
- Roisen, Michael F. MD and Mehmet C. Oz, MD. 2007. *You: Staying Young: the Owner's Manual for Extending Your Warranty*. New York, NY: Free Press.
- Silberstein, Susan, PhD. 2008. *Garbage In, Garbage Out: The Health Consequences of What We Feed Our Kids*. http://www.susansilberstein.com/ultimate/tools-and-resources.
- Silberstein, Susan, PhD. 2005. *Hungry for Health*. West Conshohoken, Pennsylvania: Infinity Publishing.com.

Web Pages:
- Center for Disease Control, accessed May 07, 2012, www.cdc.gov
- National Institutes of Health, accessed May 07, 2012, http://www.nih.gov/
- National Health Interview Survey, accessed May 07, 2012, www.cdc.gov/nchs/nhis.htm
- Office of the Surgeon General, accessed May 07, 2012, http://www.surgeongeneral.gov/
- Living Foods Institute, accessed May 07, 2012, http://www.livingfoodsinstitute.com/index.php
- Physicians Committee for Responsible Medicine, accessed May 07, 2012, http://www.pcrm.org/index.html
- Body Mass Index Calculators:
    - National Heart Lung and Blood Institute, accessed May 07, 2012, www.nhlbisupport.com/bmi/

- Center for Disease Control and Prevention, accessed May 07, 2012, www.cdc.gov/healthyweight/assessing/bmi/
- Mayo Clinic, accessed May 07, 2012, www.mayoclinic.com/health/bmi-calculator/NU00597

- Healing Daily, http://www.healingdaily.com/
- Dr. Nancy Appleton, www.nancyappleton.com
- Article on the dangers of Aspartame, http://www.321recipes.com/aspartame.html
- Web MD, http://www.webmd.com/
- The Glycemic Index Foundation http://www.glycemicindex.com/
- Center for Science in the Public Interest http://www.cspinet.org

DVDs:
- Silberstein, Susan, PhD. 2008. *Fight Cancer with Your Fork!*. Silberstein, Susan, PhD. (Alternate Title: *Kitchen Chemotherapy: Eating for Cancer Prevention And Control*). http://www.susansilberstein.com/ultimate/tools-and-resources.

Chapter 12

Illegal Substances

By twelfth grade, more than half of all teens have been offered drugs. By eighth grade, almost half have had at least one drink, and while the number of high school students who smoke is down, about 20 to 25 percent do smoke. Odds are good that your child has been offered at least one of these substances, possibly as early as fifth or sixth grade.

It's critical that parents be proactive and talk to children early about why these things are illegal. In addition, we must help them figure out what to say when friends pressure them to be cool. As bad as these substances (chemicals) are for grown-ups, they're many times worse for children and young adults. Before the age of twenty-one, your child's body is still developing, including the brain and liver.

Make it clear to your children early on—around fourth grade—that illegal activities will not be tolerated. As they get older, keep a watchful eye out for the signs. If you suspect substance abuse and do nothing, you're teaching your child that what he's doing is okay. Keep in mind that in some parts of the country, parents can be charged with a crime when their kids break the law.

If you've been teaching ethics all along, and have kept the lines of love and communication open, there's a good chance your children will avoid most law-breaking activities. You must still talk about the importance of avoidance. Burying your head in the sand and hoping for the best just doesn't work. If you don't make your opinions known, your child will assume you don't care if they try these things.

Addiction is the state of being enslaved to a substance. For children, the definition of addiction is that the substance grabs hold of you and won't let go. You'll spend the rest of your life trying to pry its claws from around your neck. (This is one time you *do* want to scare them.) Remind them repeatedly that it's easy to *not start* smoking/drinking/taking drugs, but it can be nearly impossible to quit.

When you feel your child is old enough, have him or her look at pictures of meth addicts. What meth does to the outside of your body, other addictions do to the inside (brain, liver, lungs). Ask your child if he thinks the meth addict wants to look like that. Why doesn't the addict just stop using? The short answer is that he can't.

Addiction only happens to people who say "It won't happen to me."

Drugs

The number of illicit drugs available today is overwhelming, and new ones are coming along all the time. I'll give an overview here, but for the most current information, visit the websites listed in the Appendix.

According to a survey by the National Institute on Drug Abuse (NIDA), nearly half of all twelfth graders have tried illicit drugs at least once and nearly one-fourth of them had used some sort of drug in the month prior to the survey. Even those students who didn't use drugs said drugs are readily available in school. Eighty-five percent of teens said they knew how to obtain marijuana if they wanted to.

Most parents assume that their kids won't do drugs. If Mom and Dad do suspect a problem, they often hope they're mistaken because they don't want to confront the child. It's critical that parents step up and fight the battle.

The Most Common Types of Drugs

- **Stimulants (uppers):** These cause increased heart rate and blood pressure, and may cause anxiety or heart failure. Be aware that some students take these as a study aid.
- **Inhalants (chemical vapors):** These include paint thinners, aerosol sprays, and even gasoline and propane. They may produce unconsciousness, brain damage, or even death by suffocation, as the vapors replace oxygen in the lungs.
- **Prescription drugs (prescribed to someone other than the teen):** These include opiates, nervous system depressants, or Ritalin purchased from students with ADHD.
- **Steroids (used to help build muscle):** These can cause liver damage, infertility, stunted growth, cancer, and severe acne. Continued abuse can lead to heart failure and increased aggression. Many of the side effects are irreversible.
- **Club drugs:** These include ecstasy (MDMA), Rohypnol, GHB, and ketamine. Rohypnol and GHB are known as "date rape" drugs, as they can sedate and incapacitate a victim, and can easily be added to a victim's beverage. All may become addicting.
- **Hallucinogens:** PCP, LSD, DMT, mescaline, and Foxy alter the user's perception of reality.
- **Meth and cocaine/crack:** These stimulants produce a greater "high," or sense of euphoria, than other stimulants but are incredibly addicting. Both come in powder and crystal (rock) forms, and both have severe, adverse effects on the body. In addition, users often resort to stealing from friends and family to pay for their ever-increasing habit.
- **Marijuana:** It produces an overwhelming feeling of apathy, while distorting judgment. The biggest danger with marijuana is that many teens don't consider it a real or dangerous drug.
- **Over-the-counter drugs:** These include cough medicine, diet pills, pain relievers, and sexual performance enhancers.

Some teens, in an effort to increase the effects of a drug, will combine it with other drugs or alcohol, often with deadly results.

Warning Signs to Watch For

Watch for the following in your child: mood swings, new friends, dropping grades, change in attitude or sleep habits, avoidance of their usual fun activities, change in appearance, withdrawal, secrecy about friends and activities, and inability to concentrate. Are money, valuables, or prescription drugs missing? Parents should also look for drug paraphernalia including rolling papers, pipes, and the drugs themselves. If you suspect drug use, don't be afraid to search their room. They'll complain loudly that you don't trust them, but their safety and health are more important than their anger. Many students are actually relieved to get caught. They want help, but don't know what to do.

What Parents Can Do

Start the conversations early: **drugs are bad for you**. They make you sick, they can kill you, and if you get caught you will go to jail. As your child gets older, explain that drugs are chemicals that cause changes in the body. Some drugs will start harming your body right away, while others take longer. Some are good for treating illnesses, but even these must be used with caution, since they all have side effects. That's why a doctor has to write a prescription.

Other things you can say:

- Illegal drugs are illegal for an important reason—they're bad for you. Some will start harming your body right away, others take longer. Many can kill you.
- Don't let your friends talk you into making the biggest mistake of your life. You're smarter than they are.
- My job is to protect you from bad guys, and I'll do whatever it takes to make that happen.
- If I ever suspect that you're doing drugs, you and I will be attached at the hip for a really long time—even on dates.

- Street drugs don't have standards. You never know what they've been diluted with. The same is true for buying drugs online.
- Illegal drugs make you feel good for a very short time, but will cause problems for the rest of your life. Is it worth it?
- Don't break my heart.

Many students report that they started taking drugs because "there was nothing else to do" or because "Mom and Dad don't care what I do as long as I don't bother them." Numerous studies have shown that teens whose parents talk to them regularly about values and the dangers of illegal substances have a much lower incidence of drug use than parents who don't discuss these things.

Know your child's friends. Invite them for dinner so you can talk to them. Get to know their parents and talk to them about the kids.

If you can't be home with your children after school, try to arrange some supervised activity for them. Sports, church youth groups, and after-school programs are available in many areas.

"Trust but verify." Check up on your kidlets at random times. Make sure they are where they're supposed to be.

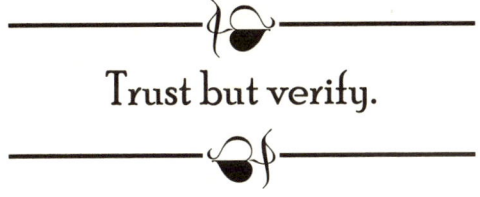

Trust but verify.

Monitor any and all prescription drugs in the home as well as over-the-counter medications. Explain your prescriptions, why you take them, and the side effects. Make it clear that it's dangerous to take someone else's medication.

Be sure to discuss date rape drugs with your daughters and how to stay safe. Girls should never leave their drinks unattended at parties. If the drink tastes funny, or they start to feel funny, they must get help *immediately*. Some of these drugs are extremely fast-acting.

Alcohol

Some parents feel it's okay if their child is "just" drinking alcohol. At least they're not doing drugs, right? Alcohol *is* a drug (and the drug of choice for young people), and a dangerous one for many reasons.

Some Statistics

- Kids who start drinking at an early age are at greater risk of alcohol dependency. For every year you *delay* the start of drinking, the risk of dependence goes *down* by 14 percent.
- Teens who start drinking before the age of fifteen are four times more likely to become an alcoholic than those who start at twenty-one or after.
- Teens who drink are more likely to have sex as well as engage in risky sexual behaviors (multiple partners, unprotected sex, etc.).
- Teens who drink are twice as likely to contemplate suicide.
- About 1,900 people under the age of twenty-one die each year in crashes where underage drinking is involved.
- Teens don't just drink, they drink to excess.
- The leading causes of death for fifteen-to-twenty-four-year-olds are car crashes, homicides, and suicides. Alcohol is a leading factor in all three.
- Teens don't understand that their body is not developed enough to process alcohol.

Warning Signs to Watch For

The signs are similar to those for drug abuse: mood swings, new friends, dropping grades, change in attitude or sleep habits, avoidance of their usual fun activities, change in appearance, withdrawal, secrecy about friends and activities, inability to concentrate, and missing money, valuables, or, of course, alcohol.

What Parents Can Do

Keeping children away from alcohol may be more difficult than avoiding drugs and smoking, since most adults have some alcohol in the home. You may want to keep the liquor in a locked cabinet as your child gets older. If they ever complain that you don't trust them, your answer is, "It wouldn't be fair of us to put temptation in front of you."

As with smoking and drugs, it's important to start discussing the dangers at an early age—as soon as they start asking for a taste of what you're drinking. "Wine (or whatever) is just for grown-ups because it can make you sick." For tweens and teens, look for teachable moments on TV and in movies. "Why do the commercials say 'drink responsibly'? What does that mean?" "Why are those kids stealing beer from their parents?" Answer: "Because they don't know it can make them sick. I'm glad you're smarter than that."

Make it easy for your child to say no in tough situations. If he wants to have a party, discuss the rules. Limit the number of guests and the time frame, so things don't get out of hand. Uninvited guests will not be allowed in. Make it clear there will be no alcohol served and have your child make it clear to the guests. Provide plenty of snacks and nonalcoholic beverages. Adults should monitor the party—pass around the food and ask if anyone needs anything. Have your child come get you (or text you) if there's a problem.

When your child goes to a party at a friend's house, you should *always* call the other parents. Ask if they plan to supervise and what their policy is on alcohol. If you don't like the answers they give you, you may have to tell your daughter she can't go. Your job is to keep her safe, not be her buddy.

Other things you might say:

Some people will want you to try alcohol so they can watch you get drunk. Do you really want to be in a position where people will laugh at you? What if they post the video? How will you feel?

Do you want to risk your future to make your friends happy?

The younger you start drinking, the greater your chance of addiction. I don't want to risk your future. (Note: The average child will insist he won't get addicted. Your answer is: How do you know? Do you have a label on you that I don't know about? Let me see it.)

Smoking

Ninety percent of people who smoke started before they graduated high school. Therefore, if you can keep your kids from starting before graduation, chances are good they will never take up the habit.

I personally never understood the appeal of smoking. It tastes bad, makes you smell bad, and it's bad for you. So why *do* kids take up smoking? Unfortunately, there are myriad compelling (to them) reasons.

- One or both parents smoke. Remember, you're their number-one role model. It also makes it easier to get cigarettes if they're available in the home. Incidentally, students whose parents smoke feel that their parents are being hypocritical when they tell the kids not to smoke. If you smoke, telling them to "do as I say, not as I do" just isn't going to work.
- Their peers smoke. If you know your child's friends are smokers, it's critical to sit him down for this talk right away. Their health is more important than a need to fit in.
- It's forbidden, therefore they want to try it. At some point, most kids hit a rebellious stage, also known as the "you can't stop me" phase.
- They feel smoking makes them look cool or at least older.
- They want to lose weight. More girls than boys take up smoking for this reason.
- They're invincible. 'Tweens and teens are famous for their "nothing bad will happen" mentality. They argue that it won't hurt to just try it, or they tell themselves that they don't smoke a lot so they won't get addicted.

Warning Signs to Watch For

Keep an eye (and nose) out for stained fingers, the smell of smoke on their hands or clothes, excessive air freshener used in their room or car, excessive use of mints or mouthwash, and missing tobacco products from the house.

What Parents Can Do

Start talking to your children early about why smoking is bad. If you yourself smoke, explain how hard it is to quit. Go online and find pictures that compare a healthy lung to a smoker's lung.

Have them talk to other kids who smoke. Have they tried to quit? What does it feel like? Most teen smokers will swear they can quit whenever they want to, so it's important to talk to someone who has actually tried quitting. Can they find even one student who *has* quit?

Do the math: a pack a day costs at least $3.50. Multiply that by 365, and it will cost almost $1,300 per year. After fifty years, they will have spent more than $63,000. If the cost of cigarettes goes up, the lifetime cost will go up accordingly. Still worth it? Where will that $1,300 a year come from, by the way?

I used to ask students, "If someone held you down and forced you to take poison, you'd probably fight it. So why would you want to poison yourself voluntarily?"

Kids think smoking looks cool, but is it really cool to smell bad all the time? There's a saying: Kissing a smoker is like licking an ashtray.

Ask if they really want to start something that will control them for the rest of their life. Is it worth a lifelong addiction and thousands of dollars to look cool for a couple of years? Are the people you're looking cool for worth it? Don't let someone else ruin your health or pressure you into a life-changing decision.

Point out that if his friends are pressuring him to smoke, they're not very good friends. You trust him to have enough respect for himself to say "no thanks."

Other Talking Points Regarding Illegal Substances

Often people drink or take drugs to forget their problems. Do the problems go away? What happens when they sober up? Are the problems still there? Can you ignore your problems forever?

We don't tell you not to drink/smoke/do drugs because we want to spoil your fun. There are some serious health risks and legal consequences involved. We love you and want you to be safe and healthy.

If I catch you, you'll be grounded for a *long* time. You'll go everywhere I go until you're old enough to be trusted. (Parents—you must be willing to follow through on this one.)

One of the first things drugs and alcohol do is affect your judgment. People often get pressured into doing really stupid things that they regret later. Don't put yourself in that position.

This is not the plan God has for you.

It's helpful to youngsters to give them some possible responses they can use when offered illegal substances:

- My parents will KILL me.
- My parents do random drug testing.
- I'm allergic.
- I don't like the taste.
- If you're my friend, you'll respect my decision.
- Why would I want to poison myself?
- Are you crazy? Do you know what that does to your body?
- Smoking/drugs/alcohol is for losers.

Brainstorm with your children to come up with some other responses.

Numerous studies have shown that teens whose parents regularly talk to them about the dangers of drugs, smoking and alcohol are significantly less likely to use illicit substances. Talk to your children today.

Part 2

Your Lesson Plans –

What to Teach at Each Stage of Development

———— 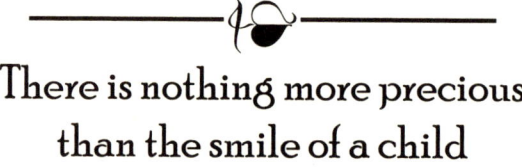 ————
There is nothing more precious
than the smile of a child
————————————

Note: There is some repetition in this section. Some topics take several years to teach and will show up in more than one age category.

AGES 1–3

- **Needs of children** – Unconditional love, safety, patience, physical contact, stability, empathy, attention, boundaries, healthy food, consistent enforcement of the rules.
- **Education** – A love of learning begins with reading. You can read them stories before they even understand the words. Children's books teach vocabulary and concepts such as colors or numbers. Focus on educational toys.
- **Life skills** – By two or three, your child can help put things away. Praise them for helping. Start teaching decision making. ("Which shirt do you want to wear?") Start teaching them the words for feelings. ("You're angry with your brother.")
- **Spirituality/religion** – Say nightly prayers and at meals.
- **Consequences** – For toddlers, life is about learning the rules. ("Tails are not for pulling. Sand is not for throwing.") Mom and Dad soon learn that rules are for testing. Be consistent in enforcing them. A time-out or tap on the hand is sufficient discipline.
- **Respect** – Toddlers won't understand what respect means, but they will understand what it means to be happy and sad. Keep the discussion focused on feelings. ("It makes people cry when you bite them.")
- **Lying** – Preschoolers can't tell the difference between reality and fantasy, and many children this age enjoy making up stories. Right now they don't understand the concept of lying. When they tell you they don't know why your flower garden looks like a minefield, stick to the facts. ("Flowers need to stay in the dirt, and the flower bed is not for children to dig in.")
- **Social skills** – "Please" and "thank you" are a good place to start. Remember to say "thank you" when they hand you something, and "please" when you want something from them.

- **Safety** – This is all about you keeping them physically safe, especially after they learn to crawl.
- **Healthy lifestyle** – Get your cherub off to a good start. Offer lots of whole grains and vegetables after they have enough teeth. *Never* offer sodas or sugary drinks. Offer water instead. Limit fast food and avoid sweets. Giving sweets to babies sets them up for health problems later on. Avoid salty snacks and fried food. Make your own baby food. (Cook vegetables, puree them in a blender or food processor, and freeze them in ice cube trays or in clumps on cookie sheets. When frozen, transfer to a zip-top bag.) Limit TV and computer viewing to less than one hour each day; both have been implicated as a cause of ADHD (attention-deficit/hyperactivity disorder).

Age 4

- **Needs of children** – Unconditional love, safety, patience, physical contact, attention, empathy, stability, boundaries, healthy food, consistent enforcement of the rules, self-worth (no name-calling or put-downs).
- **Attitude** – Parents can begin teaching the concept of choosing your attitude. Play the "I wish" game. ("I wish we never had to go to bed, but you're body needs to rest because you're growing so fast.")
- **Education** – A love of learning begins with reading. You can read them stories before they even understand all the words. Children's books teach vocabulary and concepts such as colors or numbers.
- **Life skills** – Start assigning them basic chores, such as making their bed, setting the table, and putting toys away at night. Praise them for helping. Continue with decision making. Emphasize teamwork. Model good listening skills and use "I" messages when you get angry. Teach your children to use "I" messages. Continue teaching them the words for feelings. ("You feel proud because you put the toys away by yourself.")

- **Spirituality/religion** – In addition to nightly prayers, start your child in Sunday school. Children this age are usually eager to start school.

- **Consequences** – Introduce logical consequences. ("If you don't wash your hands, you don't get a snack." "If you don't put your toys away, then you don't get to play with them tomorrow.") Start considering what motivates your child. (No TV? A time-out? Extra chores?) Catch them being good.

- **Respect** – At this age your child will soon learn he can talk back to you. Teach him which things are not okay (eye rolling, sass, defiance).

- **Lying** – Your child is learning to tell the difference between reality and fantasy, although he'll still try to make up stories. When he talks about the puppy that ate all the cookies in the jar, reply that you like his story, but that's not what really happened.

- **Social skills** – Continue with "please" and "thank you." Start working on table manners (use of cutlery, chewing with the mouth closed).

- **Safety** – Continue to look around your home for potential safety hazards.

- **Finances** – Explain that you don't always have money for treats or toys. A simple, "Sorry, there's no extra money today—maybe next time" is all the explanation your child needs, although it may not be enough to stop a tantrum. Try playing the "I wish" game. ("I wish we could fill the truck with your favorite candy!")

- **Healthy lifestyle** – Get your cherub off to a good start. Offer lots of whole grains and vegetables. Never offer sodas or sugary drinks. Offer water instead. Limit fast food, and limit sweets to special occasions, such as their birthday party. They're still learning to like healthy foods. Avoid salty snacks and fried food. Limit TV and computer viewing to less than one hour each day; encourage physical activity.

- **Illegal substances** – It's not too early to plant the seeds: drugs are bad for you. Smoking is bad for you. Drinking is bad for you. Explain that these things will make them sick and damage their body.

Ages 5–7

- **Needs of children** – Happy memories, encouragement, role models (children are now starting to learn your values indirectly), unconditional love, safety, patience, attention, empathy, physical contact, stability, boundaries, healthy food, consistent enforcement of the rules, self-worth (no name-calling or put-downs).
- **Attitude** – Gratitude for the things they have. Forgiveness, likability, confidence. Parents can continue teaching the concept of choosing your attitude. Keep playing the "I wish" game.
- **Education** – School is their job. Make sure they do their homework. Begin reading longer books to them and have them read to you. Make it clear that homework is not optional, and spell out the consequences for not doing homework. Dedicate an area for doing homework (*not* in front of the TV). Start teaching study skills by helping them memorize facts. Begin teaching organization: when homework is finished, supplies get put away and the assignment goes into the backpack.
- **Life skills** – Continue chores, teach perseverance and conflict resolution. Continue with decision making. Emphasize teamwork. Model good listening skills and use "I" messages when you get angry. Teach your child to use "I" messages. Continue teaching them the words for feelings. ("You're frustrated because you can't stay up as late as your older brother.")
- **Spirituality/religion** – Say nightly prayers, attend Sunday school, say grace at mealtime. Consider vacation Bible school.
- **Consequences** – Introduce natural consequences. ("If you forget your lunch, you will be very hungry." "When you make a mess, you clean it up.") Catch them being good.

- **Respect** – Continue to calmly correct disrespectful behavior. If you lose your temper and also become disrespectful, you'll lose credibility.
- **Lying** – To discourage lying, avoid asking "gotcha" questions. Instead of asking "Who did this?" or "Did you do ____?" when you know in fact they did, focus on solving the problem.
- **Stealing** – Parents must take immediate corrective action. Your child must return the item or pay for it, as well as apologize.
- **Social skills** – Teach him how to answer the house phone properly. For sleepovers, discuss how to be a good guest and/or host.
- **Safety** – Includes physical, emotional, and moral safety. Talk about "stranger danger" and bullies. ("If anyone makes you feel scared or uncomfortable, tell us right away. It's our job to protect you.") Lock out inappropriate TV channels and shows. Put the computer where you can see it when they're using it.
- **Finances** – Start him on a small allowance (maybe a dollar for each year of age). Explain the three-pot system. Get him a wallet or coin purse to keep his spending money in, so he can take it with him to the store. Decide if his allowance will be dependent on the completion of chores.
- **Healthy lifestyle** – Have your child help plan meals and do some cooking. Try new fruits and vegetables, and new ways of cooking them. Offer healthy dips for veggies, such as hummus, guacamole, pesto, or homemade ranch dressing. Ketchup will do in a pinch, but it's still about 50 percent sugar. Offer lots of whole grains and vegetables. Never offer sodas or sugary drinks. Offer water instead. Limit sweets to special occasions, such as their birthday party. They're still learning to like healthy foods. Avoid salty snacks and fried food. Limit TV and computer viewing; encourage physical activity.
- **Illegal substances** – Continue sending the messages: drugs are bad for you. Smoking is bad for you. Drinking is bad for you. Explain that these things will make them sick and damage their body.

Ages 8–10

- **Needs of children** – A childhood. (They want to grow up too fast.) Happy memories, encouragement, role models (children are learning your values indirectly), unconditional love, safety, patience, physical contact, stability, boundaries, attention, empathy, healthy food, consistent enforcement of the rules, self-worth (no name-calling or put-downs).

- **Attitude** – Cheerfulness, gratitude for the things they have. Forgiveness, likability, confidence. Continue teaching the concept of choosing your attitude.

- **Education** – Teach all three learning styles: visual, auditory, tactile. Give choices on when (*not* if) to do schoolwork. Start talking about what motivates him or her to do well. In middle school, buy them a small file container for returned assignments and tests. Get them a small notebook for recording assignments and a calendar to keep track of due dates. Make sure they're doing well in English. When studying for a test, look at the layout of the text and section headings. Start setting a minimum number of minutes per day for studying and homework.

- **Life skills** – Teach goal setting for school projects. Teach problem solving and ask questions such as "Can we look at this another way?" Continue chores, perseverance, and conflict resolution. Continue with decision making. Emphasize teamwork. Model good listening skills and use "I" messages when you get angry. Teach your child to use "I" messages. Continue teaching the words for feelings. ("You're disappointed you got sick the day of the party.")

- **Spirituality/religion** – Say nightly prayers, attend Sunday school, say grace at mealtime. Consider vacation Bible school.

- **Consequences** – Add consequences for not getting schoolwork done. Continue natural and logical consequences. Catch them being good.

- **Respect** – As you treat your cherubs respectfully, so will they be respectful to you. Most of the time.
- **Lying** – If lying has become a chronic problem, seek professional help.
- **Stealing** – Parents must take immediate corrective action. Your child must return the item or pay for it, as well as apologize.
- **Cheating** – This is the age kids realize that cheating in school is possible. Copying homework or peeking at a friend's answers during a test can be tempting to tweens. Explain all the reasons that cheating is wrong.
- **Work ethic** – With chores, clearly state what the parameters are, so Junior will know when he's done and can tell if he's done a satisfactory job. ("Dishes must be clean, dry, and put away. Windows must be washed inside and out, and must be streak-free.")
- **Social skills** – Start discussing the Traits of Socially Successful People.
- **Safety** – Get to know their friends and the parents of their friends. Discuss Internet bad guys. Listen to their music, and lock down the Internet when you and your spouse won't be home. Lock out inappropriate TV channels and shows. Put the computer where you can see it when they're using it.
- **Sex** – Answer questions in simple terms. Sex is something married people do when they love each other.
- **Finances** – Increase allowance each year. Discuss marketing and advertising ploys.
- **Healthy lifestyle** – Get children involved in meal preparation: peeling carrots, making salads. Try new fruits and vegetables, and new ways of cooking them. Offer healthy dips for veggies, such as hummus, guacamole, pesto, or homemade ranch dressing. Ketchup will do in a pinch, but it's still about 50 percent sugar. Offer lots of whole grains and vegetables. Never offer sodas, limit fast food, and limit sweets to special occa-

sions, such as their birthday party. They're still learning to like healthy foods. Avoid salty snacks and fried food. Limit TV watching; encourage physical activity.

- **Illegal substances** – Look for teachable moments. Discuss addiction. Lock up the liquor cabinet and your prescriptions, to avoid temptation. Children have been known to start substance abuse at this age. Teach ways to say no. Continue sending the message: drugs are bad for you. Smoking is bad for you. Drinking is bad for you. Explain that these things will make them sick and damage their body.

Ages 11–13 (Hormone Alley)

- **Needs of children** – The need to fit in. A childhood. (They still want to grow up too fast.) Happy memories, encouragement, role models (children are now starting to learn your values indirectly), unconditional love, safety, patience, attention, empathy, physical contact, stability, boundaries, healthy food, consistent enforcement of the rules, self-worth (no name-calling or put-downs).
- **Attitude** – Teach them the five-year rule: will whatever you're upset about matter five years from now? Encourage cheerfulness, gratitude for the things they have, forgiveness, likability, confidence. Continue teaching the concept of choosing your attitude.
- **Education** – School is more than just memorizing facts. It's about time management, learning to think, and solving problems. Education is something you do for yourself. Parents can use both internal and external motivators. Help your students determine their primary learning style. Help them evaluate their work before they turn it in. Teach them to take notes in class and from the book, and how to prepare for a test. When they get to middle school, buy them a small file container for returned assignments and tests. Get them a small notebook for recording assignments and a calendar to keep track of due dates. Make sure they're doing well in English. When studying

for a test, look at the layout of the text and the section headings. Encourage the use of their primary learning style.

- **Life skills** – Give more leeway in decision making (say, buying clothes). Teach goal setting for school projects. Teach problem solving and ask questions such as "Can we look at this another way?" Continue chores, perseverance, and conflict resolution. Continue with decision making. Emphasize teamwork. Model good listening skills and use "I" messages when you get angry. Teach your child to use "I" messages. Have them start describing their feelings to you as you model your listening skills.

- **Spirituality/religion** – Say nightly prayers, attend church and/or Sunday school, say grace at mealtime. Consider vacation Bible school. Involve them in the church youth group.

- **Consequences** – As you add more rules, continue to be consistent in enforcing them. Continue consequences for not getting schoolwork done. Continue natural and logical consequences. Catch them being good.

- **Respect** – As you treat your cherubs respectfully, so will they be respectful to you. Most of the time. Make sure they treat others (teachers, elders, neighbors, family members) respectfully as well.

- **Lying** – Trust them, but check up on them periodically.

- **Stealing** – If new stuff starts appearing, ask questions and read their body language. Parents must take immediate corrective action. Your child must return the item or pay for it, as well as apologize.

- **Cheating** – There may be increased peer pressure or academic pressure from Mom and Dad. Make sure your youngster is spending adequate time on homework and studying. If he seems overwhelmed with homework, speak to his teachers. Discuss the ways people cheat and how they are only cheating themselves. Explain all the reasons that cheating is wrong.

- **Work ethic** – If your child is doing odd jobs for others, talk to the employer to be sure the job is being completed satisfactorily. Discuss with your child the components of work ethic: dependability, initiative, and interpersonal skills. With chores, clearly state what the parameters are, so your child will know when he's done and can tell if he's done a satisfactory job. ("Dishes must be clean, dry, and put away. Windows must be washed inside and out, and must be streak-free.")

- **Social skills** – Discuss the concept of class, and what it means to be a lady or gentleman. Teach graciousness. Continue discussing the Traits of Socially Successful People

- **Safety** – Talk about online predators and cyberbullying. Make it clear that online harassment is illegal. If someone is bullying them, they must let you know. Listen to their music, and lock down the Internet when you and your spouse won't be home. Lock out inappropriate TV channels and shows. Put the computer where you can see it when they're using it and monitor their online profiles (Facebook, MySpace, etc.). When you give your child a cell phone, explain the rules: it must be *off* during school hours, no taking pictures in the locker room, etc. Never post compromising pictures or let others take compromising pictures of you. Taking compromising pictures or video of someone without their consent is illegal as well.

- **Sex** – Teach the mechanics, risks, and reasons for abstinence. Teach your child ways to say no.

- **Finances** – Talk about needs vs. wants. Increase allowance each year. Discuss marketing and advertising ploys.

- **Healthy lifestyle** – Encourage your child to look up new recipes and prepare them. Keep healthy snacks on hand and within easy reach. Don't buy junk food. Discuss the options at his friends' houses. If they always have cookies and milk at a friend's house, have him bake some granola bars to take over. Help him make healthy choices at lunch, whether he buys lunch or packs his own. Continue to limit TV and computer time, and encourage physical activity, especially if they're struggling with their weight. Offer lots of whole grains and vegetables. Never offer sodas, limit fast food, and limit sweets to special occasions. Avoid salty snacks and fried food.

- **Illegal substances** – Watch for the warning signs: mood swings, new friends, dropping grades, change in attitude or sleep habits, missing money or valuables, changes in appearance, secrecy about friends and activities, inability to concentrate, avoidance of their usual activities, missing pills or alcohol, even excessive use of breath mints or air freshener. Look for teachable moments. Discuss addiction. Lock up the liquor cabinet and your prescriptions to avoid temptation. Children have been known to start substance abuse at this age. Teach ways to say no. Continue sending the message: drugs are bad for you. Smoking is bad for you. Drinking is bad for you.

Ages 14–18

- **Needs of children** – The need to feel grown up. The need to fit in. Happy memories, encouragement, role models, unconditional love, safety, patience, physical contact, attention, empathy, stability, boundaries, healthy food, consistent enforcement of the rules, self-worth (no name-calling or put-downs).
- **Attitude** – Teach them the five-year rule: will whatever you're upset about matter five years from now? Encourage cheerfulness, gratitude for the things they have, forgiveness, likability, confidence. Continue teaching the concept of choosing your attitude.
- **Education** – Grades become more important, since colleges and universities will look at their grades. Get a copy of each teacher's grading criteria and/or rubric. School is more than just memorizing facts. It's about time management, learning to think, and solving problems. Education is something you do for yourself. Parents can use both internal and external motivators. Help your students determine their primary learning style. Help them evaluate their work before they turn it in. Teach them to take notes in class and from the book, and how to prepare for a test. They should have a file container for returned assignments and tests, a small notebook for recording assignments, and a calendar to keep track of due dates.

Make sure they're doing well in English. When studying for a test, look at the layout and section headings of the text.

- **Life skills** – Start teaching what to look for in a spouse; dating eventually leads to marriage. Give more leeway in decision making (say, buying clothes). Continue chores, perseverance, and conflict resolution. Continue with decision making. Emphasize teamwork. Model good listening skills and use "I" messages when you get angry. Teach your child to use "I" messages.

- **Spirituality/religion** – Say nightly prayers, attend church and/or Sunday school, say grace at mealtime. Consider vacation Bible school. Involve them in the church youth group.

- **Consequences** – As you add more rules, continue to be consistent in enforcing them. Continue consequences for not getting schoolwork done. Continue natural and logical consequences. Catch them being good.

- **Respect** – As you treat your cherubs respectfully, so will they be respectful to you. Make sure they treat others (teachers, elders, neighbors, family members) respectfully as well.

- **Lying** – Trust them, but check up on them periodically.

- **Stealing** – If new stuff starts appearing, ask questions, and read their body language. Parents must take immediate corrective action. Your child must return the item or pay for it, as well as apologize.

- **Cheating** – There may be increased peer pressure or academic pressure from Mom and Dad. Make sure your child is spending adequate time on homework and studying. If he seems overwhelmed with homework, speak to his teachers. Discuss the ways people cheat and how they are only cheating themselves. Explain all the reasons that cheating is wrong.

- **Work ethic** – When they start looking for a job, talk about the job interview, and help them write a brag sheet and resume. If your child is doing odd jobs for others, talk to the employer to be sure the job is being completed satisfactorily. Discuss with your child the components of work ethic: dependability, initiative, and interpersonal skills. With chores, clearly state what the parameters are, so he will know when he's done and can tell if he's done a satisfactory job. ("Dishes must be clean, dry, and put away. Windows must be washed inside and out, and must be streak-free.")

- **Social skills** – Discuss the concept of class, and what it means to be a lady or gentleman. Teach graciousness. Continue discussing the Traits of Socially Successful People.

- **Safety** – Driving is a privilege, not a right. Spend plenty of time practicing with your new driver. Have your teen sign a driving contract and make it clear they are not to use the phone while they're behind the wheel. Not even once. Incoming calls and texts *can* wait until they have parked the car. Talk about online predators and cyberbullying. Make it clear that online harassment is illegal. If someone is bullying them, they must let you know. Listen to their music and lock down the Internet when you and your spouse won't be home. Lock out inappropriate TV channels and shows. Put the computer where you can see it when they're using it and monitor their online profiles (Facebook, MySpace, etc.). When you give your child a cell phone, discuss the rules: it must be *off* during school hours, no taking pictures in the locker room, etc. Never post compromising pictures or let others take compromising pictures of you. Taking compromising pictures or video of someone without their consent is illegal as well.

- **Sex** – Teach the mechanics, risks, and reasons for abstinence. Teach your child ways to say no.

- **Finances** – Teach your teen how to set up a budget. When he gets a job, he may need to open another savings account for a car. Leave the retirement money alone. When he's ready, open a checking account with a debit card. Explain how to balance the account and how to be safe online. Explain the perils of credit cards. Continue to talk about needs vs. wants.

- **Healthy lifestyle** – Continue to discuss healthy options for the times they're away from home. Encourage your child to look up new recipes and prepare them. Keep healthy snacks on hand and within easy reach. Don't buy junk food. Discuss the options at his friends' houses. If they always have cookies and milk at a friend's house, have him bake some granola bars to take over. Help him make healthy choices at lunch, whether he buys lunch or packs his own. Continue to limit TV and computer time, and encourage physical activity, especially if they're struggling with their weight. Offer lots of whole grains and vegetables. Never offer sodas, limit fast food, and limit sweets to special occasions. Avoid salty snacks and fried food.

- **Illegal substances** – Some parents tell their children, "If you want to smoke, wait until you're twenty-one." By the time they *are* twenty-one, smoking doesn't seem so appealing. Watch for the warning signs of substance abuse: mood swings, new friends, dropping grades, change in attitude or sleep habits, missing money or valuables, changes in appearance, secrecy about friends and activities, inability to concentrate, avoidance of their usual activities, missing pills or alcohol, excessive use of breath mints or air freshener. Look for teachable moments. Discuss addiction. Lock up the liquor cabinet and your prescriptions to avoid temptation. Teach ways to say no. Continue sending the message: drugs are bad for you. Smoking is bad for you. Drinking is bad for you.

After Age 18

If anyone ever told you that parenting is eighteen years of hard work, they were wrong. Parenting doesn't stop when your child turns eighteen. Parenting is for life. Your children will still need advice, a shoulder to cry on, and occasionally money or a place to stay. Most importantly, they will *always* need your love.

APPENDIX

ADDITIONAL RESOURCES FOR PARENTS

WEB SITES

General:
   www.focusonthefamily.com
   www.actsofkindness.org
   www.commonsense.org
   www.kidshealth.org
   www.informedFamilies.org
   www.drugfree.org
   www.mommymealplanner.blogspot.com
   www.fabermazlish.com
   www.momster.com

Internet and TV Safety:
   www.NetSafeKids.com
   www.Wiredkids.com
   www.familysafecomputers.org
   www.protectkids.com
   www.TheTVBoss.org
   www.cyberangels.org

Financial:
   www.daveramsey.com
   www.clarkhoward.com

Learning Styles:
For anyone:
   people.usd.edu/~bwjames/tut/learning-style/stylest.html
For your children:
   www.scholastic.com/familymatters/parentguides/backtoschool/quiz_learnstyles/

BOOKS

General:
- Dobson, James C. 1996. *The New Dare to Discipline.* Carol Stream, IL: Tyndale House Publishers.
- Faber, Adele, and Elaine Mazlish. 2012. *How to Talk So Kids Will Listen & Listen So Kids Will Talk.* New York: Scribner.
- Faber, Adele, and Elaine Mazlish. 2002. *Siblings Without Rivalry: How to Help Your Children Live Together So You Can Live Too.* New York: Quill.
- Gordon, Thomas. 2000. *Parent Effectiveness Training: The Proven Program for Raising Responsible Children.* New York: Three Rivers Press.

Financial:
- Godfrey, Joline. 2003. *Raising Financially Fit Kids.* New York: Ten Speed Press.
- Howard, Clark and Mark Meltzer. 2005. *Clark Smart Parents, Clark Smart: Teaching Kids of Every Age the Value of Money.* New York: Hyperion.
- Pearl, Jayne A. 1999. *Kids and Money: Giving Them the Savvy to Succeed Financially.* New York: Bloomberg Press.

MAGAZINES

Disney's Family Fun
Family Circle
Parent & Child
Parents Magazine

INDEX

Abstinence, 223-4, 294, 297
Active listening, 92
Addiction, 157, 274, 279, 281, 293, 295, 298
Alcohol, 132, 157, 208, 278-280, 282, 295, 298
  Warning signs, 278, 295, 298
Allowance, 160, 229-241, 289, 291, 294
  And chores, 241-244
Anger, 16, 43, 95, 111, 124
Arrogance, 145, 147
Artificial sweeteners, 262
Assignment sheet, 64, 73
Attire, 192, 194
Attitude, 25-46, 173, 286, 288, 290, 292, 295, 298
  Choosing, 93, 110, 139, 156, 169, 209
  Modeling, 47,
Auditory learners, 56-58

Banking, online, 246
Blood sugar, 255, 261, 263, 267
Body language, 92, 175
Body mass index, 257
Bovine growth hormone, 259, 263
Brag sheet sample, 177
Breakfast ideas, 269
Budget, 7, 91, 233, 244
  How to create, 244-246
Bullies, 39-40, 204-205, 289, 294
Bullying, 141
  Cyber-, 216, 219-221, 294, 297

Calcium, 263, 269, 270
Cancer, 224, 251-255, 258, 259, 260, 275

Carbohydrates, 255, 259, 261, 262
Catch them being good, 117, 120, 142, 287, 288, 290, 293, 296
Cheating, 79, 149, 163-167, 291, 293, 296
Choices, 20, 79, 81-85, 290, 294, 298
  And consequences, 114, 115
  Offering, 36, 52
Chores, 75-77, 101, 267, 286, 288, 290, 293, 296
  And allowance, 241-242
  Expectations, 108-110
  To earn extra money, 78, 162, 237
Cinderella myth, 167
Class, 188-194, 197
Commitment, 79-81, 98-99, 102, 139, 225
Communication, 11, 24, 90-94, 110
  With your child, 92-94
Compound interest, 233-234
Confidence, 28, 32, 288, 290, 293, 295
  Acting as if, 34
Conflict, 107, 288, 290, 293, 296
  Avoiding, 20, 126, 128, 157, 158
  Resolution, 94-98
Consequences, 105-129, 157, 285, 287, 288, 290, 293, 296
  Choosing, 20, 105
  Escalating, 115
  Evaluating, 83, 114
  Importance of enforcing, 105-6, 119, 124, 129, 161
  Logical, 110, 120-121, 287, 290, 293, 296
  Natural, 120-121, 151, 152, 238, 288

Rules and, 107
Consistency, 107, 235, 285, 286, 288, 290, 292, 295
   Enforcement of rules, 112, 113-115, 125, 183
Cornell notes, 66
Creativity, 86-87
Credit cards, 100, 165, 230, 231, 239, 244, 297
CyberAngels.org, 81, 299
Dating, 98-100, 296
Decision making, 81-86, 114, 285, 286, 288, 290, 293, 296
Delayed gratification, 230, 231, 240
Dependability, 168, 169-171, 296
Diabetes, 251, 252, 255, 257, 259, 262
Disappointment, 25, 36-38, 95, 124, 195
Discipline, 23, 41
   How to, 112-120
   Vs. punishment, 110
Discussion questions, 86
Dr. Phil, 39, 126, 138, 194
Dress code, 84, 193
Driving, 183, 205-210, 297
Drugs, 145, 204, 274-278, 282,
   Types, 275
   Warning signs, 276

Education, 9, 47-73,
   Motivating students, 52-56
   Resistance, 49-50
   Selling the importance of, 51-52
   Sneakiness, 51
Eight-to-One Rule, 14-15
Enabling, 128-129, 167, 241
Encouragement, 53, 56, 80, 92, 127-128, 288, 290, 292, 295
English, importance of, 47, 70
Entitlement, sense of, 41, 168
Ethics, 87, 149-167
Exercise, 259, 267-268
Expectations, 23, 38, 71, 108-110, 122, 209

Fats, dietary, 253, 259-261
Fear of parenting, 126
Fear of the unknown, 23, 33
Finances, 100, 229-249, 287, 289, 291, 294, 297
Five-Year Rule, 27, 135, 292, 295
Flour, white, 261, 263
Food, 4, 56, 253-270
   As a reward, 56, 136
   Organic, 263-265
   Plant-based vs. animal, 254-255
   Problem, 261-264
Forgiveness, 43-44, 288, 290, 292, 295
Frustration, 36-38, 80, 111, 220

Goal setting, 69, 77-78, 290, 293
God, 43, 87-88, 100
Godfrey, Joline, 233
Gotcha questions, 150, 289
Graciousness, 190-191, 294, 297
Grades, 52, 54, 62, 72, 146, 295, 298
   And sports, 123
Grading scale, 71
Grammar, 70-72
Gratitude, 40-42, 288, 290, 292, 295

Harlow, Harry, 4-5
Healthy lifestyle, 10, 251-272, 286, 287, 289, 291, 294, 297
Heart disease, 251-255, 257, 259
Helping others, 88-90, 100
Honey, 262
Hosting guests, 184-185
Howard, Clark, 230, 233, 299
Hygiene, 108, 171, 191, 197

Illegal substances, 208, 273-282,
Initiative, 172, 294, 297
Internet, 5, 106, 175, 215-222, 247, 268
   Banking, 246
   Cheating, 163-164

Cyber bullying, 219-221
Inappropriate material, 196, 217-218
Postings, 38, 197, 218-219
Predators, 81, 216-217
Safety, 221-222, 291, 294, 297
Shopping, 246-247
Interviews, job, 174-176
Introductions, 184
Investing, 233, 234, 240-241

Job interviews, 174-176
Job sharing, 19-20
Journal, financial, 236

Kindness, 88, 90, 187
Kinesthetic learners, 57-59

Language, inappropriate, 118, 142, 191-192, 213, 214
Learning styles, 56-59, 66, 68, 290, 292, 295, 299
Life skills, 3, 75-103, 285, 286, 287, 290, 293, 296
Likability, 44-45
   Components of, 45
Listening, 24, 33, 90-96, 139, 185-186, 215, 286-296
   Reflective, 96-97, 135
Logical consequences, 110, 120-121, 287, 290, 293, 296
Lunch ideas, 270
Lying, 114, 149-158, 166, 285, 287, 289, 291, 293, 296
   Chronic, 157-158
   For convenience, 154-155
   Loss of trust, 150, 153, 156, 160
   Out of fear, 151-154
   Out of habit, 155-156
   White lies, 157

Manners, 8, 108, 179-185, 189, 197
   Everyday, 183-185
   Phone, 182-183
   Table, 179-181, 287
Marriage, 81, 98-103, 223, 226-227, 232, 296
Maslow, Abraham, 4-11
Master Teacher, 53-55
Maternal Deprivation Syndrome, 5
Media, 9, 125, 191, 210-214, 230
   Social, 218
Milk, 259, 263, 269
   Almond, 263
   Alternatives, 269
   Soy, 263
Mistakes, allowing, 7, 11, 22-23, 43, 53, 62, 83, 97-98, 229
Money management, 229, 232, 238, 242, 247-249
Monkeys, Rhesus, 4-5
MOPS (Mothers of Preschoolers), 16
Motivation, 146, 287, 290, 292, 295
   Educational, 48, 52-56, 72
   For consequences, 122-123
Movies, 167, 195-196, 197, 210, 213, 279
   Teachable moments, 83, 167
Music, 125, 214-215, 291, 294, 297

Natural consequences, 120-121, 151, 152, 238, 288
Needs of children, 4-11, 285, 286, 288, 290, 292, 295
Negative attention, 17, 129, 160, 196
Negative comments, 8, 15, 137
Notes, taking, 57, 59, 65-68, 292, 295
Nutrients, types of, 259-261

Obesity, 231, 257, 259, 260
   Illness caused by, 253, 259
Organic foods, 263-265
Organizational skills, 52, 63-65, 288
Orphanages, Romanian, 5
Overspending, 242-244

Pearl, Jayne A, 233, 300
Perseverance, 79-81, 168, 288, 290,

293, 296
Phone, 63, 139, 182, 200, 203, 289, 294, 297
   Cell, 63, 156, 164, 174, 183, 268
   Manners, 182-183
   Safety, 205, 207, 219
Physical safety, 5, 137, 200-204
Plant-based foods, 251, 253-256, 260, 261, 266, 267
Popularity, 44, 155
Positive reinforcement, 112, 115-118
Prayers, 42, 88, 196, 285, 287, 288, 290, 293
Proactive parenting, 4, 20-24, 110, 204, 206, 273
Problem-solving, 78-79, 97, 134, 290, 293
Processed foods, 253, 259, 261, 262, 263-264, 266
Progress Report, 51, 73
Propriety, 180, 189, 195
Protein, 254, 255, 259-260, 263, 266, 267, 269
Punishment, 6, 110-112, 121, 123, 150, 151, 153

Ramsey, Dave, 229, 231, 299
Random acts of kindness, 88
Reactive parenting, 3, 21-22, 110
Reflective listening, 96-97, 135
Religion, 87-88, 100, 224, 285, 287, 288, 290, 293, 296
Resistance to education, 49-50, 55
Respect, 55, 56, 81, 92, 131-147, 285, 287, 289, 291, 293, 296
   And difficult people, 146
   And family members, 92, 143-145
   For authority, 142
   For elders, 145
   For others, 45, 140-142, 222
   For siblings, 143-144
   Importance of, 7, 103, 132
   Modeling, 93, 95, 133-140, 152
   Self-, 145-146, 212, 222, 225

Showing, 12, 23
Resume, 90, 174, 177, 178, 296
Retirement, 100, 231, 238, 240, 248, 297
Risky behavior, 145, 206, 266
Role models, 80, 166, 280, 288, 290, 292, 295
   Importance of, 10, 11
   Negative, 125
Rules and consequences, 107

Safety, 199-227, 137, 182, 286, 287, 289, 291, 294, 297
   Bullies, 204-205
   Driving, 205-210
   Emotional and moral, 210-222
   Physical, 5-6, 200-204
Savings, 230, 231, 236, 239-241, 244-245, 247, 248
Self-confidence, 81, 145-146, 147
Self-esteem, 6, 29, 32, 121, 145, 205, 226
   Benefits of, 146, 237
   Destroyers of, 8, 10, 14, 111, 257
Self-fulfilling prophecy, 13, 14, 31, 115, 151
Self-respect, 145-146, 212, 222, 225
Senioritis, 72
Sex, 81, 199, 211, 212, 222, 223-227
Sexting, 86
Shyness, 23, 28-35, 184
   Causes of, 29
   Strategies, 29-35
Sign language, 13
Signal words, 67
Sleep, 4, 5, 136, 257, 268
Sleepovers, 86, 155, 185, 289
Smoking, 54, 252, 259, 280-281
   Discussion items, 281-282
   Signs of, 281
Snack ideas, 264-267, 270
Social media, 218
Social skills, 8, 179-198, 285, 287, 289, 291, 294, 297

Socially successful people, 185-188
Soy, 261, 263, 266, 269, 270
Spending money, 41, 235, 289
Spending, online, 246
Spirituality, 87-88, 285, 287, 288, 290, 293, 296
Spouse, choosing, 98-103
Standard American diet, 253-254
Standards, 113, 189, 194-197
Stealing, 158-162
STEP, 16
Student loans, 232
Study skills, 62-69, 288
Studying, 50, 51, 55, 62, 65
   For a test, 68-69
Sugar, 253, 256, 261-262, 263, 266
   And diabetes, 255, 259
   And cancer, 259

Teachable moments, 83, 139, 197, 212, 226, 279, 292, 295, 298
Teasing, 6, 10, 27, 39-40, 140, 141, 191, 204
Texting, 55, 92, 183, 207-208, 220, 268
Three pot system, 233, 238-241, 289
Time management, 52, 63, 65, 156, 292, 295
Touch deprivation, 5
Traits of the socially successful, 185-188
Trust, 45, 101, 133, 217
   Of parents, 6, 110
   Loss of, 51, 137, 150, 153, 156, 162
   Respect and, 139-140
TV, 83, 195, 202, 211-214

Unit pricing, 243

Vegetarianism, 267
Verbal abuse, 111, 136, 137
Visual learners, 56-58
V-chip, 213-214

Water, 4, 200, 201, 258, 265
Weight, 252, 256-258, 259, 267, 280, 294, 298
White lies, 157
Work ethic, 167-174, 291, 293, 296
Working parents, 18-20

Yelling, 11, 14, 110, 111,
   Harmful effects of, 14, 111
   How to change, 112, 135-138

When you're a parent,
the days are long,
and the years are short.
— Anonymous

Our health always seems
much more valuable
after we lose it.
— Anonymous